SERIES 7 MANUAL
ML7·ML7-R·SUPER 7

IAN BRADLEY

# SERIES 7 MANUAL
## ML7· ML7-R·SUPER 7

**Special Interest Model Books**

**Special Interest Model Books Ltd**
P.O. Box 327
Poole,
Dorset BH15 2RG

First published 1973 by Model and Allied Publications
Revised edition 1977
Second edition 1982
Reprinted 1990, 1997, 2007

ISBN 978-0-85242-775-0

Typeset by Computer Photoset Ltd, Birmingham
Printed and bound in Great Britain by Biddles Ltd, King's Lynn, Norfolk

# Contents

## SERIAL NUMBER

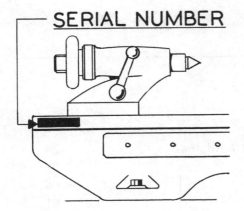

## SERIAL NUMBER

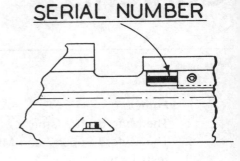

## RE-LOCATION OF SERIAL NUMBERS

OVER THE years the serial numbers have been re-located on the bed of the lathes. Originally the numbers were stamped on the rear shear at the tailstock end of the bed. Now the numbers are to be found on the front shear at the headstock end of the bed. See Fig. above.

Should the serial number of the quick change gearbox be needed this will be found on the inner end of the box as seen in Fig. right.

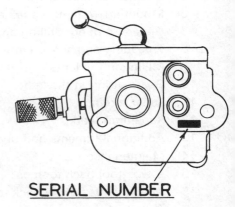

## SERIAL NUMBER

# Foreword

THIS BOOK was first published in 1973 and revised again in 1977. During that period a number of modifications and amendments have been made to the lathe and its equipment, the process having been continued to date. Consequently it has been thought timely to again revise the book bearing in mind that its contents must be of value not only to those readers who are fortunate enough to have the latest type of Myford lathe, but also to those who possess early machines of the same make. This has involved moving some items from the Appendix to positions in a relevant chapter where they would be most readily significant.

The aim of this book on Lathe Work is to give practical assistance and to serve as a guide to all users of Metal Working Lathes.

The book will, I hope, be used as a workshop companion rather than kept only as a work of reference.

No useful purpose would be served here in dealing with the history and development of the lathe; these are matters that have had full consideration elsewhere. Nor will any elementary facts concerning the lathe receive treatment as these, too, can be found in many books that are available.

It is thought, therefore, that those who may find the book of service are already aware of these elementary points, and that to repeat them here would be guilty of time wasting.

Instead, I shall be dealing straight away with the Myford Series Seven Lathe, its use, and the many items of equipment that have been provided for it. Myfords themselves provide a handbook for every machine they sell, so this should be consulted on matters of detail concerning maintenance.

Although the methods set out and the accessories described apply largely to Myfords lathes, I have, at the same time, tried to make this book of real service to every lathe worker.

I should like to record my appreciation of the help furnished by the many engineers, technicians, manufacturers, and others who have given freely of their time and knowledge in the preparation of this book.

*Hungerford*                    I.B.

# CHAPTER ONE

# The Myford ML7 Lathe

MYFORD LATHES have for many years been pre-eminent in the amateur field, where their excellence was quickly recognised by many knowledgeable workers. Early types of lathe made by Myford were smaller than those we shall be considering, but they formed the basis for the development of the ML7 lathe that is the subject of this manual.

The professional worker, also, has found that the ML7 lathe meets many of his requirements, the more so when the many additional fitments that have been introduced came to his notice.

## The Basic Lathe

In order to clarify the construction of the simple screw-cutting lathe the reader is invited to examine the illustration Fig. 1.1 showing its various parts with their names. If this diagram is read in conjunction with

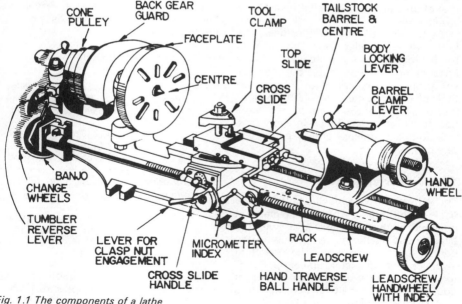

*Fig. 1.1 The components of a lathe*

the many photographic illustrations in the book, the exact location of these parts in the Myford lathe will be apparent.

## THE MYFORD ML7 LATHE

On its introduction perhaps one of the more appealing characteristics of the Myford ML7 lathe, both to the professional and to the amateur, was its self-contained layout. When almost every other small lathe needed a motor driven line shaft and a separate countershaft to drive it, Myford arranged the driving motor on a platform directly behind the headstock, the drive being taken from the motor by means of a V-belt to a small countershaft placed over the mandrel. Corresponding pulleys on both the mandrel and the countershaft permitted a second V-belt to effect the final drive to the headstock itself. These arrangements may be seen in Fig. 1.2 depicting the motor and countershaft layout similar to that of an early ML7 lathe in the author's workshop.

As a result of this compactness, the lathe, when installed, does not depend for its location on the position of any lineshafting in the shop, but can be set at any convenient place that is well lit. It can be mounted on suitable benching, or on one of the range of steel lathe cabinets that are available. In every case the compact driving arrangements are retained.

## The Motorising Unit

The unit comprises a bracket bolted to the back of the lathe bed, a motor platform attached to this bracket and a swinging head providing the means of setting the correct belt tension when the operating lever is pulled against its limit stop. Pushing the lever away from this position, of course, eases the belt tension, and it is in this slack position that the lever should

be when the lathe is not in use.

The motor platform also swings on a hinge set in the bracket, its position being controlled by a slotted tie bar enabling the motor position to be secured once the correct belt tension has been found. Belt guards are provided; that covering the motor-to-countershaft belt being fixed whilst the guard protecting the final drive belt is hinged on the swing head so as to allow belt changing to be carried out. The belts used are:

Motor-to-countershaft $\frac{3}{8}$in. V-belt 34$\frac{7}{16}$in. inside length;
Countershaft-to-mandrel $\frac{1}{2}$in. V-belt 23in. inside length.

## Electric Motors

The electric motors fitted to Myford ML7 lathes are either $\frac{1}{3}$h.p. 3 phase or $\frac{1}{2}$h.p. single phase machines running on a 230–240 50 cycle single phase supply. Motors suitable for a 60 cycle single phase electrical supply, however, are available. The headstock spindle speeds are as in the following table:

**Headstock Spindle Speeds**

| Headstock belt position | 1$\frac{7}{8}$-in. dia. motor pulley (*standard*) | |
|---|---|---|
| | Ungeared | Geared |
| 1 | 200 (246) | 35 (43) |
| 2 | 357 (438) | 62 (76) |
| 3 | 640 (785) | 110 (135) |

| Headstock belt position | 2$\frac{1}{2}$-in. dia. motor pulley | |
|---|---|---|
| | Ungeared | Geared |
| 1 | 273 (338) | 47 (58) |
| 2 | 487 (600) | 84 (103) |
| 3 | 870 (1,070) | 152 (187) |

These speeds are based on a single phase 50 cycle AC motor speed of 1,420–1,450rpm and a single phase 60 cycle AC

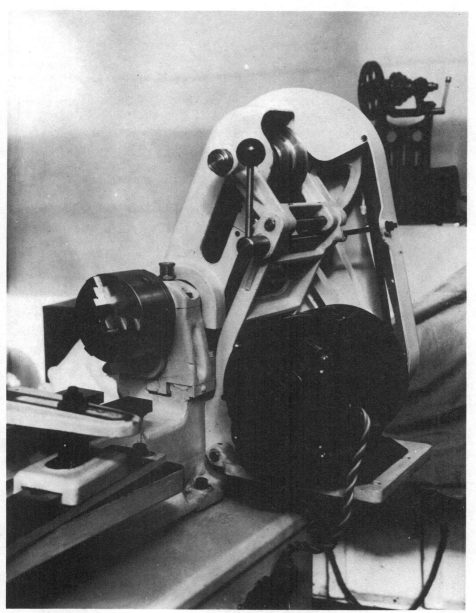

*Fig. 1.2 The motorised drive*

*Fig. 1.3 The motorised unit*

motor speed of 1,750rpm, in the case of the latter the speeds are shown in brackets.

It should be noted that single phase electric motors do not take kindly to much stopping and starting. If the work for which the lathe is intended is likely to involve this then the Countershaft Clutch Unit Cat. No. 1466 should be fitted. The motor can then be left running while the mandrel rotation is controlled by the clutch.

## The Clutch Unit

As has already been mentioned, the continual stopping and starting of single phase alternating current electric motors is, in the long run, detrimental to them. The solution to this difficulty is to fit the lathe with a clutch, set on the countershaft between the motor and the lathe headstock, enabling the user to start and stop the mandrel while keeping the motor running continuously.

The Myford Clutch Unit No. 1466 was designed to provide such a facility. An examination of the illustration Fig. 1.4 will show that the unit provides a self-contained assembly immediately interchangeable with the standard countershaft fitted to the lathe.

The clutch is of the internal expanding type comprising a pair of shoes, similar to those fitted in an automobile brake system, that can be caused to expand and

*Fig. 1.4 (right) Clutch unit*
*Fig. 1.5 (below) Parts of the Clutch unit*

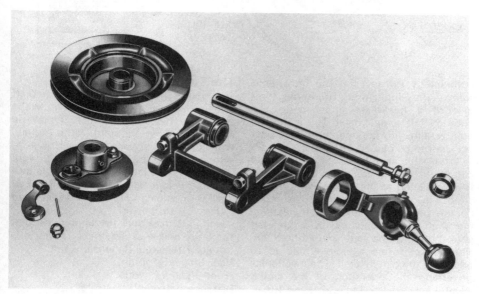

*Fig. 1.6 The actuating mechanism*

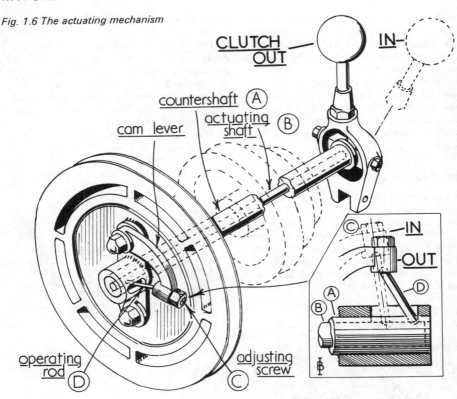

## The Lathe Bed

contract by the lever at the right-hand side of the clutch unit. The shoes form part of a backplate attached to the countershaft spindle itself. This spindle is hollow, allowing the operating or actuating shaft to be passed through it.

When the user needs to engage the clutch, the actuating shaft is pulled and a lever attached to the cam expanding the shoes is moved upwards. The connection between the lever and the actuating shaft at one end and in a threaded socket fitted to the cam lever at the other. The socket forms a simple method of adjusting the clutch itself. The mechanics governing the operation of the clutch control are depicted in Fig. 1.5 and 1.6.

The bed is made from a close-grained cast iron and is heavily ribbed to withstand any twisting to which it may be subjected. The standard lathe admits work 20" long between centres. However, a long bed machine that will take work 32" long is available and the bed length is therefore adjusted accordingly. The bed itself is depicted in Fig. 1.7 and sectioned in Fig. 1.8 (opposite).

Fig. 1.8 may give the impression that the lathe bed is symmetrical. In fact it is not so. The actual dimensions are:

Rear Shear $1\frac{3}{8}''$ wide
Front Shear $1\frac{3}{4}''$ wide
Distance between Shears $1\frac{3}{8}''$

## The Headstock

The headstock (Fig. 1.9) is a self-contained unit secured to a seating machined on the lathe bed itself. The unit comprises a casting containing the two bearings for the mandrel, the housing for the back gear assembly with its operating lever, and the bracket for the tumbler gear cluster mounted on a stud to the left of the main casting.

The headstock bearings are formed in two halves, from Glacier T.1. anti-friction alloy, set in the headstock casting. The two bearing halves are held down by caps, adjustable shims being placed between the facings machined on the caps and the corresponding machined faces on the main casting.

The bearings are lubricated by drip-feed lubricators screwed directly into the bearing caps. These hold sufficient oil for continuous running and may be adjusted for the most economical use of the lubricant.

The mandrel assembly consists of the spindle itself upon which is mounted the 65-tooth back gear, sometimes called the bull wheel, the cone pulley assembly comprising the pulley itself with the small pinion for the back gear and the 25-tooth gear that drives the change wheel assembly through the tumbler gear system.

When required the bull wheel and the small back gear pinion can be locked together to provide the direct drive for the lathe spindle. The method of locking the two gears together is depicted in Fig. 1.10. As will be seen a steel key having gear teeth machined upon it slides in a recess milled in the face of the bull wheel. When it is desired to lock the gears together the cap screw is loosened and the key lowered until it is firmly in mesh with the cone pulley pinion. The key is then secured once more by the cap screw. To free the bull wheel reverse the process.

## The Tailstock

The tailstock Fig. 1.11 is composed of two main assemblies, the body in which the mechanism is housed, and a base plate supporting the body, and upon which it can slide when it is necessary to adjust the tailstock for the purpose of taper turning.

The barrel is bored No. 2 Morse taper and clear through $\frac{19}{32}$in. diameter. It is engraved with graduations of $\frac{1}{16}$in. spacing, enabling drilling depths to be read off directly, and has a maximum travel of $2\frac{3}{4}$in. On machines with metric graduations the spacing is 1mm.

The tailstock with base as a combined unit is clamped to the lathe bed by means

*Fig. 1.7 The lathe bed*

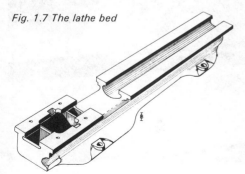

*Fig. 1.8 Section of the lathe bed*

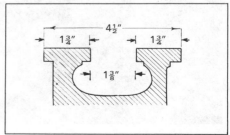

*Fig. 1.9 The headstock*

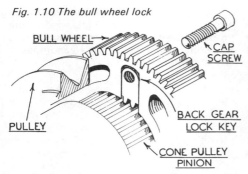

Fig. 1.10 The bull wheel lock

BULL WHEEL

CAP SCREW

PULLEY

BACK GEAR LOCK KEY

CONE PULLEY PINION

of an eccentric lock operated by a lever whilst the barrel itself is secured against movement when required by the thumb lever.

The locking mechanism for the tailstock barrel is depicted in the illustration Fig. 1.12. The lock itself consists of a pad bolt and a bush, located in a chamber machined in the tailstock body and straddling the tailstock barrel itself. These parts 'float' in the chamber, which they fit closely; they can be made to grip the barrel when the thumb lever is operated

Fig. 1.11 The tailstock

and draws the stud through the bush. The body of the tailstock is aligned by a tenon machined towards the front of the base casting itself. Two screws, set each side of the body and abutting a lug formed as a part of the tenon, serve to move the body across the base for taper turning and to return it to its original position approximately once the turning operation has been completed.

In order to ensure that the tailstock retains its alignment at all times the base is fitted with an adjustable gib strip. This is adjusted by two screws and locked by screws engaging each end of the gib.

Earlier models of the ML7 tailstock had the tenon sited at the rear of the base. The arrangement is illustrated in Fig. 1.13. In this instance the tenon is a steel key made a firm fit in the base and a running fit in the tailstock body itself.

The Tailstock Barrel Lock has been altered and is not now as illustrated in Figs 1.12 and 1.13 whilst the position of the lock has remained unchanged at the front of the tailstock its configuration is currently as depicted in the accompanying illustration.(Fig. 1.14).

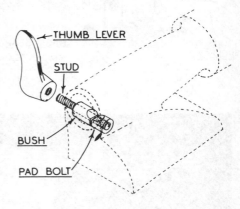

Fig. 1.12 The tailstock barrel lock

Fig. 1.13 Early model tailstock to show tenon position

## The Carriage

The carriage is an assembly that controls the movement of the turning tool along or across the face of the work. It comprises the saddle, the cross slide and the top slide. The saddle itself has an apron that houses all the necessary controls; the cam-and-lever assembly actuating the clasp nut together with the quick traverse hand wheel and its attendant gearing that engages the rack secured to the face of the lathe bed.

## The Saddle

The saddle lock is illustrated in Fig. 1.15. enabling any shake to be removed from its movement along the bed. There is also a simple locking device built into the rear of the saddle allowing the operator to secure the saddle against movement when needed.

## The Saddle Lock

The saddle lock is illustrated in Fig 1.15. It comprises a locking bolt passing through a lug on the rear right-hand wing of the carriage and engaging an eccentric pad situated in a seating machined in the rear saddle strip. The pad is free to move in the strip and make contact with the shears of the lathe bed. So, when the locking bolt is tightened, the pad is drawn into firm contact with the bed thus effectively locking the carriage against movement.

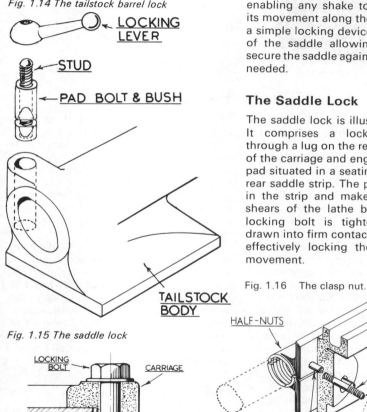

*Fig. 1.14 The tailstock barrel lock*

LOCKING LEVER

STUD

PAD BOLT & BUSH

TAILSTOCK BODY

*Fig. 1.15 The saddle lock*

LOCKING BOLT — CARRIAGE

LATHE BED

REAR SADDLE STRIP

ECCENTRIC LOCK PAD

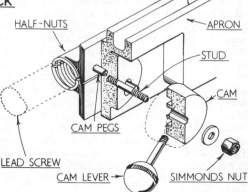

Fig. 1.16   The clasp nut.

HALF-NUTS

APRON

STUD

CAM

CAM PEGS

LEAD SCREW

CAM LEVER

SIMMONDS NUT

*Fig. 1.17 The leadscrew hand wheel*

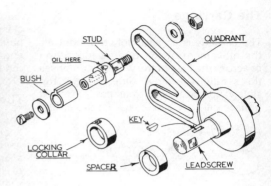

*Fig. 1.18 Method of mounting change wheels*

## The Apron

The apron is suspended from the front of the carriage, being secured to it by cap screws. In addition to the housing of the hand wheel and clasp nut assemblies the apron, on its forward end face, has a short leadscrew guard secured to it. This fitment serves to prevent unwanted swarf chippings from falling on the leadscrew and being trapped by it so damaging the threads of the clasp nut.

The clasp nut comprises a pair of half-nuts working in slides machined on the rear face of the apron, and opened and closed by a cam-and-lever assembly on the apron front face. The nut itself is fairly well protected by virtue of its location. However, as an added protection, the leadscrew guard is extended inwards to afford cover for the half-nuts in case some swarf should penetrate to them. The parts of the clasp nut assembly are illustrated in Fig. 1.16. The half-nuts are thrown in and out of engagement by means of a pair of cam pegs projecting through the apron casting and making contact with a cam located on the front of the apron. The cam rotates on a fixed stud screwed into the apron itself and is held in place by a washer and self-locking nut.

## The Leadscrew

The leadscrew with which the clasp nut engages is ¾in. diameter and has eight threads to the inch Acme form. It is carried in a pair of bearing housings with 'Oilite' bushes; these are secured to the front of the lathe bed. In normal circumstances the leadscrew is supplied with a distance collar and 'SIMMONDS' nut to keep it in place, a thrust collar being used to take up end play.

As an alternative to this method a hand wheel Fig. 1.17 can be supplied. The wheel is engraved on its periphery in divisions of 0·001in., a pointer fitted to the front edge of the lathe bed being used to read off the required measurement. This indexing device is most useful when milling in the lathe or when carrying out facing operations needing an exact measurement.

## Change Wheels

In order to provide a power drive to the carriage the leadscrew is driven from the mandrel through a system of change wheels mounted on a bracket at the headstock end of the lathe (Figs. 1.18 and 1.19). The bracket is slotted so that combinations of change wheel can be

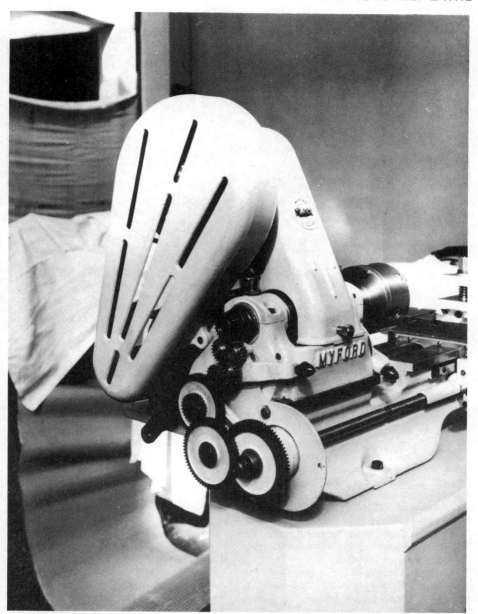

*Fig. 1.19 Change wheels*

*Fig. 1.20 The Myford quick change gearbox*

accommodated and adjusted for mesh. In addition the bracket can be rotated around the leadscrew in order to bring the change wheels into mesh with the mandrel gearing. The change wheels are mounted on studs attached to the quadrant and able to be moved along slots machined in it. The studs are secured by nuts at the back of the quadrant. The studs are hardened, and oil is introduced externally when wheels are mounted. The wheels or gears themselves are carried on bushes long enough to hold a pair of wheels at a time, the bushes having integrally machined keys to couple the two wheels together.

On the leadscrew the change wheels are located by a locking collar and a spacer that can be set either side of the change wheels as necessary, the drive from the wheel to the leadscrew being

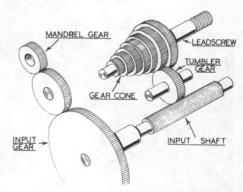

*Fig. 1.21 Principles of a quick change gearbox*

through a woodruff key.

In order to provide for the various combinations of gear given in the table fixed to the inside of the change gear guard, two sets of the stud assembly are provided.

## Tumbler Gearing

The change wheels do not mesh directly with the mandrel, but with gearing called tumbler gearing mounted on a lever attached to the end of the headstock casting. This arrangement allows the leadscrew to be reversed in its rotation so changing the direction of the carriage itself.

## The Quick Change Gearbox

For many users the time taken to set up a train of change wheels is of no moment. To others, however, this is a matter of some importance and cannot be tolerated. The quick change gearbox illustrated in Fig. 1.20, enables the operator immediately to set the leadscrew drive so that any of the thread pitches or feeds available can be cut without delay.

The gearbox itself operates on the principle propounded many years ago in America by the Norton Company. Basically the device comprises a box containing a pair of shafts mounted in bearings and parallel one to the other. The upper shaft is connected to the leadscrew and has mounted upon it a cone of gears while the lower shaft, called the input shaft, has gear teeth running its full length. A tumbler gear carried in a selector enables the two shafts to be geared together, the ratio of the gearing being dependent upon which gear in the cone has been selected.

The tumbler gear is, of course, always in mesh with the gear on the input shaft which is, in turn, driven from the mandrel through a train of gears. In the diagrammatic representation (Fig. 1.21) there are seven gears in the cone, so seven rates of feed to the leadscrew are available. If a simple alteration is made to the ratio of the gears driving the input shaft from the mandrel then a further seven rates of feed are available making a total of fourteen feeds. Add a simple reversible

gear system between the input gear and the input shaft, consisting of two pairs of gears that can be selected by a lever operating a dog clutch between each pair, then the ratio is again doubled bringing the final number of ratios available to twenty-eight.

In the gearbox fitted to the Myford lathe the tumbler gear selector is seen on the front of the box while the lever that operates the dog clutch is on the top.

## The Cross Slide

As befits a small lathe, the cross slide, apart from supporting the top slide, is designed to be used as a boring table. The standard slide has a travel of 5in. and some 36 sq. in. of surface area. A long cross slide is obtainable; this is 1⅝in. longer than the standard slide and has an extra T-slot which, if used for mounting the Myford No. 1468 toolpost, leaves ample room for the workpiece.

The feedscrew is carried in an outrigger bearing secured to the face of the slide itself and engages a renewable nut set in the front wall of the saddle. It is fitted with a ball handle and a micrometer dial. The dial which is also used with the top slide, is of a light colour. For this reason it is somewhat difficult to read, but can be much improved by first blackening the dial by stove enamelling, then carefully scraping the tops of the numbering and division marks till they stand out clearly. The result of the treatment is illustrated in Fig. 1.22.

## The Top Slide

The top slide is the mounting platform for the turning tools and also for the 4-tool turret to which reference will be made in a later chapter. The top slide travel is 2½in. and the whole top slide can be swung 63° each side of zero. The base of the slide is engraved in degrees and is secured to the cross slide by a pair of bolts set in the front T-slots.

The limits of top slide swing have led some workers to make modifications that will allow the slide to approach an angle of swing much wider than is normally obtainable. Figs. 1.23 and 1.24 demonstrate one solution. Here the top slide has been provided with a sole plate that enables the additional angularity to be realised but also lifts the slide high enough for the feedscrew ball handle to clear the cross slide fittings themselves.

The sole plate is shown inverted in the second illustration, where it will be seen that it is held down to the cross slide by counterbored screws engaging strips set in the two front T-slots while the top slide is secured by a pair of nuts with washers running on special cheese headed bolts passed through the sole plate.

One must point out, when using standard tools, however, that this device does upset the setting of the lathe tool on the centre line of the work. However, by

*Fig. 1.22 (right) Modified micrometer dial*

*Fig. 1.23 (below) Top slide with sole plate set over 15°*

employing small tool bits, say $\frac{5}{16}$in. cross section, this difficulty can be overcome.

## The Tool Clamp

The tool clamp arrangements (Fig. 1.25) were specially designed to accommodate the Myford quick setting tools to which

*Fig. 1.24 Underside of sole plate to show fixing*

we shall refer later. The clamp itself is a malleable casting held down by a nut running on a stud set in the top slide itself. The clamp has a spherical seating machined in it allowing a corresponding spherical washer to be used to seat the nut. An adjusting screw, fitted with an 'elephant's foot' pad to save marking the surface of the top slide, is set in the clamp so that it can be aligned to grip the turning tool firmly. A spring surrounds the stud and bears on the underside of the clamp holding it up when adjustment to tool height is being made. A pin is set in the foot of the stud to prevent it turning when the nut is turned.

## The 'Tri-Leva' Speed Selector

When a single belt is used to transmit power from one 3-step pulley to another it follows that time must be lost in

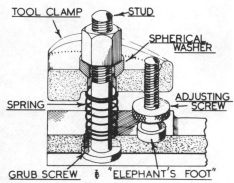

*Fig. 1.25 The tool clamp*

effecting a belt change. If these belt-and-pulley arrangements form part of a lathe intended for production, the delay in carrying out the belt change, and so a speed alteration in the mandrel, may be unacceptable.

To overcome the difficulty Myford Ltd.

25

*Fig. 1.26 The Tri-Leva speed selector*

have introduced the 'Tri-Leva' Speed Selector. This device makes use of three individual driving belts any of which can be brought into contact with the appropriate pair of pulleys by simply depressing any one of the selector levers seen in the illustration Fig. 1.26. The makers point out that when making a speed change it is not even necessary to disengage the speed already in use. The mechanism of the 'Tri-Leva' does that for one.

With all three levers depressed the lathe mandrel is held with sufficient firmness enabling operations, such as hand tapping or marking out, to be performed. Partial depression of any of the levers allows the drive to be slipped when tapping or using button dies in the lathe.

With all levers in the disengaged position the mandrel is completely isolated from the drive and is free to rotate for such operations as setting up the work, using the dial indicator, or marking out when needed. The device is also suitable for use with the ML7B lathe.

It should be noted that the Tri-Leva attachment is only suitable for use with the ML7 lathe. The attachment makes use of three driving pulleys and the ML7 lathe is the only machine made by Myford that has a 3-step mandrel cone pulley that matches the pulleys fitted to the Tri-Leva attachment.

# CHAPTER TWO

# The Myford Super 7 & ML7-R Lathes

THE SUPER 7 (Fig. 2.1) is based on the ML7 lathe. While it has many features in common with that tool there are a number of points of difference between the two machines. These concern the following major assemblies:

(1) the headstock (2) the mandrel (3) the tailstock (4) the motor drive assembly (5) the top slide (6) the cross slide and top slide micrometer dials.

## The Headstock

The illustration Fig. 2.2 shows the various parts of the modified mandrel assembly for the Super 7. The mandrel which is

*Fig. 2.1 The Myford Super 7 lathe*

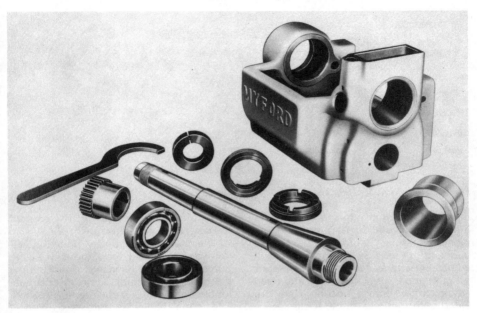

*Fig. 2.2 Part of the Super 7 headstock*

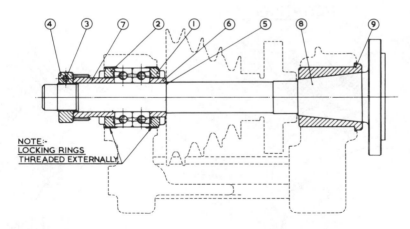

*Fig. 2.3 Section of the Super 7 headstock*
*(1) G 2340 adjusting ring  (2) G 2340 adjusting ring  (3) cap screw (2BA × ¾in)  (4) A 2056*
*adjusting collar  (5) spindle shoulder  (6) A 2055 distance sleeve  (7) A 1995 30-tooth gear*
*(8) A 1992 headstock spindle  (9) A 3609 Spindle bearing (front)*

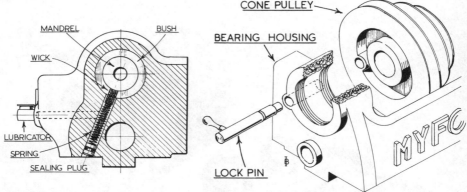

Fig. 2.4 The wick lubricating system          Fig. 2.5 The cone pulley lock

hardened is carried at its working end in a bronze bush, and in its outer end in a pair of angular contact ball races as depicted in Fig. 2.3. The mandrel is fully adjustable and is designed to operate at a high speed. Early models of the head-stock with a bronze bearing were provided with the large oil reservoir seen as part of the headstock casting; later machines now have a wick lubricating

system for the front bearing. The parts of the device are illustrated in Fig. 2.4.

The mandrel cone pulley in the Super 7 is reversed, having the large step at the outer end of the headstock, and is provided with an oil nipple to ensure adequate lubrication to the cone pulley bearing. The cone pulley is furnished with a locking device for use if the mandrel needs to be held stationary for any

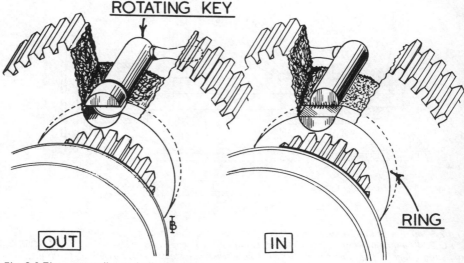

Fig. 2.6 The cone pulley to bull wheel lock

reason, when replacing chucks for example. The lock comprises a pin passing through the headstock casting and passing into a drilled hole formed in the cone pulley itself (Fig. 2.5).

## The Bull Wheel

The bull wheel attached to the mandrel is the major element in the back gear or mandrel reduction gear assembly. The method of locking the wheel to the cone pulley differs from that used in the ML7 lathe. The key engaging a gear forming part of the cone pulley assembly used in the ML7 lathe, and needing an Allen key for its engagement, has been superseded by a rotatable key provided with a spring detent. The key has a short lever attached to it so that it can be finger controlled and rapidly brought in or out of engagement with a ring attached to the cone pulley gear. The parts of the device are illustrated in Fig. 2.6. Half a turn is needed to throw the lock in or out of engagement, the spring-loaded ball detent being employed to hold the device after engagement or disengagement.

*Fig. 2.7 ML7 B tumbler gear*

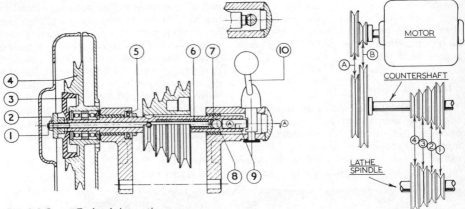

Fig. 2.8 Super 7 clutch in section

Fig. 2.9 Diagram of belt combinations

## The Tumbler Gearing

The two pinions mounted on the tumbler gear lever are made from Tufnol, a fabric substance impregnated with synthetic resin. This material is silent in operation so virtually eliminating the noise produced by tumbler gearing. The pinions run on hardened pins attached to the lever controlling the engagement of the tumbler gearing.

The layout of the gearing is similar to that used on the ML7 lathe. But, whereas this lathe has steel gear wheels as standard and Tufnol gears as an optional extra, the ML7B is fitted with fabric gears as standard equipment. The tumbler gearing and gear wheel arrangements are illustrated in Fig. 2.7.

## The Motor Drive Assembly

Basically the arrangements for the self-contained motor drive are similar to those made for the ML7. They are, however, more sophisticated, embodying as they do total and positive enclosure of all the belting involved. In addition, a modified and somewhat advanced clutch unit is

**Headstock Spindle Speeds**
(1420/1450 r.p.m. Full Load Speed Motor)
Spindle Speeds with 1750 r.p.m. (60 Hz A.C.)
Motor in Brackets

| Motor Drive Belt Position | Headstock Drive Belt Position | Ungeared | Geared |
|---|---|---|---|
| A | 1 | 2105 (2525) | — |
| A | 2 | 1480 (1775) | — |
| A | 3 | 1050 (1260) | 135 (162) |
| A | 4 | 740 (890) | 95 (114) |
| | | | |
| B | 1 | 600 (720) | 77 (92) |
| B | 2 | 420 (505) | 54 (65) |
| B | 3 | 300 (360) | 39 (47) |
| B | 4 | 210 (250) | 27 (32) |

fitted as standard equipment. This clutch is of the cone type and is of metal-to-metal construction; its component parts are depicted in the sectional illustration Fig. 2.8.

The coned clutch plate (3), is brought

into engagement with the drive pulley (4) by a spring (6). A cam shaft, operated by a ball handle (10) engages the push rod (1) running through the drive shaft (7). Contact between the cam shaft and the push rod is maintained by a ball (8) and a push bar (9).

A word of warning here, a clearance of from 0·005in. to 0·010in. must be allowed between the end of the push bar and the face of the cam *when the clutch is* *engaged.* If this clearance is not observed the clutch will slip and damage may be done to the contact faces of the cone and the drive pulley. The adjustment to obtain clearance is carried out by screwing the push rod further into the clutch plate (3) finally securing it by means of the nut (2) once the adjustment has been made. The push rod is provided with a screwdriver slot at its outer end to enable the adjusting to be carried out.

*Fig. 2.10 The tailstock for the Super 7*

Both the countershaft drive and the motor pulleys are twin units, each having a pair of V-grooves for the driving belt. The diameter of these grooves is such that the belt can be moved from one groove to the other without hindrance. The use of two-step pulleys has resulted in fourteen mandrel speeds according to the accompanying table and the diagram Fig. 2.9.

## The Tailstock

The Super 7 tailstock (Fig. 2.10) is of a different pattern to that used on the ML7. The new tailstock is of the ejector type; that is to say centres, chucks and drills mounted in the tailstock are automatically ejected or released when the tailstock barrel is wound inward. This takes place when the inner end of the barrel feed-

screw makes contact with the taper shank of whatever equipment is mounted in the tailstock.

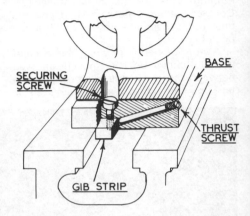

Fig. 2.11 The tailstock gib strip adjustment

Fig. 2.12 The Super 7 micrometer dials

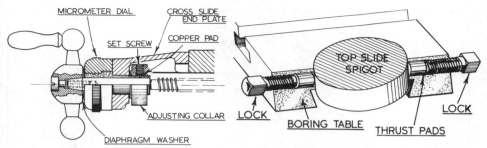

Fig. 2.13 Mechanism of the micrometer dial

Fig. 2.14 Method of locking the top slide set over

In addition, the feedscrew itself is provided with a thrust bearing to reduce, if not completely remove, all the frictional loading imposed by a drilling operation. When a large drill is being used for long periods, this load can be very high and can easily lead to fatigue on the part of the operator.

Both the barrel lock and the eccentric assembly locking the tailstock to the lathe bed are the same as those used on the ML7. The gib strip adjustment, while basically the same as that of the ML7 has some minor modifications. These are depicted in the illustration Fig. 2.11.

The above remarks apply to older machines. For some time now the gib strip arrangements for both the ML7 and Super 7 have been identical.

## Cross Slide and Top Slide Micrometer Dials

The micrometer dials Fig. 2.12 are adjustable so that they can be set to zero when required. They turn on a sleeve forming part of the feedscrew end float adjusting mechanism, and are friction loaded so that, while they turn freely enough for setting purposes, they do not move independently of the feedscrew itself.

This friction loading is imparted by a

Belleville or diaphragm washer placed between the end of the sleeve and the back of the ball handle. These details are depicted in the illustration Fig. 2.13 showing the mechanism in section.

## The Top Slide Mounting

Unlike the mounting and securing of the top slide on the ML7 boring table, the Super 7 top slide is capable of rotation through 360° and may be locked at any point on the circle. The method of locking the top slide is illustrated in Fig. 2.14. The top slide has a machined spigot of large diameter which projects into a hole formed in the boring table. A pair of lock screws with thrust pads are set at 180° to one another each side of the boring table. When pressure is applied to the lock screws the pads are forced against the spigot thus securing the base of the top slide of which the spigot forms part.

It should be noted that the top slide spigot trough shown diagrammatically parallel sided, is in fact tapered in order to prevent the slide from rising up under load.

Myford have pointed out that whilst it is theoretically possible to rotate the top slide through 360° users should be made aware that this total movement cannot be used in practice because, in

35

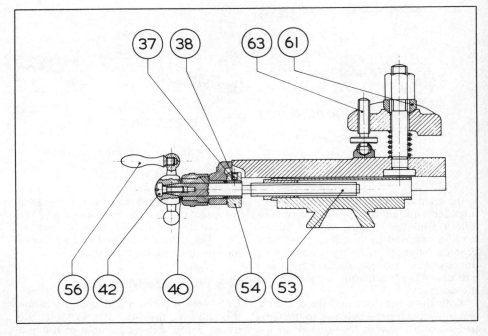

*Fig. 2.15 Top slide (37) Pad adjusting collar (38) socket set screw (40) Diaphragm washer (42) Ball Handle securing screw (53) Feed screw (54) Adjusting Collar (56) Ball handle assembly (61) Spherical washer (63) Adjusting screw assembly*

certain positions, the feed screw ball handle tends to foul the cross slide extension bracket.

It should also be noted that the bearing surface of the top slide spigot is, in fact conical and not cylindrical, as might be inferred from Fig 2.14. In this respect it resembles the arrangement made for the Myford ML10 lathe.

The two hardened steel thrust pads that secure the top slide against involuntary movement in relation to the cross slide are handed. It is essential, therefore, that, if for any reason they are removed, they are replaced in their original position. If by any chance they are reversed it may well be quite impossible to

withdraw them again without damage to the saddle assembly; so the need for great care is readily understood.

Production of the ML7 lathe has now ceased and is replaced by the ML7-R machine.

This lathe is similar to a Super 7 but without the countershaft clutch which can be fitted as an extra if required. The machine has the ML7 carriage.

The Super 7 lathe is similar to the ML7-R but has the countershaft clutch. In addition the following extras are built into the machine:

Graduated Leadscrew Handwheel, Sensitive Tailstock with ball thrust to the Barrel Feedscrew. Quick-setting Index

Dials for the slide rest feed screws. Power Traverse to the Cross-slide. Large Boring Table.

The letter B following the Machine Reference number denotes the fitting of the Quick Change Gearbox for the lead-screw drive.

Both lathes are obtainable as long-bed machines i.e. admitting 31 in. between centres as opposed to the standard admission which is 19 in. between centres.

*Fig. 2.16 ML7-R lathe*

# CHAPTER THREE

# Installation

IT IS NOT THE INTENTION of the author to enlarge overmuch on the details of installation. These are matters covered quite fully by the booklet issued with each lathe by Myford Ltd. which should be consulted on points of detail.

However, a few words on the subject, and of mounting the lathe in particular, can hardly be avoided. Obviously, the quality of the mounting will depend very much on how much one is prepared to spend on it. The cheapest support for a lathe is a wooden bench. But it must be emphasised that strength is the essential ingredient here. It is quite useless to mount machine tools on benching that is flimsy or decrepit; not only on account of the lack of safety and the damage that

collapse must inevitably cause, but also because of its effect on the accuracy of the lathe.

Material for wooden benching must be well seasoned or trouble will no doubt arise when the bench is put into service.

The author prefers free-standing benches since they offer some flexibility when planning a workshop or when some alteration in its layout has to be made.

A typical example suitable for the mounting of machine tools, or for use as a fitting bench, is illustrated in Fig. 3.1. The material sizes there given are those used in the author's workshop.

When mounting lathes on wooden benching a word of warning must be uttered. Unless steps are taken to prevent

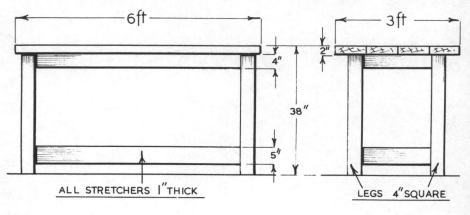

*Fig. 3.1 Free standing machine bench*

*Fig. 3.2 a-b Tray top cabinet*

Fig. 3.3 The industrial stand

*Fig. 3.4 Self-contained coolant equipment*

it the feet of the lathe bed may be pulled into the bench as the fixing bolts are tightened. The result, inevitably, would be to distort the lathe bed and destroy the machine's accuracy. To avoid this a substantial steel plate should be placed on the bench top and the lathe set on this. Myford point out that the drip tray available from them will serve very well for the purpose.

## Cabinet Stands

Undoubtedly, the most satisfactory way of supporting a bench lathe, for in essence that is what both the ML7 and Super 7 are, is to mount it on a cabinet stand specially designed for the purpose. Two types are available. The first, depicted in Fig. 3.2 is the Tray Top Cabinet Stand No. 20/038 and is fitted with cork mats to the cabinet shelves, a deep tray and raising blocks to prevent interference by the edge of the tray with the operator's hands.

The second type available is the Industrial Stand No. 1486 (Fig. 3.3). This stand has a deep tray suitable for use with coolant equipment which can be built

into the base of the stand. An isolating switch and electrical control panel are fitted. The door seen below the panel covers a locker to contain essential equipment for use on the lathe.

## Suds and or Coolant Equipment

As we shall see later the provision of adequate coolant supplies is of some importance, particularly to the industrial user. Without it the machining of some materials would be a virtual impossibility. Most conveniently the coolant system can be built into the cabinet stand. Alternatively the self-contained coolant equipment 1488/A illustrated in Fig. 3.4 can be used alongside a cabinet stand if this arrangement seems more convenient.

## Levelling the Lathe

The makers point out that it is of the utmost importance to make sure that the lathe is truly level when it is set in place. They give detailed instructions for doing so in the booklet already referred to. Before embarking on the process of levelling, however, make sure that the lathe itself, whether on a bench or set on a cabinet stand, is provided with a firm foundation. Wood flooring however, unless set on a concrete base, is not usually ideal foundation material.

Many years ago the author had as a workshop one of those excellent sectional wooden buildings, designed primarily for garden purposes, having its floor framing set on a series of brick pillars disposed about the edge of the floor frame. To have set a lathe to work on such an unsure foundation would have been futile. The brick pillars left a considerable gap between the floor and the ground, the only possible solution being to cut a hole of sufficient size in the floor so that a concrete block to carry the lathe could be cast in place. As will be seen from the illustration Fig. 3.5 the block projected well into the ground itself, so the lathe mounted on it was well supported. However, if the sectional wood building had been intended for use as a workshop in the first place, it might have been possible that both the flooring and its supports could have been sufficiently strengthened to support a lathe from the outset. It also follows that when lathes are to be used in upstairs locations, the siting of them needs to be chosen with some care.

## Checking the Levelling of the Lathe

In order to find out whether or not the lathe has been set level, a simple check that can be made is to take a cut across a test piece held in the chuck. The method used is depicted in the illustration Fig. 3.6. The test piece, a length of mild steel some 4in. to 6in. long and about 1in. diameter is first machined to the shape shown. Then without using the tailstock *light* cuts are taken, followed by measurements to determine if any difference exists between the two ends of the component. The amount removed should not be more than from 0·002in. to 0·004in. and, of course, no alteration to the cross slide setting must be made between the machining of one end of the test piece and the other. If no difference is discernible then the lathe has been set level. However, differing measurements at either end indicate the

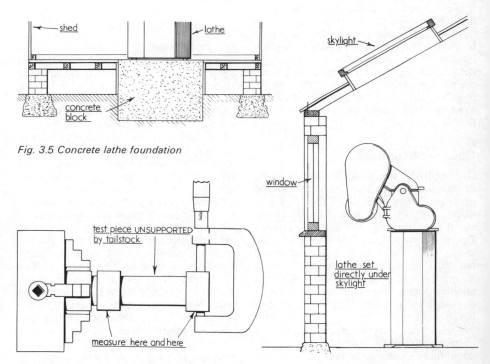

*Fig. 3.5 Concrete lathe foundation*

*Fig. 3.6 Method of checking the levelling*

*Fig. 3.7 Lighting the lathe*

lathe is not level and requires packing. This packing is placed under the foot of the lathe bed at the tailstock end. If the collar at the outer end of the test piece is larger than that near the chuck extra packing will be needed under the *front* of the foot. If the collar is smaller, place the packing under the *back* of the foot.

## Lighting the Lathe

The importance of adequate lighting when working at a lathe cannot be disputed. Whenever possible advantage should be taken of any natural light there is, placing the lathe close to a window for example. If the building can be adapted

*Fig. 3.8 (left) The safe work light*

*Fig. 3.9 (below) Low-voltage electric lighting*

to provide top light as well, the natural illumination will be greatly enhanced. In this connection the sheets of corrugated plastic material on the market are a simple means of providing for overhead lighting. They are often readily interchangeable with existing roof material so the work of providing for this form of light is then not a difficult matter.

Fig. 3.7, depicts the lathe sited so that it has both top light and lighting from the front. It will be seen that a box skylight provides lighting from above. Such a fitting needs to be made with great care in order to ensure that no rain leakage over the lathe can take place. While the window can be made to open, the skylight should preferably be fixed in order to ensure a water-tight condition.

*Artificial Lighting*. In addition to natural light it is inevitable that some form of artificial lighting will be needed, indeed in some instances it may be the only light available. Treatment of other than electric lighting would be superfluous so it is light from electrical sources that will be considered.

The use of fluorescent lighting has many attractions, but it must be emphasised that, in certain circumstances when used in connection with moving machinery, a stroboscopic effect is produced by it. This phenomenon gives the impression that the machinery is stationary when in fact it is not. If fluorescent light is applied directly to the lathe the danger is clear.

It is best then to use it for general illumination and to employ normal lighting directly over the lathe and other machine tools.

Of late years low-voltage lighting has found favour in some industrial undertakings. The energy required is derived from a small transformer set close to the light source, and the voltage is such that the lathe operator cannot receive an electric shock when using a light fitting

attached directly to the machine.

A typical piece of equipment for the purpose is the Safe Work Light, Myford No. 60/023 illustrated in Fig. 3.8. The output from the transformer housed in the metal box seen to the left of the light fitting is 40 watts at 25 volts. The arm of the fitting attached to the back of the lathe is in three articulated parts enabling the operator to set the light at the most convenient position for work. The lamps illustrated in Fig. 3.9 may be of interest to readers. They incorporate discarded headlamp reflectors such as are usually obtainable at the local garage. The fittings allow the reflectors to be adjusted for angle and are made to accept small bayonet cap lamp holders. Laboratory clamps serve to attach the lamps to a standard bolted to the back of the lathe, using the machined face that is to be found there.

The lamp bulbs employed are of the twin contact type providing 36 candle power at 20 volts. Two in use at a time, and run from the low-voltage system in the author's workshop, provide adequate illumination.

## Electrical Systems

Details of the electrical equipment used in connection with Myford lathes are given in the handbook supplied with each machine. The switchgear available is suitable for either 440 volt 3 phase 50 cycle AC systems or for a 240–250 volt single phase 50 cycle AC supply. The motors provided from the works are:

| For ML7 | | | |
|---|---|---|---|
| | 3 phase | $\frac{1}{3}$h.p. | 1,420/1,450r.p.m. |
| | Single phase | $\frac{1}{2}$h.p. | 1,420/1,450r.p.m. |
| For Super 7 | | | |
| | 3 phase | $\frac{1}{2}$h.p. | 1,420/1,450r.p.m. |
| | Single phase | $\frac{3}{4}$h.p. | 1,420/1,450r.p.m. |

The switchgear fitted to the lathe varies according to the type of machine involved. For the most part drum type reversing switches are supplied mounted on a specially designed bracket attached to the cabinet stand. The ability of the lathe to be reversed is occasionally of some advantage, so any motors bought independently, and when wired correctly, should have terminal connections that will permit this.

For those whose electrical supply is based on a frequency of 60 cycles per second there are of course suitable motors to be had. Their purchase is, perhaps, better undertaken in the localities where a 60 cycle frequency is standard.

Mention must also be made of the 2-speed electric motors available. These provide 6 speeds for the ML7 mandrel ungeared both forward and in reverse. These motors need a special switch for their control and this will need to be specified when ordering.

It should also be noted that the fitting of a 2-speed motor reduces the swing in the gap to $9\frac{1}{4}$in. diameter.

*Earthing.* Too much emphasis cannot be placed on the importance of making sure that the lathe is properly earthed. In many instances the lathe is connected to the electrical mains by a plug-and-socket combination. Provided a three core cable is fitted correctly to the plug and the earth wire of this cable is secured to its appropriate terminal, both in the plug and on the lathe itself, all should be well. If there is any doubt, however, the matter must be referred to a qualified electrician for resolution.

Lathe motors to be connected directly to the electrical mains should always have this connection made by a competent and qualified wireman.

# CHAPTER FOUR

# Lathe Tools

## Chip Formation

WHEN A TOOL is used to cut metal in the lathe, the pressure set up on the cutting edge and face of the tool causes what is termed 'plastic flow' in the material and, as the stress increases, the metal chip is separated by a shearing action.

The initial stage of plastic flow is represented diagrammatically in Fig. 4.1(A) and the way in which this leads to the formation of a continuous ribbon or chip is shown in (B) and (C).

Ductile metals, steel, and some kinds of brass for example, come off from the tool in a long, continuous chip, but when machining brittle metals, like cast iron, the chips are usually separated in the form of flakes.

The shearing stress is greatest when heavy cuts are taken, and becomes less as the cut is reduced. Light finishing cuts, producing a thin metal chip, set up comparatively little stress in the material and this results in a good, smooth finish being imparted to the work.

The tool's cutting edge must always be kept really sharp if the tool is to cut efficiently and machine the work accurately.

To enable a lathe tool to cut to the best advantage, the angles at the tip, forming the cutting edge, must be correctly proportioned.

## Clearance Angles

When the cutting edge is in contact with the work, the tip of the tool below the cutting edge must be ground away to give cutting clearance, so as to prevent this part of the tool rubbing against the work. Front clearance, as represented in Fig. 4.2(A), is given to enable the tool to be fed either directly into or across the work, and the side clearance, (B), allows the tool to be traversed along the work and to cut freely without rubbing. For ordinary turning, the angles formed by both these clearances usually range from 5° to 10° but the greater the clearance angle, the more will the cutting edge be thinned

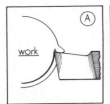  

*Fig. 4.1 Action of tool on work*

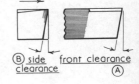

*Fig. 4.2 Front and side clearance*

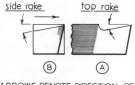

ARROWS DENOTE DIRECTION OF CUT

*Fig. 4.3 Top and side rake: front rake (A) (B) and (C)*

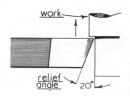

*Fig. 4.4 Relief angle*

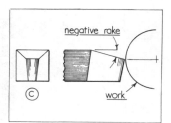

and its strength reduced from lack of support.

## The Rake Angle

Where the surface of the tool is laid back so as to slope away from the cutting edge, the tool will cut more freely as the shearing action is more pronounced, but the slope or rake, as it is termed, must not be made too steep or the cutting edge will become too weak to withstand the normal cutting pressure. Top rake Fig. 4.3(A) enables steel to be cut more freely when the tool is fed directly into or across the work as in parting off operations. Side rake, (B), promotes free-cutting where traversing cuts are taken along the work with the ordinary knife tool. The actual angles used in ordinary turning practice vary in accordance with the duty required of the tool and the nature of the material being machined.

When machining some varieties of hard bronze, there may be difficulty in preventing chatter and keeping the tool from digging into the material. For this work, the tool will often cut better if given a negative front rake as represented in (C).

The rake and clearance angles in common use are set out in the accompanying table.

## The Relief or Trail Angle

If too great a length of the tool's cutting edge is in contact with the work during machining, chatter is liable to develop and the finish and accuracy of the work will then suffer. The amount of relief necessary and the actual length of the cutting edge will depend largely on the rigidity of the lathe as well as on the stiffness of the work-piece, but as shown in Fig. 4.4 a relief angle of some 20° will usually be found sufficient.

## MATERIALS FOR LATHE TOOLS

*Carbon or Tool Steel.* Tools made of carbon steel can be sharpened to a very keen edge for producing highly-finished

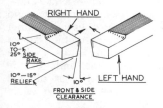

*Fig. 4.5 The knife tool*

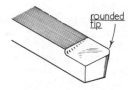

*Fig. 4.6 Knife tool with rounded tip*

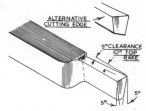

*Fig. 4.7 The parting tool*

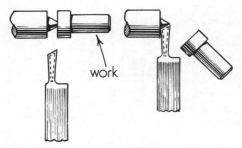

*Fig. 4.8 Obliquely ground parting tool*

work, but the material is not so resistant to wear and becomes blunted more quickly than alloy steel. Carbon steel including silver steel in the annealed or softened state can readily be filed to shape, and hardening and tempering require no great skill or special equipment.

*High-Speed Steel.* This is an alloy steel usually incorporating tungsten up to some 18%. Tungsten steel tools need special, exact heat-treatment for hardening in order to obtain the most efficient machining, but the details of this treatment vary with different brands of alloy steel. Although a really keen edge may be difficult to obtain, tools made of these steels are stronger and retain their sharpness well even when taking heavy cuts in tough materials.

*Tungsten Carbide Tipped Tools.* Tools having a tungsten carbide tip brazed on to a steel shank are extremely resistant to wear and the effects of heat when machining at high speed. The cutting edge is also but little affected by the surface scale and sand found adhering to iron casting. This tip material is rather brittle and may be fractured if subjected to sudden shock, but its great advantage is that by its use the speed of machining can be greatly increased without damaging the cutting edge, and re-sharpening is necessary at much longer intervals than when alloy steel tools are employed.

Tungsten carbide has an affinity for steel and, when machining this metal, the tip may in time become cratered or pitted, so that the cutting edge breaks away. Tungsten carbide tools must be ground on a special kind of abrasive wheel, and the cutting edge needs finishing afterwards on a plastic wheel or hone impregnated with diamond dust.

## TURNING TOOLS

*The Knife Tool.* Fig. 4.5 the right-handed tool is used for traversing towards the lathe headstock, and the left-handed form is ground to cut in the reverse direction. This is the most useful tool for all general turning, and serves for facing as well as for taking traversing cuts. For all light machining, front and side clearance angles of 10° can be used, and the side rake angles can be made as great as 25° for machining mild steel.

The tip of the tool should not, after grinding, be left with a sharp point, as this is easily fractured and, besides, the work will be ringed when the area of the cutting edge is so small. Instead, the extreme tip is either rounded on the oilstone as shown in Fig. 4.6 or the cutting edge is honed with a small flat. A tool with a rounded tip is more suitable for taking both traversing and facing cuts.

For machining brass, the side rake should either be omitted or reduced to an angle of about 5°.

Free cutting materials, like aluminium alloys, impose very little strain on the cutting edge and this enables a rake angle of up to 30° to be used to promote rapid machining. For making these and other lathe tools, short lengths of high-speed steel, ground on all four sides, can be obtained and, where the ends of the material are ready-formed to an oblique angle, much work will be saved when grinding the tools to shape.

*The Parting Tool* (Fig. 4.7). For forming

grooves or cutting off material, the parting tool is fed directly inwards with a steady, plunging cut. Top rake is, therefore, used to promote free-cutting in steel, but this rake may cause the tool to dig-in and jam when machining brass or similar alloys. As illustrated, the raked surface of the tool should terminate in a hollow curve to curl the chip and carry it clear of the work. Front clearance is necessary to enable the tool to cut inwards, but this clearance should be restricted to 5° or so in order to maintain the strength of the cutting edge.

A small clearance is also ground on the two sides of the tool and, in addition, the two flanks of the tool may be relieved behind the cutting edge to prevent rubbing.

When parting off the use of a suitable coolant is a great advantage. If this can be supplied as a continuous stream so much the better; for this will not only cool the tool and the work, but will also promote the free passage of swarf from the kerf formed by the tool itself.

Do not be over cautious when parting off since this is likely to promote chatter, but keep up a steady rate of feed to ensure that the tool cuts continuously.

To reduce the cutting pressure and prevent chatter, the cutting edge is made as narrow as possible, consistent with adequate strength.

## 'Eclipse' Parting Tool

Short lengths of high-speed steel, ground with side clearance are manufactured for use as parting tools when held in a suitable tool holder.

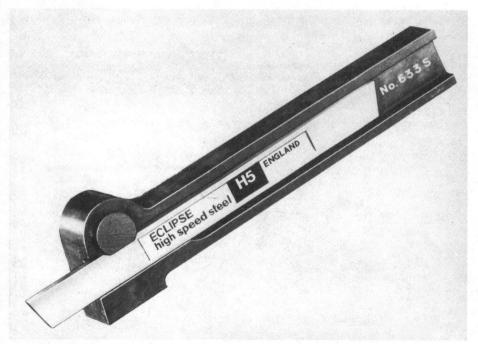

*Fig. 4.9 The Eclipse parting tool*

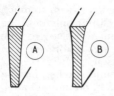

Fig. 4.10 Bevel and
hollow ground blades

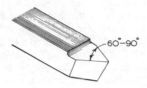

Fig. 4.11 The V-tool

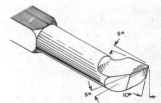

Fig. 4.12 The boring tool

Experience shows that parting off operations are facilitated by mounting the tool upside-down in a back toolpost secured to the rear of the cross slide. If the cutting edge of the parting tool is ground obliquely, as illustrated, parts such as washers can be parted off cleanly, but the tool must be fed further inwards in order to reface the end of the stock before severing the next component.

*The 'Eclipse' Parting Tool Holder.* Messrs James Neill and Company of Sheffield have made a parting or cutting-off tool holder especially for use on small lathes such as the Myford ML7. This tool holder, Eclipse No. 633S, is designed to hold a high-speed steel blade $\frac{1}{16}$in. wide by $\frac{5}{16}$in. deep. The shank of the tool is $\frac{5}{16}$in. wide by $\frac{9}{16}$in. deep, having an overall length of $3\frac{11}{16}$in. It can therefore be used in other lathes or machines such as the shaping machine which have American slotted-pillar toolposts.

*Cutting-off Blades.* High-speed steel

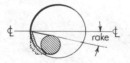

Fig. 4.13 Checking
boring tool clearance

Fig. 4.15 Boring bar with small cutter bits

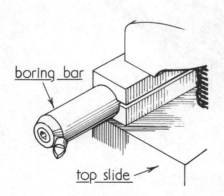

Fig. 4.14 The boring bar on top slide

Fig. 4.16 Alternative mounting for boring bar with small cutter bits

cutting-off blades are obtainable in either *bevel section* as shown at (A) in Fig. 4.10 or *hollow ground* as at (B) in the same illustration. The hollow ground blade is that fitted to the 'Eclipse' cutting-off tool holder as it has the advantages of increased side clearance so valuable where light section blades are in use.

*The V-Tool.* This tool is used for machining V-grooves and for chamfering the edges of the work. For the latter purpose, the V-tip is usually ground to form an included angle of from 60° to 90°. Clearances are formed on the two sides of the 'V' and top rake may also be given for machining cast-iron or steel parts. To increase the strength of the tool, it is advisable to remove the sharp point at the apex of the 'V' on an oilstone. For machining the coned heads of countersink screws, the V-tool should be set to cut an included angle of 90° on the stock, and for chamfering washers the tool is usually ground to an included angle of approximately 80°.

*The Boring Tool.* The size of the tool and the length of the shank behind the cutting edge will vary in accordance with the diameter and depth of the bore machined in the work. The head of the tool must be ground to give adequate clearance below the cutting edge when the tool is mounted at centre height. This clearance can be checked by entering the tool in a hole in the drill gauge of the same diameter as the machined bore (Fig. 4.13).

The shank of the tool should be made as rigid as possible in order to withstand whipping under the pressure of the cut. For some purposes, it is more convenient to use a short boring bar in which a small cutter bit is mounted (Figs. 4.14–4.16); this will enable the overhang of the tool to be kept at a minimum.

*Screw Cutting Tools.* For cutting external V-threads, a V-tool is used having adequate clearance on its two sides, but the clearance on the forward side is made greater as the helix angle or slope of the thread must be taken into account. The included angle at the tip is ground to 55°, 60°, or 48° for forming Whitworth (55°), Cycle Standard, American and Metric ISO (60°) or BA threads (48°) respectively. If top rake is given to the tool, it will cut more freely, but the angle of the finished thread will be less than intended. A correction, to cut the thread to the standard angle, can be made by increasing the V-angle so as to offset the loss arising from the presence of top rake.

Internal V-threads are cut with a tool similar to a pointed boring tool and, again, the included angle of the V-point must be equivalent to the angle of the

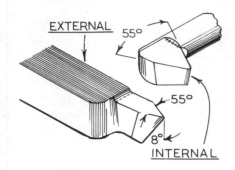

*Fig. 4.17 Screw cutting tools*

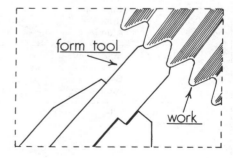

*Fig. 4.18 Screw cutting form tool*

standard thread, and a correction must also be made if the top rake is used.

*Form Tools.* Form tools are largely used in production engineering for machining components quickly and accurately to shape. The screw cutting form tool illustrated in Fig. 4.18 is taking a plunging cut directly into the work.

## Mounting Tools

It is of the greatest importance that the tool should be rigidly and securely mounted so that it will neither spring nor shift its position when cutting. For all ordinary turning and boring, the tool should be set with the cutting edge at exactly centre height. An easy way of setting the tool correctly is to take a light facing cut over the end of the work; if the tool is set too low, a central pip will be left, and if the tool is above centre a rub mark will show at the centre of the work. When the height setting of the tool is correct, it will cut freely and cleanly right up to the work centre.

## The Tool Height Gauge

The importance of setting the turning tool at centre height must always be emphasised. If one is prepared to waste time on it the correct setting can be found by trial and error. Far better, however, to use

| Table of Tool Angles | | | | |
|---|---|---|---|---|
| *Tools* | *Materials* | *Front Clearance Degrees* | *Side Clearance Degrees* | *Rake Degrees* |
| *Knife* | Mild steel | 5–10 | 5–10 | 15–25 |
| | Cast iron | 5–10 | 5–10 | 10–15 |
| | Brass | 5–10 | 5–10 | 0– 5 |
| | Aluminium | 5–10 | 5–10 | 20–30 |
| *Parting* | Mild steel | 5 | 2– 5 | 0–10 |
| | Cast iron | 5 | 2– 5 | 0–10 |
| | Brass | 5 | 2– 5 | None |
| | Aluminium | 5 | 2– 5 | 0–15 |
| *V-Tool* | Mild steel | — | 5–10 | 5–15 |
| | Cast iron | — | 5–10 | 5–10 |
| | Brass | — | 5–10 | 0– 5 |
| | Aluminium | — | 5–10 | 10–20 |
| *Boring* | Mild steel | 5° or more in bore | 5–10 | 5–15 |
| | Cast iron | | 5–10 | 5–10 |
| | Brass | | 5–10 | None |
| | Aluminium | | 5–10 | 10–15 |
| *Screw-Cutting* | All | — | Leading edge 10°. Trailing edge 5° | None |

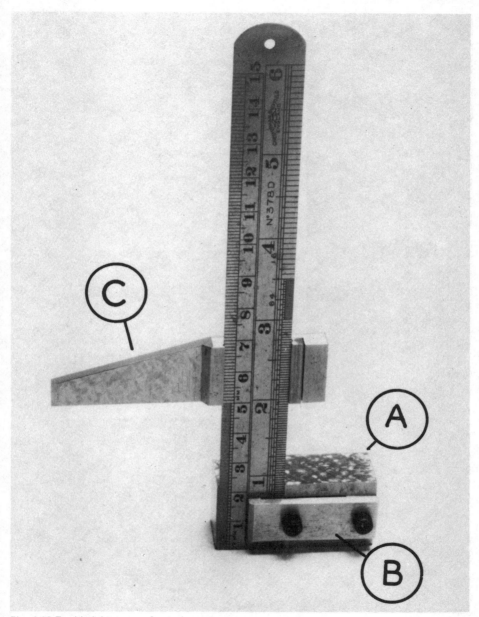

Fig. 4.19 Tool height gauge: front view

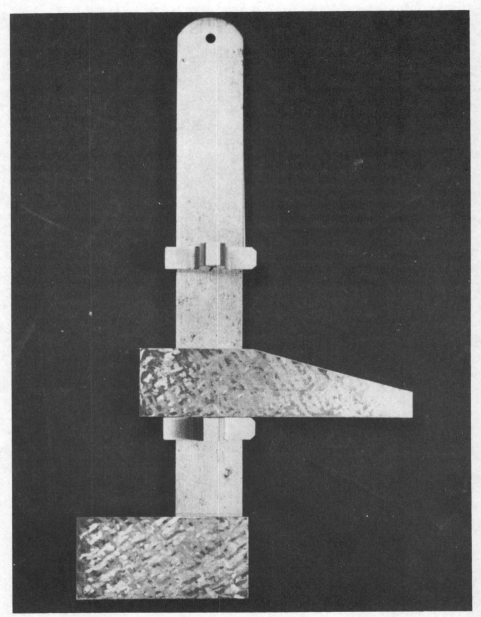

Fig. 4.20 Tool height gauge: modified

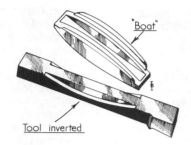

*Fig. 4.21 Myford patent lathe tools*

a simple gauge like that depicted in Fig. 4.19, for, once set, the gauge can be stood on the cross slide and the turning tool packed up until its cutting edge makes contact with the blade of the gauge.

A 6in. rule forms the basis of the device. This is set in a base (A) to which it is held by the clamp plate (B). The blade (C) can be slid up and down the rule and locked at a point representing the centre height of the lathe; the setting required can be found by reference to a lathe centre placed in the headstock spindle.

For those who have lathes of differing centre heights in the workshop the modification illustrated in Fig. 4.20 will enable the height gauge to be used on two separate lathes. The modification comprises the addition of two small clamps that can be attached to the rule and set at points enabling the blade, when brought into contact with them, to register the centre heights of the lathes involved. As shown in the illustration the gauge is set for use with the ML7 and ML10 lathes in the author's workshop.

## Quick Setting Tools

With the standard form of tool clamp, the height of the tool is adjusted by inserting

*Fig. 4.22 Myford patent lathe tools provide secure mounting*

packing strips, but there is no need for these when Myford quick-setting lathe tools are used. These tools are supplied in all the standard forms already described.

As shown in the accompanying illustration Fig. 4.21, rapid and accurate adjustment of the height setting is obtained by forming annular grooves both in the shank of the tool itself and in the boat-shaped base piece on which the tool rests.

This form of construction allows the point of the tool to be tipped either upwards or downwards, so that the cutting edge is readily set to the correct height. When the tool clamp is tightened, the large area of contact between the tool and its base will thus ensure a rigid and secure mounting for the tool. The clamping plate of the Myford tool holder rides on a spherically curved washer which serves to maintain evenly distributed clamping pressure on the tool. The adjusting screw fitted to the clamp plate is furnished with a swivelling foot that always stands upright and so does not damage the surface of the top slide.

Myford quick-setting tools, high-speed steel with welded or tungsten carbide tipped $\frac{1}{2}$in. square require the tool boat 107Z on the ML7 or Super 7; $\frac{3}{8}$in. square, high-speed steel, butt welded only, require 108Z tool boat for ML7 and Super 7. The different sets are so made that when a NEW tool is set to centre height the shank is roughly horizontal.

A criticism of the quick-setting tools

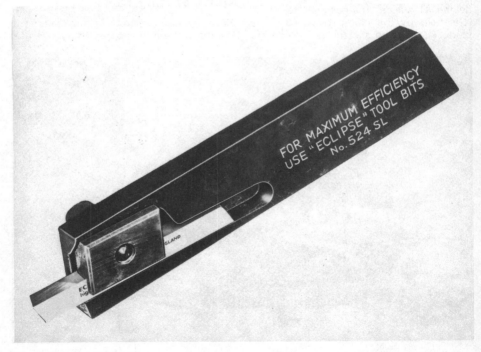

Fig. 4.23 Eclipse tool holder

has been made, that when they are re-ground the action of setting them to height alters their rake and clearance angles. If this is so it indicates that the tool has been sharpened by grinding its TOP—an alto-gether too common a practice. Not only does this weaken the tool but it also reduces the area available to conduct heat away from the tool point.

In the case of a knife tool, sharpening by grinding mostly off the front and to a lesser extent off the flank, merely licking the top will maintain angles, strength and heat-conducting area. The same remarks also apply to a V-tool where grinding the flanks and just licking the top will have the same effect.

It is worthy of note particularly for those who are newcomers to lathe work, that as supplied the quick-setting tools have correct recognised clearance and rake angles. This enables the novice user to start work immediately without having to grind a cutting tool from the solid, a practice with which he can hardly be expected to be familiar.

## Tool Holders

Tool holders are also made for holding cutters consisting of a short length of round or square high-speed steel, but these holders are apt to lack the rigidity of the solid tools already described. One advantage of using a small, removable cutter is that it can be more readily re-sharpened, as less metal has to be removed during grinding.

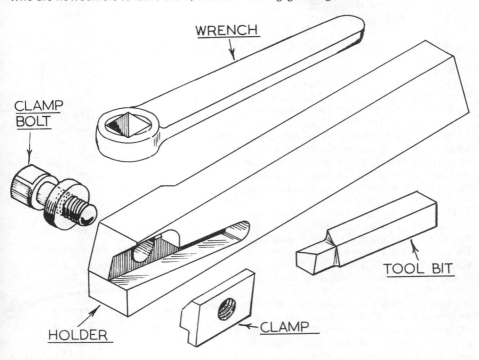

WRENCH

CLAMP BOLT

TOOL BIT

HOLDER

CLAMP

*Fig. 4.24 Exploded view of Eclipse holder*

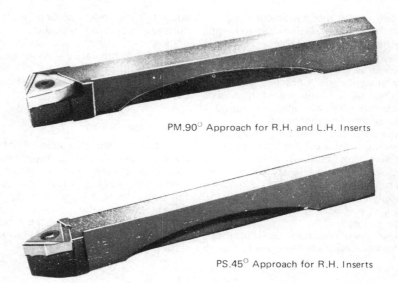

PM.90° Approach for R.H. and L.H. Inserts

PS.45° Approach for R.H. Inserts

*Fig. 4.25 Myford quick-setting tools with throw-away carbide tips*

As an example the tool holder illus-trated in Fig. 4.23 and dismantled in Fig. 4.24, the Eclipse' No. 514SL, is made by Messrs. James Neill & Co. of Sheffield and designed for lathes up to $3\frac{1}{2}$in. centres. It has a shank $\frac{5}{16}$in. by $\frac{3}{4}$in. cross section and will accommodate tool bits of $\frac{3}{16}$in. section by 2in. long. As with the 'Eclipse' parting tool holder described earlier it is of a size that can also be used in an American type toolpost.

Round boring bars, fitted with an inset cutter, are usually carried in a split holder of square section, so that they can be securely clamped in the toolpost and set with the least possible overhang.

As most turning operations need the use of more than one tool, time will be saved if the tools can be quickly changed as required. The Myford turret attachment replaces the standard form of tool clamp and will carry four tools, each of which can readily be brought into operation on slackening the clamp handle.

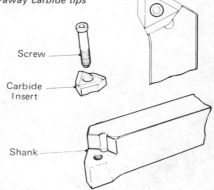

Screw

Carbide Insert

Shank

*Fig. 4.26 Tool holder has only three parts: Shank, Insert and Screw*

*Fig. 4.27 Tool Boat*

A ratchet stop mechanism, housed within the turret body, enables the individual tools to be accurately located for repetition work at any one of the right stations provided. The mechanism of the turret is fully protected against the entry of swarf and the height setting of the tools cannot be upset by chips lodging under the turret base. The attachment is fully described in Chapter 12.

The tungsten carbide tools illustrated in Fig. 4.25 have been introduced by Myford Ltd. to meet the needs of those who require equipment enabling them to machine some of the more difficult materials.

In common with the other quick-set tools obtainable from Myford Ltd. these devices are seated in a tool boat so that they can readily be set at the correct height for the turning operation.

The tool holder is provided with carbide inserts that have six separate cutting edges each ground to the correct rake and clearance angles. There are three cutting surfaces on each side of the insert which may be turned to bring a fresh edge into play when necessary. The inserts may be turned over and locked in place when one side of the insert has all its edges blunted.

As will be apparent from the illustration two forms of tool are available. The first, akin to the knife tool, has a 90 degree approach and is obtainable either right- or left-handed.

The second tool has a 45° approach and is fitted with right-hand inserts. Practical use of these carbide tools has shown that they are particularly useful when machining aluminium alloy. This material

*Fig. 4.28 Detail of Myford quick-set tool*

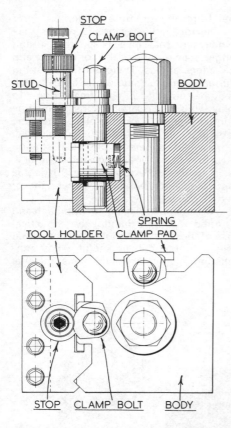

STOP
CLAMP BOLT
STUD
BODY

SPRING
TOOL HOLDER   CLAMP PAD

STOP   CLAMP BOLT   BODY

Fig. 4.29 Section and plan view of the Myford Dickson toolpost

tends to weld itself to the cutting edge of steel tools thus spoiling the finish of the work surface. This does not occur when a tungsten carbide tool is used.

## The Myford Dickson Quick Change Tool Post

There can be little doubt that rapid interchangeability of tooling is of the greatest importance when repetition work is being undertaken. Indeed interchangeability is

valuable at any time particularly when the tools themselves can be assured of being at centre height.

The Myford Dickson Quick Change Toolpost, illustrated in Fig. 4.28, has been designed to supply tooling equipment that ensures precise repeatability. It is easily fitted and reduces setting time by eliminating the need for tool packing.

Only a single bolt fixes the toolpost to the top slide whilst the height of the tool is simply adjusted by the knurled sleeve on the toolholder. The toolpost is supplied with two holders for square section tools, one boring bar holder for round section tools and one parting off holder complete with 5% Cobalt High Speed Steel Blade. In addition a pair of operating wrenches are included in the equipment.

*The Toolpost.* The toolpost itself is a steel block machined with vertical slideways that enable the tool holders to rise and fall in order to adjust tool height. The adjustment is obtained from the knurled sleeves that are provided with collars to engage corresponding grooves machined in the clamp bolts themselves. The sleeves, in some publications called the stops, rise and fall on a 2BA stud set in each tool holder. The sleeves are locked by 2BA cap screws set axially in them and abutting the outer ends of the studs in the tool holders. The latter have tenons machined in them and are shaped so that they fit into corresponding angular seatings in the toolpost where they are restrained by a clamp pad actuated by an eccentric bolt (Fig. 4.29). The toolpost is very easy to use. Setting a tool at centre height is only a matter of slackening the tool holder clamper device, then raising or lowering the tool holder till the tool point is correctly set. Thereafter the tool holder is again secured and the stop or sleeve locked. When this procedure has been followed, a tool holder may be removed or replaced in a matter of seconds with a positional error not exceeding 0·0003in.

# CHAPTER FIVE

# Sharpening Lathe Tools

FOR ACCURATE MACHINING and to produce well finished work it is essential to use properly sharpened lathe tools. Increasing feed pressure to force a blunt tool through the work can only result in bad workmanship.

In using the freehand method of grinding, with the tool applied to the wheel while supported on a flat grinding rest, care must be taken not only to grind the tool to the required angle, but also to leave a flat unbroken ground surface. When the flat side-face of the wheel is used, the tool is guided largely by touch and the angle ground is checked either by eye or by employing a gauge. Practice is required to obtain accurate grinding by this method.

If the tool is applied to the periphery of

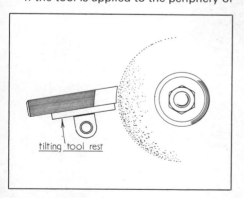

Fig. 5.1 Tool applied to the periphery of the wheel

the wheel as shown in Fig. 5.1 the ordinary form of tilting tool rest will guide the tool more accurately. The rest is tilted so that the tool points above the centre of the wheel and the setting can be varied experimentally to grind the tool face to the finished angle required.

As the face of the tool is then hollow ground it is advisable not to use a grinding wheel of small diameter, for a cutting edge formed at the meeting of two deeply concave surfaces will be lacking in strength. Remember that the grinding wheel must always run in a direction towards the finished edge of the tool.

## The Angular Grinding Rest

An easier and more accurate method of grinding a tool to an exact angle is to use a rest that can be set to the corresponding angle. Accurate grinding then becomes almost automatic, and the face of the tool is left truly flat. An adjustable angular rest, fitted to an electric tool grinder is illustrated in Figs. 5.2 and 5.3. The rest is easily set to grind to the tool angle required by means of a sheet-metal gauge of the kind shown in Figs. 5.4 and 5.5.

When using this type of rest, a narrow parting tool, for example, can be ground without difficulty, but where there is no angular guidance, the tool may not be given the proper clearance angles, and any irregularity of the ground surfaces will weaken a slender tool.

*Fig. 5.2 Angular rest*

Fig. 5.3 Angular rest

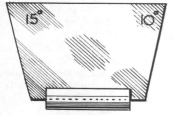

Fig. 5.4 Angle template

## Cooling the Work

In commercial practice, overheating of the tool is prevented by playing a copious, high-pressure jet of water on the grinding wheel, for a slow stream is ineffective and may even cause cracks to form in the cutting edge. Cooling the tool by dipping it in water may also cause surface cracks to appear in the metal at the thin cutting edge. Dry-grinding will give good results,

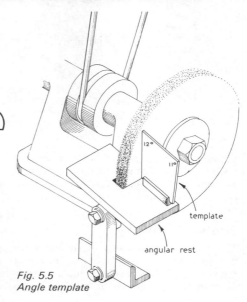

Fig. 5.5
Angle template

*Fig. 5.6 Star wheel dresser*

*Fig. 5.7 Diamond dresser*

graded for size by a screening process.

For rough-grinding small lathe tools, a grit size of from 28 to 40 is suitable, and a wheel having a finer grit of from 60 to 80 is afterwards used for finish grinding. In these wheels, the abrasive grains are incorporated in a vitrified or silicate bonding material. The tenacity of this bonding material, termed the grade, should be such that the abrasive grains are shed as they become blunted, so that fresh, sharp grains are left exposed.

## Care of Grinding Wheels

For accurate grinding, the wheel must run truly. Out-of-truth running can be corrected by trueing the wheel with a diamond tool of the kind illustrated in Fig. 5.7. This tool is supported on the grinding rest and is then carefully worked by hand in a straight line across the wheel face. After a wheel has been in use for some time, it may become glazed and cease to cut efficiently as the abrasive grains lost their sharpness.

To remove the blunted grains and expose the underlying sharp grains, the wheel is treated with a star-wheel dresser of the kind shown in Fig. 5.6.

The dresser is applied to the wheel in the same way as the diamond tool, but its action is more to clean and renew the surface of the wheel, instead of actually cutting through the abrasive grains like the diamond tool.

Sometimes, by pressing a tool too heavily against the wheel, the surface of the wheel becomes loaded with metal particles. Here, again, the surface of the wheel is renewed and its cutting properties restored by applying the star-wheel dresser.

Always see that the grinding wheel is securely mounted on the spindle, in accordance with the manufacturer's instructions, and that it is set to run at the recommended speed.

provided that the tool is holding contact with the wheel for only a short time, and that the tool is then given an interval to cool.

## Grinding Wheels

There are several well-known makes of abrasive wheels available for grinding small tools. The abrasive grains incorporated in the substance of the wheel are

Fig. 5.8 Lathe tool honing jig

Fig. 5.9 Method of clamping the jig

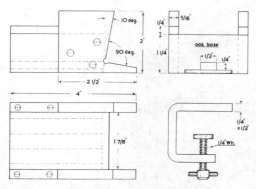

Fig. 5.10 Detail of the lathe tool honing jig

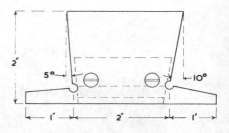

Fig. 5.11 Double-ended honing jig

## Honing Tools

After a tool has been ground, its cutting edge may still be too rough to give a high finish to turned work. An oilstone should, therefore, be used to remove any grinding burrs and to give the cutting edge a smooth keen finish. Always hold the tool flat on the stone so as not to round the edges and thereby reduce the clearance and rake angles. A useful jig for honing the end-face of the tool is illustrated in Figs. 5.8 to 5.11. The jig is clamped to the bench and, with the tool held firmly against the wooden base, the oilstone is worked to and fro across the end of the tool.

The steel side members serve as guides for the stone, and at one end are formed at an angle of 5° and at the other to 10° to suit parting tools as well as knife tools.

## Sharpening Twist Drills

Twist drills can be sharpened by freehand grinding, but to grind the two lips exactly level and precisely to the angles illustrated requires practice.

To grind a drill quickly and accurately, and without having to depend on a gauge for checking the lip angles, a drill grinding jig is usually employed. Some commercial tool grinders are equipped with a jig of this kind, or the jig may be obtained separately and fitted to an existing machine.

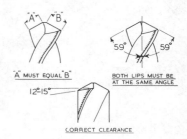

Fig. 5.12 Twist drill angles

When drilling from the lathe tailstock, a correctly ground drill should always be used; for if the two lips of the drill are not symmetrical, the drill will not follow a straight path in the work and will form an over-size hole.

# CHAPTER SIX

# Mounting Work In The Lathe

THE COMMONLY USED METHODS of mounting work in the lathe are; either in a chuck or collet, between the lathe centres, on the face plate and on the saddle. For this purpose, various accessories are employed, and these will be described together with their methods of use.

## TYPES OF CHUCKS

### The Four-Jaw Independent Chuck

As each jaw can be adjusted independently of the others, this is the most generally useful type of chuck, and it should be chosen where only a single chuck is specified for the lathe. The independent chuck is narrower in the body than the corresponding self-centring chuck, and the reduced overhang allows a comparatively large and heavy chuck to be fitted.

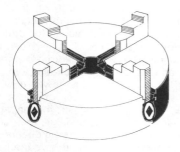

*Fig. 6.1 the 4-jaw independent chuck*

In addition, symmetrical work can readily be set to run truly in the 4-jaw chuck, and a greater gripping power is sustained, particularly when mounting irregularly shaped parts. As the jaws are reversible for inside or outside holding, only one set of jaws is needed.

### The Self-Centring Chuck

Although these chucks are sometimes manufactured with either two or four jaws, the 3-jaw pattern is by far the most useful for general work requiring the gripping of round bars and symmetrical parts. The jaws all move together when the chuck key begins to turn and normally maintain concentricity to within 0·003in. However, the self-centring chuck has not the gripping power and the wide adaptability of the independent chuck. The simultaneous movement of the jaws is effected by incorporating in the body of the chuck a hardened steel disc, rotated by a toothed pinion when the chuck key is turned. This disc bears on its front face a spiral thread or scroll that meshes with the curved teeth machined on the back of the chuck jaws. The jaws cannot be reversed owing to the curvature of the teeth, and so a second set of jaws is provided as an alternative, for gripping on the outside of large work.

Some makes of self-centring chucks have a more elaborate form of scroll to

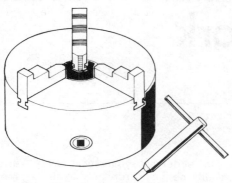

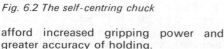

*Fig. 6.2 The self-centring chuck*

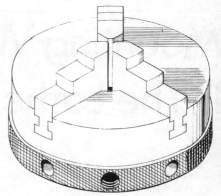

*Fig. 6.3 The lever-scroll chuck*

afford increased gripping power and greater accuracy of holding.

Instead of a square thread being formed on a flat disc, as in the previous example, a V-thread is used and the scroll is made in the form of a hollow cone.

This mode of construction allows the gripping pressure to be transmitted in a direction at right angles to the faces of the threads. In addition, to obtain greater accuracy, the V-form of thread can be finish-ground after the hardening process.

One disadvantage of this type of chuck, when fitted to a small lathe, is that the greater depth of the body necessary to accommodate the conical scroll results in increased overhang. Moreover, when turning a number of components to a constant length, it may be found necessary to locate the parts by means of stops set in the chuck body, in order to keep the work from being drawn inwards as the jaws are closed. Again, if the diameter of the work-pieces varies, the accuracy of the machining may be upset by the angular travel of the jaws.

## The Lever-Scroll Chuck

The construction of these chucks is much simplified by omitting the gear drive and, instead, the scroll is turned directly by means of a tommy bar engaging holes drilled radially in the knurled periphery. These small chucks have but little gripping power and are intended only for light work, but their rapid action and reduced overhang are an advantage for some purposes. In some makes of these chucks the jaws are made in two parts, with a base portion to engage with the scroll, and a removable gripping piece that can be reversed for inside or outside holding.

## Chucks Fitted with Soft Jaw Blanks

Manufacturers can usually supply self-centring chucks fitted with unhardened jaw blanks that can be machined in place to give exact centring at any particular setting. Owing to the difficulties in the manufacture of the scroll, the accuracy of a self-centring chuck varies for different positions of the jaws. Soft jaws can also be machined to hold work that cannot be gripped in jaws of the standard form.

When machining the jaws, they are first set to the diameter of the work-piece, and the backlash in the scroll mechanism and jaw guides is then taken up by loading the jaws in the direction of the applied grip. For this purpose, a recess is machined in the front part of the

68

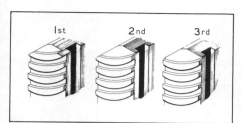

*Fig. 6.4 Changing the jaws of a self-centring chuck*

jaws to take a ring, against which the jaws are opened or closed, as the case may be, during the machining operation on the gripping surfaces of the chuck jaws.

## Changing the Jaws of a Scroll Chuck (Fig. 6.4)

Turn the key until all the jaws cease to move outwards, and after withdrawing the jaws clean them carefully and put them in a safe place away from chips. If in a new chuck the jaws are tight in their slots, they can be removed by tapping lightly with a piece of wood.

To replace the jaws:

(1) Set No. 1 slot uppermost;
(2) Turn the scroll back until the end of the thread is just clear of the slot;
(3) Insert No. 1 jaw and, if necessary, tap it tightly with a piece of wood until it bottoms on the scroll thread;
(4) Turn the scroll forward a short distance to engage the thread;
(5) Repeat for No. 2 and No. 3 jaws in that order.

## Setting Work in the Independent Chuck

When mounting irregularly-shaped parts, the work is set so that the essential portion runs truly. Grip the work lightly with all four jaws and use the rings on the chuck face as a rough guide for centring.

Rotate the lathe mandrel slowly and mark the high-spot on the work with the lathe tool or with a piece of chalk steadied against the toolpost. Release the jaw opposite to the high-spot and tighten the opposing jaw. If the high-spot lies between two jaws, correct one pair of jaws at a time. When the centring is correct, with the work supported against the chuck face, tighten all the jaws firmly.

## Accurate Centring

Mount the dial test indicator in the toolpost and, on turning the mandrel by hand, note the total run-out recorded. Next, with the indicator showing the maximum reading, adjust the chuck jaws to set the work back for a distance equal to half the total run-out. Finally, check the centring and correct any remaining error in the same way.

## Setting Off-set Work

Setting is usually carried out with reference to a centre punch mark or a drilled centre on the work surface.

Chalk the surface of the work and then scribe a circle on the rotating work with a pencil held against the toolpost. Any eccentricity of the punched centre in the scribed circles will then show in what way the chuck jaws must be adjusted to obtain true running. For greater accuracy, the setting can be checked by using a centre-finder (Fig. 6.5), which consists of a pointed rod universally pivoted at one end. When the point of the rod is engaged in the punched centre and the mandrel rotated, the far end of the rod will describe a circular path if the centring is inaccurate. Where the part has to be centred from a circle scribed on the work face, the surface gauge is placed on the lathe bed and its scriber is used as an

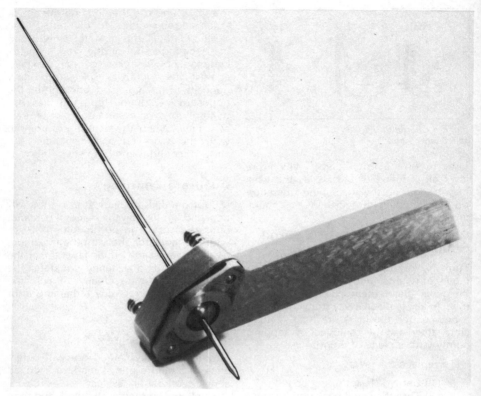

*Fig. 6.5 The centre-finder or 'wobbler'*

indicator when setting the marked circle to run truly (Fig. 6.7).

## Setting to Marked Lines

Where an arc, denoting a machining dimension, has been scribed on the work and no centre mark is present, the surface gauge is again used to set this arc to run truly. Alternatively a 'sticky pin' can be used for the same purpose.

## The Sticky Pin

The 'sticky pin' is a device well-known to the professional worker who uses it as a simple and inexpensive substitute for the scriber set in the surface gauge. It consists in nothing more than an ordinary sewing pin set in a piece of plasticene and applied to the work in hand after mounting it at some convenient point.

In the operation first described the 'sticky pin' could be attached to the turning tool in the manner illustrated.

## Centring Square Stock

This material can be quickly centred in the 4-jaw independent chuck by first centring a length of round rod having a diameter equal to the distance across the flats of the

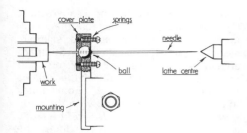

*Fig. 6.6 Using the 'wobbler'*

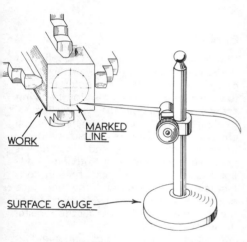

*Fig. 6.7 Setting to marked lines*

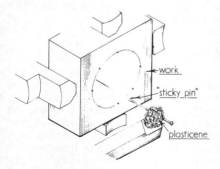

*Fig. 6.8 The 'sticky pin'*

square bar. The round rod is then released by slackening two adjacent jaws and the square bar gripped by moving the same two adjacent jaws in the reverse direction.

## Distortion

Owing to the pressure of the chuck jaws, frail work, such as rings and thin-walled cylindrical parts, may be found to be untrue when removed from the chuck after machining. When possible, therefore, grip the work by some rigid part. To avoid the work being forced back in the chuck during machining, bed the part against the body of the chuck or against the jaw faces. If necessary, place a collar or distance piece between the work and the chuck body to save having to tighten the jaws excessively.

## General

To obtain a secure hold, the work should, if possible, be gripped by the whole length of the chuck jaws. Gripping the work by the tips of the jaws throws a great strain on the jaw slots and on the actuating threads; overtightening may then make the jaws permanently bell-mouthed and useless for accurate or even safe holding.

When roughing out short pieces of large diameter material the tailstock should be used to support the workpiece. In this way much of the load engendered by the turning operation is transferred to the tail-stock thus relieving not only the chuck but the mandrel itself.

Gripping work of larger diameter than the chuck body should be avoided, as only a portion of the jaw thread is then engaged with the scroll or adjusting screw, and the end teeth may well be broken off the jaws. Rough or irregular work should not be held in the self-centring chuck, except for operations

71

requiring only a light grip; where possible provide an even gripping surface by first machining the work in the independent chuck. If the jaws are fully tightened and do not seat evenly, the chuck may be damaged. Chucks that are fitted with serrated jaws, and so have a better grip with less jaw pressure, are less susceptible to damage in this way. Never apply additional leverage to the chuck key in an attempt to increase the grip on the work.

## FITTING CHUCKS

### Method of Mounting

Chucks as usually supplied, require an adaptor or backplate for the purpose of mounting them on the mandrel nose.

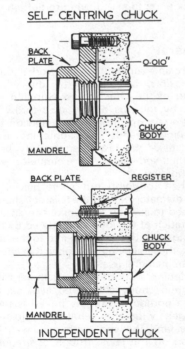

Fig. 6.9 Back for self-centring and independent chucks

A concentric register and a square back face with tapped holes enable the chuck to be accurately located and securely mounted on the backplate. Standard chucks can be obtained ready mounted on a backplate, or machined backplates can be supplied separately. Some types of chucks can be supplied with the body portion bored and threaded to fit directly on the spindle nose; this reduces the amount of overhang and allows a large independent chuck to swing in the bed gap without the jaws fouling the bed shears.

### Backplates

Chuck designs vary as to the location of the register face at the back of the body; consequently, backplates differ in form to correspond, but the holes for the fixing screws are usually in the register facing. Backplates for use with geared scroll chucks normally make contact with the outer or bolting face, and clearance is provided at the inner face. With independent and lever scroll chucks, bolting contact is as a rule made with the inner face of the body, and the outside diameter of the backplate then serves as the register diameter (Fig. 6.9).

In some forms of large independent chuck it is possible to reverse the position of the backplate flange so as to reduce the overhang of the chuck when mounted on the spindle nose.

### Fitting a Backplate

Before mounting the partly machined backplate casting on the lathe mandrel for machining the chuck seating, make sure that the spindle nose is clean and well-lubricated. Clean the threaded portion of the backplate by brushing with paraffin and, at the same time, remove any burrs.

Screw the backplate firmly on to the

nose, and check for even contact at the register face by applying marking paste. If necessary, the register face of the back-plate should be lightly scraped to obtain full contact. Machine the register diameter with a pointed knife tool to a push fit in the chuck body. Face off the register to give at least 10 thousandths of an inch bottom clearance in the recess of a chuck having an outer register or bolting face.

With the backplate still in place on the spindle, check both the register diameter and the bolting face for true running with a test indicator. Next, mark with the lathe tool the pitch circle for the holes to receive the securing screws. Remove the backplate and mark out the positions of the screws by stepping out the centres on the marked pitch circle with the dividers.

This applies to scroll chucks where the screws are inserted from the back, and the holes should be drilled to allow $\frac{1}{32}$in. clearance for the screws.

Independent chucks usually have the fixing screws inserted from the front and screwed into the backplate. Clamp the backplate in the chuck with toolmaker's clamps and then drill the backplate to a depth of $\frac{1}{16}$in. or so, with a drill fitting closely the holes in the chuck body.

Next, drill all holes to the tapping size and then tap. Before inserting the screws for the final assembly, thoroughly clean the parts and remove any burrs with a scraper to ensure that the backplate seats correctly in the chuck.

## Mounting and Removing Chucks

Before mounting a chuck, make sure that both the spindle nose and the face of the backplate are clean and free from chips and are lightly oiled.

First, if it is perchance in place, remove the tapered centre from the mandrel; then screw the chuck on to the nose and finish with a smart jerk to seat the chuck securely. Do not attempt to fit the chuck with the lathe running as this may cause serious damage to the threads or may jam the chuck on the spindle; to say nothing of physical injury to the operator that may result from the practice. To remove the chuck, hold the belt drive stationary with the left hand, and with the right pull sharply on the chuck key. If necessary, lock the lathe mandrel by engaging the backgear wheels and then pull on the chuck key or strike it with the inside of the hand. If these methods fail to loosen a tightly fitting chuck, proceed as follows:

Engage the lowest speed of the back-gear drive and free the bull wheel. Place a hardwood block on the rear bed in the path of the jaws. Pull sharply on the driving belt to turn the mandrel in the reverse direction, so as to strike the jaw against the wooden block.

When removing or replacing a chuck take great care not to damage the threads of the backplate or spindle nose.

A piece of wood placed on the lathe bed may save damage should the chuck be allowed to slip from the grasp.

## Care of Chucks

Chucks when not in use, should be protected against the entry of dust or swarf. Always stand the chuck upright on its jaws so as to stop chips from the interior falling on to the threads of the backplate.

When drilling or boring a through hole, prevent the entry of chips into the chuck mechanism by plugging the body with a piece of rag or cotton wool. If the jaws stick in their slots, they can be removed by tapping lightly with a piece of brass or wood. Sticking of the jaws indicates that the chuck needs stripping and cleaning.

Wash and brush the parts with paraffin and then apply oil or thin grease before assembly. Excess of oil tends to collect dust and chips which may clog the mechanism. As a lubricant, light grease, unlike oil, is not readily thrown out by centrifugal force at high speeds. Chuck jaws are not interchangeable; when new jaws are required, the complete chuck should be returned to the manufacturers. Never leave the key in the chuck socket, for a nasty accident might then occur if the lathe were inadvertently switched on.

## Collet Chucks

These chucks give very accurate centring of round material or the arbors of milling cutters, and the greatly reduced overhang is a further advantage. The outside of the chuck body is tapered to fit the Morse taper machined in the lathe mandrel. As the body is split, it can contract and grip the work when the chuck is pressed into the mandrel taper.

In the Myford patent collets, Figs. 6.10 and 6.11, the chucks are pressed in by means of a knurled ring that screws on to the mandrel nose. This ring engages in a groove machined in the end of the collet and enables it to be readily withdrawn. A special tubular extractor is supplied for removing the collets from the ring.

If a collet is to remain accurate, it must not be forced to hold oversize or irregular

Fig. 6.10 The Myford collet chuck

work, nor must it be contracted for more than a few thousandths of an inch below its nominal holding capacity. Although collet chucks can exert considerable gripping pressure, they should never be tightened excessively in an attempt to prevent slip.

When fitting these chucks, it is important to clean both the outside of the body and the internal bore, as well as the mandrel taper.

Once a collet has been strained or damaged by misuse, it can no longer be relied on to hold accurately.

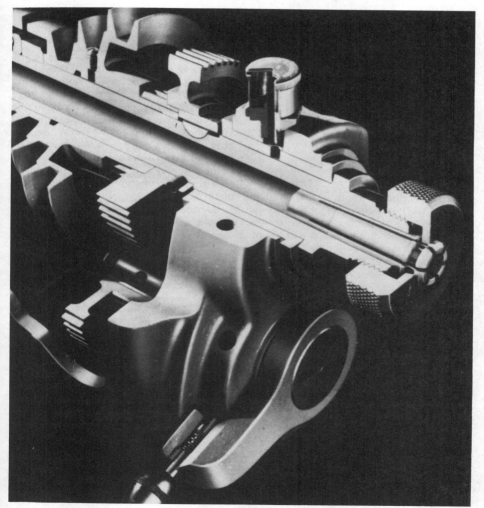

*Fig. 6.11a The Myford collet chuck in place*

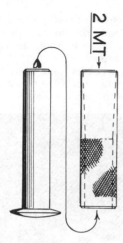

*Fig. 6.11b The collet closer*

## Collet Closer

The collet closer, which is depicted in Fig. 6.11b, has been designed to assist the user to insert, and remove, collets from the closing ring supplied with them. It consists of two parts; a tube having the same taper bore as the lathe mandrel and an extractor to eject the collet from the tube.

To use the device when placing a collet in the closing ring; set a collet in the tube, thread the ring over the collet then eject it from the tube leaving the collet in place. To remove the collet from the ring push the tube over the collet, withdraw the closing ring then push the collet out of the tube.

The device is seen in use in Fig. 6.11a.

For Myford lathes having a No. 2 Morse taper mandrel, standard collets are supplied with a holding capacity ranging from $\frac{1}{16}$in. to $\frac{1}{2}$in.

## Drill Chucks

Drilling a work-piece held in the lathe mandrel chuck can readily be carried out when the drill is held in a drill chuck fitted to the tailstock. For this work, a key chuck having a capacity up to $\frac{1}{2}$in. will hold the drill securely and with the necessary accuracy. The chuck is mounted on a tapered arbor fitting the tapered bore of the tailstock barrel.

## The Jacobs Chuck

In the past there has been a number of chucks designed for holding drills in the tailstock or elsewhere. Most of these have gone out of production leaving only the chuck illustrated in Fig. 6.12 at the head of the list. The Jacobs chuck is obtainable in several sizes notably with capacities of $\frac{3}{8}$in. and $\frac{1}{2}$in. maximum. Many Jacobs chucks are designed for a minimum holding capacity of zero and all are of the highest quality and accuracy, a characteristic that few of their competitors could claim.

Jacobs chucks are fitted on taper shanks made to close limits by the firm themselves, so purchasers should employ

*Fig. 6.12 The Jacobs chuck*

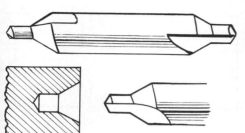

*Fig. 6.13 Action of the centre drill*

these fitments when using these chucks in the lathe or drilling machine.

## Mounting Work between the Lathe Centres

To support the work, a mounting centre is first drilled at either end, and these two centres must be in line to ensure accurate machining of the part. The centre should be drilled with a centre drill so as to form

seatings with an included angle of 60° to match the conical lathe centres. The hole formed by the pilot portion of the centre drill affords clearance for the actual point of the lathe centre, and also forms a small oil reservoir (Fig. 6.13).

Centre the work in the chuck and face the end square. Mount the centre drill in the tailstock drill chuck and, with the lathe running at high speed, drill the centre to the required depth.

If the work projects so far from the chuck that its outer end lacks rigidity, the fixed steady should be used to afford additional support; this will also relieve the strain on the mandrel bearings (Fig. 6.14). The method of using the steady is described in the section on General Turning, Chapter 7.

The removable mandrel centre is unhardened, and, if the point is worn or runs out of truth, the coned portion can be remachined by setting over the topslide

*Fig. 6.14 Using the fixed steady when centre drilling*

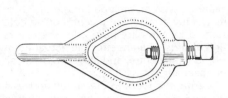

Fig. 6.15 The lathe carrier

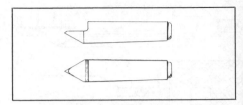

Fig. 6.17 The half-centre

to an angle of 30° with the lathe axis. For this purpose, run the lathe at high speed and use a pointed tool set at exactly lathe centre height.

The tailstock centre is hardened and when worn, must be reground in a machine. Always clean the centres and their tapered housings before fitting. The work mounted between centres is driven by a carrier (Fig. 6.15) attached at the end next the mandrel. To prevent the carrier slipping—an important point when screw cutting—a small flat can be filed on the work to give a bearing for the carrier clamp screw.

Mount the catch plate on the mandrel

Fig. 6.16 Securing the lathe carrier

nose, and set the driving dog to engage the tail of the carrier. If the carrier tends to knock against the driving dog during machining, bind the two together with a loop of wire or cord (Fig. 6.16).

Before starting the turning operation, oil the back centre and adjust it to allow the work to revolve freely but without shake. Readjust the centre from time to time to take up wear, or to allow for expansion as the work becomes heated. If the point of the tool is obstructed by the ordinary pattern of tailstock centre when turning work of small diameter, a so-called half-centre should be fitted. This centre is formed with a flat on the coned end, so that the tool can be fed inwards nearly to the centre line (Fig. 6.17).

## Mounting Work on the Faceplate

The faceplate supplied with the lathe is accurately fitted to the mandrel and is machined to run truly. If there is any doubt as to the true running, this can be readily checked with a test indicator. Should the surface of the faceplate have to be trued at any time, a light cut can be taken with a tungsten carbide tipped tool while the lathe is running on the slow, direct speed.

Before deciding that remachining is necessary, carefully examine the mating surfaces of the mandrel nose and the faceplate bore. Clean the threads and the register surfaces carefully to remove

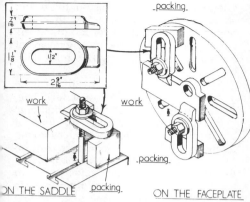

*Fig. 6.18 Myford faceplate clamps*

## Attaching the Work to the Faceplate

To prevent rocking and possible shifting of the work during machining, it is important that the work face applied to the faceplate should be quite flat. The most convenient way of mounting the work is to use bolts passing right through both the component and the faceplate slots. The projecting bolt ends carrying the nuts should be behind the faceplate so as not to interfere with the machining operations. When direct bolting is not possible, the work may be secured by means of clamps or faceplate dogs. These clamps are supplied in sets of four as a standard accessory for the Myford lathe (Fig. 6.18). A piece of thin card or blotting paper placed between the work and the faceplate will give a more secure fixing. Do not tighten the clamp bolts excessively, for the faceplate may then be distorted if the work is not quite flat.

any particles of swarf. Remove with a scraper, or a fine file, any burrs that may have been set up by misuse or by careless handling. When the faceplate has been refitted on the mandrel, check the running again with the test indicator.

*Fig. 6.19 Faceplate clamps*

Faceplate clamps of the plain type need packing to elevate them so that they lie parallel with the work. It is possible however, to devise a faceplate dog or clamp that is adjustable and so dispenses with packing.

This clamp is illustrated in Fig. 6.19 alongside the standard Myford product. The adjustment is provided by a hexagon headed screw that makes contact with the surface of the faceplate. Note that it is the *head* of the screw that makes contact. If the point is used the faceplate may be indented.

The bolting face of some components lies at right-angles to the surface to be machined; for example, when boring the gudgeon pin holes in a piston, the piston stands on end. An angle plate is, therefore, bolted to the faceplate for mounting the component, and it is secured by means of a clamping plate held by two bolts (Fig. 6.20).

Some work-pieces are of too delicate a nature to be secured to a faceplate, for example, without some additional help. This commonly takes the form of blocks or strips that are themselves bolted firmly to the faceplate, and that abut on the work so that they take up the thrust of the tool. This procedure avoids having to exert a bolting force that might otherwise distort a fragile work-piece.

Angle plates are supplied as accessories

*Fig. 6.20 Boring gudgeon pin seatings*

*Fig. 6.21 Balancing work on the Faceplate*

*Fig. 6.22 Securing the work to the boring table*

in three sizes, and one of these is specially designed for use on the faceplate. For mounting large work in this way, the special 9in. diameter faceplate may be found necessary.

## Setting the Work

As described in connection with the independent chuck, the work can be centred from a punch mark, or from a centre drilled hole, by using a centre-finder. A part can also be set to run truly by applying the test indicator to an external or an internal machined surface.

## Balancing the Work

After the part has been securely bolted in place, and before machining is started, the work should be balanced if it is of irregular shape or is set off centre.

The driving belt is slackened so that the mandrel can turn freely to allow the heaviest part of the work to settle downwards.

A counterweight, such as a lathe change wheel, is then bolted at the top of the faceplate Fig. 6.21. The amount or the position of the weight is altered until the faceplate on being spun shows no tendency to stop in any one position.

Where the work revolves at high speed, correct balancing is essential for accurate machining and this also relieves the load on the mandrel bearings.

## Mounting Work on the Lathe Saddle

When the lathe top slide has been removed, the cross slide forms a large, T-slotted boring table on which work can be mounted for machining (Fig. 6.22).

The work is usually clamped to the cross slide by means of T-headed bolts

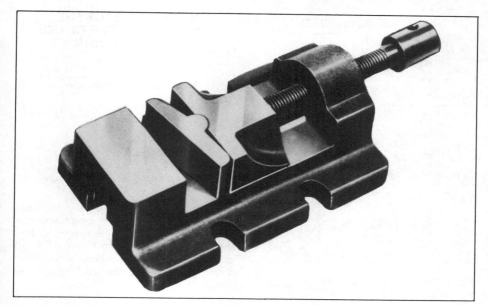

*Fig. 6.23 The Myford machine vice*

engaging in the table T-slots. T-bolts, either 3in. or 6in. in length, are supplied in sets of four as standard accessories. For mounting large work, a bridge-piece or clamping plate may be needed to span the part, but the clamp nuts must then not be too heavily tightened or the unsupported T-slots may be damaged or the work distorted.

Small work can be readily held in the Myford machine vice (Fig. 6.23) which is designed for bolting to the cross slide.

This vice has jaws $1\frac{5}{8}$in. in width and $\frac{3}{4}$in. deep, and it can also be mounted on the lathe faceplate or on the vertical slide. Work can also be set up on an angle plate bolted to the cross slide, in the way described for the faceplate.

The vertical slide is largely used for mounting work on the lathe cross slide, and a height adjustment and feed is then obtained in addition to the two horizontal settings given by the cross slide and leadscrew feeds. A full description of setting up and using the vertical slide is given in the section on milling in the lathe.

## Errors in the Use of the Self-Centring Chuck

It may not be out of place to draw attention to certain faults that may occur when a self-centring chuck is used. The first of these errors is illustrated at (A) in Fig. 6.24. If a narrow component such as a cylinder cover is gripped by the small spigot machined upon it the jaws of the chuck will tend to be tipped, and in time, strained out of square if the practice is repeated.

Instead, a ring of the same diameter as the spigot is placed toward the back of the chuck jaws so that, when the jaws are closed on the work, they will not be pulled out of square.

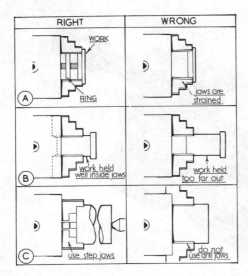

| RIGHT | WRONG |
|---|---|

Fig. 6.24 Errors in the use of the
self-centring chuck

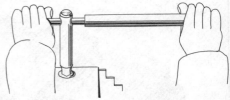

Fig. 6.25 A cardinal fault in chuck usage

Finally do not be tempted to increase leverage of the chuck key by means of a piece of tube placed over the cross bar. The practice depicted in Fig. 6.25 is all too prevalent in industry and is a certain recipe for damaging the accuracy of the chuck.

The second fault is depicted at (B). This should be self-evident. If the work is held in the way shown, the chuck jaws will again be strained, so to avoid this, make sure that the work is gripped by as much jaw surface as possible.

The third error concerns the use of the inside jaws for holding large diameter components or stock. If the procedure adopted at (C) is followed, the number of threads at the back of the jaws in contact with the chuck scroll can be reduced to a point where there is a real danger of the jaw threads being strained or even torn out. Instead, use the step jaws and support the work by the tail-stock.

## Aligning and Centring the Work

The face of the work is set vertical by means of a try-square resting on the lathe bed or cross slide. The work is aligned squarely across the lathe axis by setting the work face against a rule or parallel strip held in contact with the face of the chuck or faceplate. Both these settings can be readily checked with the test indicator mounted in the mandrel chuck. A punch mark formed on the work surface can be centred with reference to a pointed rod held in the lathe chuck. A bored hole or an external machined surface is readily set to run true by mounting the test indicator in the chuck and then rotating the mandrel by hand.

# CHAPTER SEVEN

# General Turning, Drilling & Boring In The Lathe

THE TOOLS USED for ordinary turning operations were described in Chapter 5, and the various ways of mounting the work in the lathe were dealt with in Chapter 7.

The methods employed when machining a short shaft held in the chuck will serve as an example of ordinary turning practice. If the work is mounted in the chuck with considerable overhang, or if it is of slender form, additional support should be provided by engaging the tailstock centre, otherwise the cutting pressure may spring the work and cause chatter and irregular machining.

## Centre Drilling the Work

A bearing for the tailstock centre is formed by having a centre drill mounted in the tailstock drill chuck Fig. 7.1. Where the diameter of a part held in the chuck has

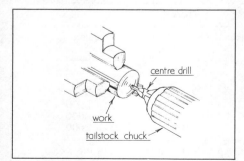

*Fig. 7.1 Centre drilling the work*

to be reduced, the usual practice is first to face the end of the work, so that the tool will engage smoothly when traversing cuts are taken along the work surface. If a right-hand knife tool is used, this will serve for both the facing and the surface turning operations.

Not only must this tool be properly ground and have a sharp cutting edge, but it should be mounted in the toolpost at the height of the lathe centre. The tool is, therefore, set as nearly as can be judged at the correct height, and a light facing cut is taken across the end of the work; this will show at once if the cutting edge of the tool is at centre height, for if the edge is either above or below centre, a pip or projection will be left at the centre of the work. It must now be decided at what speed the lathe should be run, at what rate the tool should be traversed along the work; and what depth of cut should be taken.

## Turning Speeds

The lathe should be run to give the correct surface speed for the particular piece of work being machined, cutting speeds are expressed in feet per minute, measured at the work surface. For example, if the work is 2in. in diameter, the surface or circumference will measure approximately 6in. or $\frac{1}{2}$ft, so that where the lathe speed is 100r.p.m. the surface speed of the work will be 50ft per minute.

Not only does the appropriate cutting speed vary with the kind of material being machined, but this speed will also, in part, depend on the material of which the tool is made. The following table sets out the cutting speeds for the metals in common use:

The standard Myford lathe has six mandrel speeds, ranging from 35r.p.m. to 640r.p.m. and these will cover all ordinary workshop requirements, but variations of this range are available where specially ordered.

For most purposes, where the exact calculated speed is not included in the standard form of drive, the next lowest speed should be used.

It will be noticed that the speed for machining steel with tungsten carbide tools has not been given; the reason for this omission is that, although these tools will take heavy cuts in this material, when fine cuts are taken, the cutting edge is apt to be cratered and fractured owing to the affinity tungsten carbide has for steel.

## Rate of Traverse

In the Myford lathe, the leadscrew, when rotated by the train of change wheels (Fig. 7.2), is used to traverse the saddle on closing the leadscrew clasp-nut. The finest feed obtainable with the standard set of change wheels, is 0·0037in. for each revolution of the leadscrew, but if an extra wheel, having 95 teeth, is fitted to the lathe quadrant, a still finer feed of 0·0025in. can be obtained.

## Fine Feed Tumbler Gear

The Tumbler Gear illustrated in Fig. 7.3 is applicable to the ML7 only. The similar gear for the Super 7 and ML7R lathes has 30 and 12 teeth.

## MYFORD FINE FEED TUMBLER CLUSTER

This fitment is an immediate replacement for the standard cluster gear on the tumbler reverse pin. It comprises a pair of gears machined from a single piece of material and will provide fine feeds down to 0·0018in. for each revolution of the headstock spindle.

These very fine feeds are used where a part, such as a small crankshaft, has to be machined to a high finish, with a tool having a narrow cutting edge, so as not to spring the work.

When roughing out work a coarser

| Maximum Cutting Speeds in Feet per Minute | | | |
|---|---|---|---|
| Materials | Tools | | |
| | Carbon Steel | H.S. Steel | Tungsten Carbide |
| Mild steel | 50 | 100 | — |
| Carbon steel | 25 | 50 | — |
| Cast iron | 30 | 60 | Up to 400 |
| Bronze | 60 | 120 | Up to 1,000 |
| Brass | 100 | 200 | Up to 1,000 |
| Aluminium | 150 | 300 | Up to 1,000 |

To apply the table, divide the cutting speed by the circumference of the work measured in feet; this gives the lathe speed.

*Fig. 7.2 Clasp-nut lever*

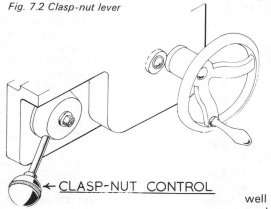

← <u>CLASP-NUT CONTROL</u>

| 12 TEETH | 25 TEETH |

*Fig. 7.3 Myford fine feed tumbler gear for ML7 lathe*

feed can be used, but the surface will, as a rule, then be less well finished, and a finer rate of feed may be required for the finishing cut.

The fine feed cluster may also be used with Myford Lathes that are fitted with a gearbox. It must be emphasised, however, that this practice naturally alters the effective feeds and these will not be as indicated on the gearbox.

At this point it may not be out-of-place to remind readers that no thread pitch should be attempted that is coarser than the pitch of the lead screw namely 8 to the inch. If such a procedure is anticipated it should be remembered that this involves the lead screw rotating faster than the lathe mandrel with the possibility of damage to the change wheels and their attendant mechanism.

## Depth of Cut

To save the trouble of altering the arrangement of the gear wheels, a fine or moderately fine feed can be used for all general turning, and the rate of cutting is then speeded up by merely increasing the depth of cut taken. Although the Myford lathe is of very rigid construction, and is well adapted for taking heavy cuts, the work itself may not be sufficiently rigid to withstand the strain, and irregular machining with poor finish may result. However, where the work is held in the chuck, the rigidity of the mounting can be greatly increased by engaging the tailstock centre; moreover this will also relieve the lathe mandrel bearings of much unnecessary strain when heavy cuts are taken. On the whole it is better to take moderately deep cuts of 40 to 60 thousandths of an inch in steel, and to finish the surface with a light cut of only a few thousandths of an inch in depth. In addition, when machining steel, the tool will cut more freely, and a better surface finish will be obtained if a plentiful supply of cutting oil is fed to the tool by means of either coolant equipment, a drip-can or a brush.

Where the work has to be turned to an exact diameter, reference to the graduated index fitted to the feedscrew of the cross slide will be found a great help.

After a preliminary cut has been taken, the diameter of the work is measured with a micrometer to ascertain how much surplus metal has to be removed; half this figure in thousandths of an inch, added to the reading on the index will then show what the final index reading should be to finish the work to size.

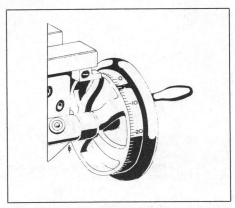

*Fig. 7.4 Leadscrew index wheel*

## Turning to Length

Where, for example, a shoulder has to be turned at an exact distance from the end of the work, the leadscrew index will be found of great value, both in saving time and in ensuring accuracy. (Fig. 7.4).

## Leadscrew Index (1430)

The leadscrew index illustrated is graduated in thousandths of an inch, and can be fitted as a standard accessory to the Myford lathe.

To traverse the tool for an exact distance along the work, the leadscrew, with the clasp-nut engaged, is turned to bring the index to its zero position, and the end of the work is then faced by using the stop slide to put on the cut. The saddle can now be backed away by turning the leadscrew and, after the cut has been adjusted, the automatic feed is employed to traverse the saddle. Meanwhile, the revolutions of the leadscrew handle are counted, allowing $\frac{1}{8}$in. for each turn, and when the leadscrew index registers the number of thousandths of an inch required to complete the length of the cut, the feed is disengaged.

After the saddle has been moved to the right to clear the work, the feed is reset, and the machining is continued until the shoulder has been formed to the full depth required. It is advisable to stop the preliminary cuts a little short of the finished length, so that the shoulder can be machined truly flat and square by taking a final facing cut.

## Machining Work Between Centres

The method of preparing and mounting the work is described in Chapter 7. If the work is long or slender, and is liable to spring away from the tool, the depth of cut must be reduced, and a tool with a narrow cutting edge should be employed. Should the work spring during machining, it will not be finished parallel.

Springing can be checked by using the travelling steady (Fig. 7.5) so as to give continuous support to the work close to the tool. When the end of the work next the tailstock centre has been turned for a short distance to run true, the pads of the steady are brought into contact with the turned surface immediately behind the tool. If the steady bears on the work where it runs out of true, the work as a whole will be inaccurately machined. After each passage of the tool over the work, the steady must be reset and, at the same time, the setting of the tailstock should be adjusted to allow for wear and for heating of the work causing expansion.

Until the work has been machined to run truly, it is advisable to lock the cross slide during the passage of the tool.

## Machining the End of Long Work

When drilling the end of a long shaft with a centre drill to form a bearing for the tailstock centre, the end of the work must first be faced square.

Fig. 7.5 Travelling steady in use

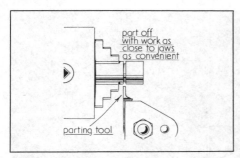

part off with work as close to jaws as convenient

parting tool

*Fig. 7.6 Parting off*

To support the overhanging end of the shaft during machining the fixed steady is secured to the lathe bed and the pressure pads are adjusted to bear evenly on the work, and without deflecting it from the lathe axis. Keep the pads well oiled to prevent scoring of the work.

The fixed steady is also used in the same way when drilling and tapping a long shaft, gripped and truly centred at its other end in the 4-jaw chuck.

## Parting off

With a rigidly constructed lathe, and a properly ground tool, parting off offers a quick and easy method of cutting off parts to length while the material is held in the chuck. The Myford quick-setting parting tool will be found most convenient in use, as the cutting edge can be so readily set to the correct heights, and in addition, the tool mounting is very rigid. Suitable lengths of high-speed steel, ground to shape and ready for use, can also be obtained from the tool merchant; these tools in the smaller sizes have a cutting edge only $\frac{1}{16}$in. in width to afford easy penetration into the work.

When using the parting tool, in order to gain rigidity, the work should be set to project as little as possible beyond the chuck jaws (Fig. 7.6).

The cutting edge is set at exactly centre height, and the tool is aligned parallel with the face of the chuck.

The tool will cut more freely if a top rake of some 10° is used when machining steel, but for brass top rake should be omitted, to save the tool from digging into the work.

The lathe may be run at the speed appropriate for the diameter of the work-piece, as in ordinary turning, but if chatter develops the mandrel speed should be reduced until a continuous coiled shaving is produced. Plenty of cutting oil should be fed to steel parts with a small brush.

The speed reduction should only be to the next lower speed. If chatter still persists the tool grinding and setting should be checked. If no cure is then effected examine the lathe spindle for end-float and slackness in the journals; the slides should also be examined and adjusted if play is found.

It is probably worthwhile reminding readers that, to part off successfully, the tool feed must be continuous and firm.

In the event of the tool digging in and jamming in the work, the tool clamp should be slackened and the tool carefully withdrawn, for if, following a jam, the lathe mandrel is turned backwards by hand, the tip of the tool may be broken.

## THE MYFORD BACK TOOLPOST NO. 1468 AND LONG CROSS SLIDE NO. 1467

Parting off is considerably eased if the tool is mounted at the back of the lathe upside down. The loads imposed by the operation of parting off are then reversed and the angular faces of the cross slide and saddle forced into more intimate contact so eliminating, or at least reducing, possibility of chatter.

The Myford Back Toolpost No. 1468 illustrated in Fig. 7.7 has been designed for such a purpose. It comprises a solid

*Fig. 7.7 The Myford back tool post No. 1468 mounted on the long cross slide No. 1467*

block of mild steel having a tenon machined on its underside to engage one of the T-slots of the cross slide. A simple long bolt holds the toolpost in place whilst a pair of square headed sets screw secure the parting tool itself.

The tool itself sits on a 'boat' having a curved underside that fits a correspondingly curved slot, machined in the body of the toolpost. The boat is thus capable of rocking in either direction to depress or elevate the point of the parting tool until this has been set at centre height.

While the Myford back toolpost can be used with the standard cross slide, it is best mounted on the Long Cross Slide No. 1467 seen in the illustration. In this way more room is available between the top slide and back toolpost, as well as between any tools mounted in them.

## Drilling in the Lathe

Drilling in the lathe can be carried out with the drill either held in the headstock chuck or mounted in the tailstock drill chuck.

## Drilling from the Headstock

When the drill is gripped in the self-centring chuck, the concentricity may not

*Fig. 7.8 Drilling on the saddle*

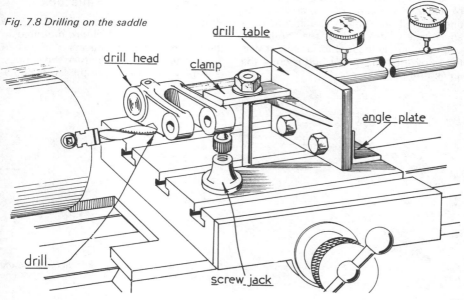

drill table

drill head

clamp

angle plate

drill

screw jack

be sufficiently exact for really accurate work, and in this event the 4-jaw chuck should be used to enable the drill to be correctly set. However, the mandrel collet chucks, previously described, will not only ensure sufficiently accurate centring, but the small size of the fitting and the reduced overhang will be found an additional advantage. Drills, mounted in this way, can be used to bore holes in components secured to the lathe saddle in the manner previously described, and the work can then be fed to the drill by traversing the saddle with the leadscrew handwheel (Fig. 7.8).

The operation illustrated is an actual example and is the set up used some years ago when machining the head casting of the *Model Engineer* Drilling Machine.

The work was located on the column of the drilling machine itself, the column being secured to the machine's work table by an angle plate that had been previously machined for the purpose.

Alignment was checked, as may be observed, by means of a dial indicator, and vertical adjustment carried out by a small screw jack. When the work had been accurately located for drilling it was held down by the T-slot bolt seen in the illustration.

The more usual way of drilling from the headstock is to support the work against the tailstock, so that the tailstock feed can be used for feeding the work to the drill. For this purpose, the work can be supported by a drilling pad carried on a tapered arbor fitting into the tailstock barrel. These pads, as shown in the illustration, (Fig. 7.9) are made in two patterns; the one flat faced for ordinary work, and the other machined with a V-slot for centring round material on the drilling axis. When a heavy part is being drilled against a flat-faced pad, it is advisable to support the work on a packing block standing on the lathe bed; otherwise, the component may slip downwards and throw the drill hole out of line (Fig. 7.10).

In this kind of drilling, the lathe is really doing the work of a drilling machine, but the drilling machine has the advantage that on its horizontal table heavy work does not tend to become displaced.

## Drilling from the Tailstock

When using this method of drilling, the drill is held in a drill chuck mounted in the tailstock barrel by means of a tapered arbor. The holding capacity of the chucks, is usually $\frac{3}{8}$in. or $\frac{1}{2}$in., but the larger chuck

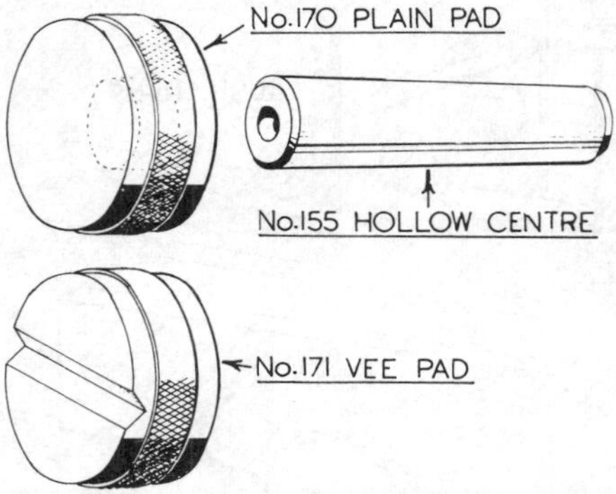

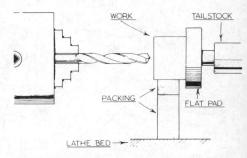

Fig. 7.9 Hollow centre E155 drill pads E170, E171

Fig. 7.10 Drilling work supported against the flat pad

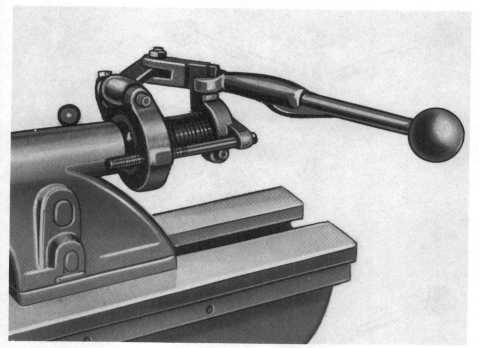

*Fig. 7.11 Lever tailstock attachment No. 1440*

is the more useful. A typical example of this mode of drilling, is drilling axially a length of rod held in the mandrel chuck when making small bushes, collars, or washers, and here, again, the Myford mandrel collet chucks will be found particularly convenient when machining a batch of small parts.

Although, for ordinary work, the drill can quite well be fed forward by means of the tailstock barrel screw, the lever operated tailstock attachment illustrated in Fig. 7.11 will be found an advantage for repetition work, or where sensitive feed for small drills is required, together with an adjustable stop for setting the depth of the drilling. Sometimes difficulty is experienced in drilling a hole truly central and in alignment with the axis of

the work, but this need not be so if the operation is carried out methodically. In the first place, a centre drill is used to form a true start for the cutting lips of the drill, and if, in addition, the centre drill has an $\frac{1}{8}$in. diameter pilot, this will drill a true-running guide hole for a pilot drill. This pilot drill of $\frac{1}{8}$in. diameter is then entered in the work for the full distance required. If a large hole is being drilled, one or more additional pilot drills may be used before the sizing drill is finally entered.

For drill of $\frac{1}{4}$in. in diameter, or less, the lathe should be run at its fastest speed, as this will help the drill both to cut freely, and to maintain a straight path in the work. For accurate drilling, the drill must be sharp and the lips must be correctly ground.

Fig. 7.12 The Cowell lever feed tailstock

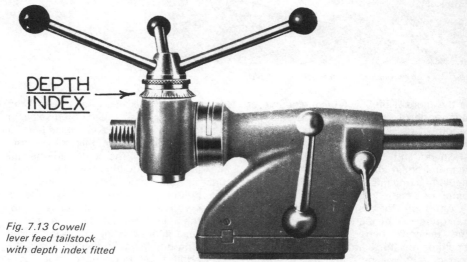

DEPTH
INDEX

Fig. 7.13 Cowell
lever feed tailstock
with depth index fitted

## THE COWELL LEVER FEED TAILSTOCK ATTACHMENT

E. W. Cowell of Watford have, for many years now, made a lever feed tailstock attachment for the Myford ML7 lathe.

The device illustrated in Fig. 7.12. Early models, of which this is an example, had no depth gauge dial, but later and present production includes an adjustable index collar fitted around the hub to which the feed levers are attached (Fig. 7.13).

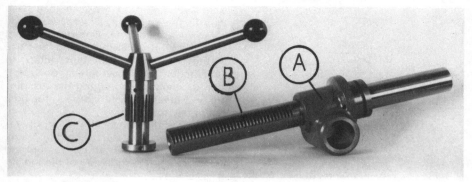

*Fig. 7.14 Cowell lever feed tailstock; the component parts*

The attachment is designed to be an immediate replacement for the mechanism of the standard ML7 tailstock. All that is needed, when fitting the device, is to remove the existing tailstock barrel, hand wheel and thrust plate and replace them by the individual parts seen in the illustration Fig. 7.14, these comprise the gear box (A), the tailstock barrel (B) and the feed lever and gear assembly (C). The gearbox is retained in place by the thrust plate supplied by Myford and is retained in the correct radial location by a special long headless screw passing through the gearbox casting into an appropriate existing tapped hole in the tailstock body itself.

The feed levers are attached to a hub on which gear teeth are machined. These engage a corresponding rack cut on the

tailstock barrel itself. The hub is located endwise by the screwed collar seen at its lower end.

## Boring in the Lathe

For this purpose, the work is either held in the mandrel chuck or is secured to the boring table of the lathe saddle.

## Boring Work in the Chuck

Where a bore has to be machined in a solid piece of material held in the chuck, the surplus metal should first be removed by drilling from the tailstock. Although a correctly centred hole may be drilled in this way, it is advisable to leave some two thousandths of an inch, or more, of surplus metal for removal by the boring tool that follows. To keep chips out of the internal working parts of the chuck when the bore is carried right through the component, the bore of the chuck should be carefully packed with rag or cotton wool before the work is mounted in place.

The type of boring tool selected will depend partly on the size of the bore, and also on its depth, but boring tools suitable for all ordinary work have already been described.

The cutting edge of the boring tool

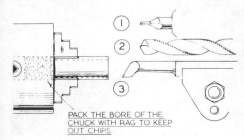

PACK THE BORE OF THE CHUCK WITH RAG TO KEEP OUT CHIPS

*Fig. 7.15 Boring work in the chuck*

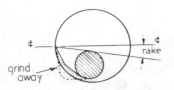

Fig. 7.16 Setting the boring tool (providing clearance)

should be set at centre height, so that the tool has proper clearance and can cut freely (Fig. 7.16).

Where a slender tool is used for machining small or deep bores, the tool should be mounted with the least pos-

sible overhang, and the feed may have to be increased by only a few thousandths of an inch at a time, in order to avoid chatter and irregular machining. The use of the cross slide feed screw index, in conjunction with micrometer or caliper measurements taken during the machining, will greatly assist in forming the bore accurately to size.

Towards the end of the sizing operation, only very light cuts should be taken, in order to reduce the cutting pressure and thereby eliminate springing of the tool.

## Boring Work on the Faceplate

It is not always possible to hold work in the chuck for boring purposes. For one thing, the very shape of the work itself

Fig. 7.17 Boring a connecting rod on the faceplate

may preclude such a thing, for another a chuck mounting may not be sufficiently accurate for the work in hand.

Take the connecting rod depicted in Fig. 7.17 for example. This was a built-up component needing both eyes to be machined parallel so each was bored in turn with the work bolted to the faceplate and clamped against packing that will ensure the work remaining square.

A weight placed opposite the work was used to ensure the work rotated in balance; this has been removed when photographing the set up.

## General Turning, etc.

The component illustrated in Fig. 7.18 is another example of a component that

*Fig. 7.18 An automobile steering arm*

could only be mounted on a faceplate.

The part, a steering arm from a small racing car, was secured to the faceplate in the manner depicted in Fig. 7.19.

In both illustrations (Figs. 7.17 and 7.19) notice that bolt heads only face towards the operator. This ensures that no projection could interfere with the placing of the boring tool itself or come foul of the topslide.

*Fig. 7.19 The steering arm set up on the faceplate for boring*

## Boring Work on the Lathe Saddle

When the work is secured to the lathe boring table, as described in the previous chapter, boring and facing operations can be carried out with a short boring bar, or boring head, mounted on the lathe mandrel. This method has to be used where the bore does not run right through the component, and the tailstock cannot, therefore, be used to give additional support to the tool. When, for example, boring an open-ended cylinder secured to the boring table, a boring bar can be mounted between the lathe centres, and the cutter is then set at the correct radius to machine the bore to the required diameter.

The Myford boring bar illustrated Fig. 7.20 is supplied with three cutters of different lengths, to enable the cutting radius to be varied over a wide range.

When the boring bar is mounted between the lathe centres, a lathe carrier of the type previously illustrated, is secured to one end of the bar, and is driven by the dog attached to the mandrel catch plate. After the work-piece has been finally located, the lathe cross slide must be locked to prevent any movement of the slide during machining.

For the actual machining operation, the tool is set to take a cut of moderate depth, but if the work-piece consists of an iron or bronze casting, the tool should be adjusted to cut well below the hard surface skin, or the cutting edge may quickly become blunted. The surface speed, taken at the cutting edge of the tool, will, as in ordinary turning, depend

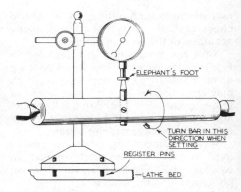

Fig. 7.21 Using the dial indicator to set the cutter

both on the nature of the material and on the size of the bore, but until the whole surface has been tooled, a slow speed is advisable to keep the tool from jumping when meeting surface irregularities. To obtain a uniform passage of the tool over the work, the automatic saddle traverse should be employed. At the end of each cut, the tool will have to be reset, so to project further from the boring bar, and to obtain an accurate setting, it is best to use the dial test indicator (Fig. 7.21). For this purpose, the indicator is mounted on the pillar of the surface gauge and, with the base standing on the lathe bed, the base register pins are pushed down so as to locate the indicator against the bed shear.

If the lathe mandrel is now turned by hand in the reverse direction, the cutter, as it passes the contact point of the indicator, will give a reading on the dial after adjustment of the surface gauge has been made. The scale of the indicator dial is then set to the zero position.

After a cut has been taken, the diameter of the bore is measured to determine how much surplus metal remains to be removed. This enables the cutter to be reset against the test indicator, so that a final cut can be taken of the exact depth needed to bring the bore to the finished diameter.

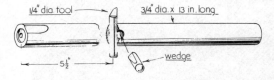

Fig. 7.20 The Myford boring bar DBE 228

# CHAPTER EIGHT

# Threading & Screw Cutting In The Lathe

### Threading from the Lathe Tailstock

WORK MOUNTED ON the lathe mandrel can be threaded with a tap or die guided by the tailstock. This method of threading is not so accurate or as reliable as screw cutting the thread with a lathe tool traversed automatically by the leadscrew, but it is sufficiently accurate for many purposes.

### Threading with a Die

The circular die is mounted in a tailstock die holder (Fig. 8.1) and the tapered shank of the holder is engaged in the tail-stock barrel. Some die holders are fitted with a draw-bar to prevent the shank turning and possibly damaging the tapered bore of the tailstock barrel. Die

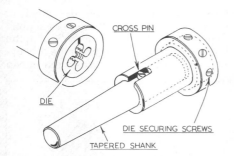

*Fig. 8.1 The tailstock die holder*
*Myford 1435/36*

holders are supplied in two sizes, to take either $\frac{13}{16}$in. diameter or 1in. diameter circular dies. The shank of the Myford die holder is fitted with a cross-pin sliding in a slot cut in the die-head; when the pin reaches the end of the slot, the die is free to revolve and ceases to cut. When starting the thread, the die is engaged with the work by feeding it forward with the tailstock; but once the die has obtained a good hold, it will continue to cut automatically as the lathe mandrel is turned (Fig. 8.2).

### Tapping

Except in the smaller sizes, good quality taps usually have a centre drilled in the end of the shank. This centre can be used to locate the tap against the tailstock centre with the tap held in a tap wrench (Fig. 8.3). The lathe mandrel is now locked and the tap is fed into the work or the tap wrench is held stationary and the mandrel is turned by hand.

As the tap wrench is turned and the tap travels forward, the tailstock centre must be kept in contact with the shank centre in order to maintain the tap in alignment.

If the tap becomes hard to turn, after it has entered for some distance, the work can be removed from the lathe and the tapping finished in the bench vice. The squareness of the tap in the hole can be checked by again gripping the work in

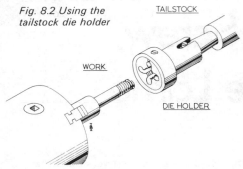

Fig. 8.2 Using the tailstock die holder

TAILSTOCK

WORK

DIE HOLDER

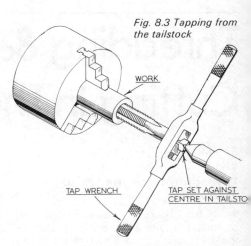

Fig. 8.3 Tapping from the tailstock

WORK

TAP WRENCH

TAP SET AGAINST CENTRE IN TAILSTO

the chuck and turning the lathe mandrel. Where the shank of a small tap has no drilled centre the tap can be gripped in the tailstock drill chuck and the lathe mandrel pulley carefully turned by hand. The tailstock should be unclamped to enable it to slide forward as the tap enters the work.

Another method is to attach a tap wrench or carrier to the tap shank just short of the threads. The chuck jaws are then closed on the shank, but leaving the tap free to turn. After clamping the tailstock to the lathe bed, the thread is cut by engaging the tap in the work and turning the tap wrench to and fro. In all threading operations on steel, a plentiful supply of cutting oil should be maintained on the work.

## SCREW CUTTING

### The Standard Whitworth Thread

This thread form is also used for British Standard Fine threads, the Standard

Brass and also for British Standard Pipe threads, and *Model Engineer* fine threads.

The included angle of the thread is 55°, and the pitch is the distance between two adjacent thread crests. The vertical depth of the thread, measured from crest to root, is equal to the pitch multiplied by 0·64. Both the crests and the roots of the threads are rounded.

Well-fitting male and female threads should make good contact on the flanks of the threads, and in ordinary work contact at the crests and roots is unnecessary.

### The Screw Cutting Tool

Screw cutting tools are described in Chapter 4. The tip of the tool is slightly rounded to form a radius at the root of the thread and also to strengthen the tool tip. A plain V-tool will not round the thread

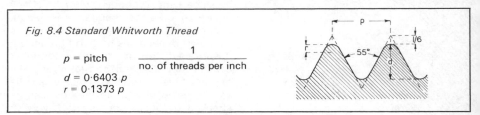

Fig. 8.4 Standard Whitworth Thread

$p$ = pitch $\dfrac{1}{\text{no. of threads per inch}}$

$d = 0\cdot6403\,p$
$r = 0\cdot1373\,p$

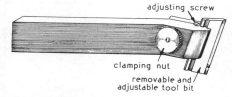

*Fig. 8.5 Screw cutting form tool*

crests, so this tool is followed by a hand-chaser or a die to finish the thread to the standard form. The thread can be machined to the correct radius at both root and crest by using a formtool Fig. 8.5, but a separate tool is required for each thread pitch cut.

## Preparing the Work

Short work can be held in the chuck and should be supported by the tailstock centre. Shafts are usually mounted between centres and driven by a carrier from the mandrel driverplate. A flat or a shallow drill hole should be formed on the end of the shaft to afford a secure seating for the carrier. If the carrier slips during machining, the thread may be spoilt. For both external and internal screwcutting, the surface to be threaded is first turned true and parallel. A groove or recess turned in the work will afford clearance for the tool at the finish of the thread (Fig. 8.6[A] and [B]).

## Setting up the Wheel Train

The arrangement of the change wheels and the method of setting up the drive are shown in the accompanying charts.

The underlying principle is that, for each turn of an 8t.p.i. leadscrew, the mandrel turns for one eighth of the number of threads per inch to be cut. Threads that are a simple multiple of the leadscrew pitch—16:24:32—therefore, require the mandrel wheel to have $\frac{1}{2}:\frac{1}{3}:\frac{1}{4}$ the number of teeth of the leadscrew wheel, and the size of the intermediate coupling wheels is then immaterial.

As shown in the charts, a compound wheel train may be used where the reduction ratio of the drive is a fractional figure, or where the ratio is too high to be covered by a simple train.

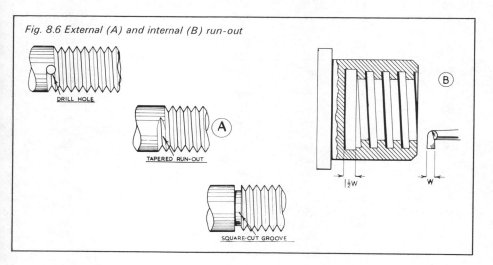

*Fig. 8.6 External (A) and internal (B) run-out*

| | | | INCH PITCHES | | | | |
|---|---|---|---|---|---|---|---|

| T.P.I. | Feed per rev. | Driver | 1st Stud | | 2nd Stud | | Lead screw | Set-up |
|---|---|---|---|---|---|---|---|---|
| | | | Driven | Driver | Driven | Driver | | |
| 8 | ·1250″ | 20 | IDLE 75 WHEEL | | | | 20 | 1 |
| 9 | ·1111″ | 40 | IDLE 60 WHEEL | | | | 45 | 1 |
| 10 | ·1000″ | 40 | IDLE 60 WHEEL | | | | 50 | 1 |
| 11 | ·0909″ | 40 | IDLE 60 WHEEL | | | | 55 | 1 |
| 12 | ·0833″ | 40 | IDLE 50 WHEEL | | | | 60 | 1 |
| 14 | ·0714″ | 20 | IDLE 70 WHEEL | | | | 35 | 1 |
| 16 | ·0625″ | 20 | IDLE 70 WHEEL | | | | 40 | 1 |
| 18 | ·0556″ | 20 | IDLE 70 WHEEL | | | | 45 | 1 |
| 19 | ·0526″ | 40 | 38 | 20 | IDLE 55 WHEEL | | 50 | 2 |
| 20 | ·0500″ | 20 | IDLE 70 WHEEL | | | | 50 | 1 |
| 22 | ·0455″ | 20 | IDLE 70 WHEEL | | | | 55 | 1 |
| 24 | ·0417″ | 20 | IDLE 70 WHEEL | | | | 60 | 1 |
| 25 | ·0400″ | 40 | 50 | 30 | IDLE 45 WHEEL | | 75 | 2 |
| 26 | ·0385″ | 20 | IDLE 70 WHEEL | | | | 65 | 1 |
| 28 | ·0357″ | 30 | 35 | 20 | IDLE 50 WHEEL | | 60 | 2 |
| 32 | ·0313″ | 30 | 40 | 20 | IDLE 55 WHEEL | | 60 | 2 |
| 36 | ·0278″ | 30 | 45 | 20 | IDLE 55 WHEEL | | 60 | 2 |
| 40 | ·0250″ | 30 | 50 | 20 | IDLE 55 WHEEL | | 60 | 2 |
| 44 | ·0227″ | 20 | 55 | 30 | IDLE 50 WHEEL | | 60 | 2 |
| 46 | ·0217″ | 20 | 46* | 30 | IDLE 45 WHEEL | | 75 | 2 |
| 48 | ·0208″ | 20 | 60 | 35 | IDLE 45 WHEEL | | 70 | 2 |
| 52 | ·0192″ | 20 | 50 | 25 | IDLE 55 WHEEL | | 65 | 2 |
| 54 | ·0185″ | 20 | 45 | 20 | IDLE 55 WHEEL | | 60 | 2 |
| 60 | ·0167″ | 20 | 50 | 25 | IDLE 55 WHEEL | | 75 | 2 |
| 64 | ·0156″ | 35 | 40 | 20 | 60 | 30 | 70 | 3 |
| 72 | ·0139″ | 25 | 50 | 30 | 45 | 20 | 60 | 3 |
| 80 | ·0125″ | 25 | 50 | 35 | 70 | 30 | 75 | 3 |
| 88 | ·0114″ | 30 | 40 | 25 | 55 | 20 | 75 | 3 |
| 92 | ·0109″ | 20 | 46* | 30 | 50 | 20 | 60 | 3 |
| 96 | ·0104″ | 30 | 40 | 20 | 60 | 25 | 75 | 3 |
| 104 | ·0096″ | 20 | 50 | 30 | 60 | 25 | 65 | 3 |
| | ·0087″ | 20 | 55 | 30 | 60 | 25 | 65 | 3 |
| 112 | ·0089″ | 25 | 50 | 30 | 60 | 20 | 70 | 3 |
| 120 | ·0083″ | 20 | 50 | 30 | 60 | 25 | 75 | 3 |
| | ·0058″ | 20 | 55 | 25 | 60 | 20 | 65 | 3 |
| | ·0043″ | 20 | 60 | 25 | 65 | 20 | 75 | 3 |
| | ·0037″ | 20 | 65 | 25 | 70 | 20 | 75 | 3 |
| | ·0018″ | 12** | 65 | 20 | 70 | 20 | 75 | 3 |

## METRIC PITCHES

| Feed per rev. millimetres | Driver | 1st Stud | | 2nd Stud | | Lead screw | Set-up |
|---|---|---|---|---|---|---|---|
| | | Driven | Driver | Driven | Driver | | |
| 0·20 | 21* | 50 | 30 | 60 | 21* | 70 | 3 |
| 0·25 | 30 | 40 | 21 | 60 | 21 | 70 | 3 |
| 0·30 | 21 | 60 | 45 | 50 | 21 | 70 | 3 |
| 0·35 | 35 | 40 | 21 | 50 | 21 | 70 | 3 |
| 0·40 | 21 | 50 | 21 | IDLE 60 WHEEL | | 70 | 2 |
| 0·45 | 45 | 40 | 21 | 50 | 21 | 70 | 3 |
| 0·50 | 21 | 50 | 45 | 40 | 20 | 60 | 3 |
| 0·60 | 21 | 50 | 45 | 40 | 30 | 75 | 3 |
| 0·70 | 21 | 50 | 21 | IDLE 60 WHEEL | | 40 | 2 |
| 0·75 | 45 | 40 | 35 | 50 | 21 | 70 | 3 |
| 0·80 | 21 | 50 | 45 | IDLE 40 WHEEL | | 75 | 2 |
| 0·90 | 45 | 25 | 21 | 40 | 21 | 70 | 3 |
| 1·00 | 45 | 40 | 21 | IDLE 50 WHEEL | | 75 | 2 |
| 1·10 | 45 | 50 | 55 | 40 | 21 | 75 | 3 |
| 1·20 | 45 | 25 | 30 | 50 | 21 | 60 | 3 |
| 1·25 | 45 | 40 | 21 | IDLE 50 WHEEL | | 60 | 2 |
| 1·30 | 65 | 25 | 21 | 40 | 21 | 70 | 3 |
| 1·40 | 45 | 25 | 35 | 50 | 21 | 60 | 3 |
| 1·50 | 21 | 50 | 45 | IDLE 35 WHEEL | | 40 | 2 |
| 1·60 | 45 | 25 | 21 | IDLE 55 WHEEL | | 75 | 2 |
| 1·75 | 45 | 20 | 35 | 50 | 21 | 60 | 3 |
| 1·80 | 30 | 40 | 45 | 25 | 21 | 50 | 3 |
| 2·00 | 60 | 40 | 21 | IDLE 55 WHEEL | | 50 | 2 |
| 2·25 | 45 | 40 | 60 | 40* | 21 | 50 | 3 |
| 2·50 | 45 | 30 | 21 | IDLE 50 WHEEL | | 40 | 2 |
| 2·75 | 55 | 20 | 30 | 40 | 21 | 50 | 3 |
| 3·00 | 45 | 25 | 21 | IDLE 60 WHEEL | | 40 | 2 |
| 3·50 | 60 | 20 | 35 | 40 | 21 | 50 | 3 |

**LEADSCREW 8 THREADS PER INCH**
*Not a standard Gear. Available as an extra.

**12 tooth Tumbler Cluster Gear available as an extra.

The tumbler reverse lever should not be shifted during thread cutting operations, as such movement may alter the position of the headstock spindle relative to the lead-screw, thereby causing split threads.

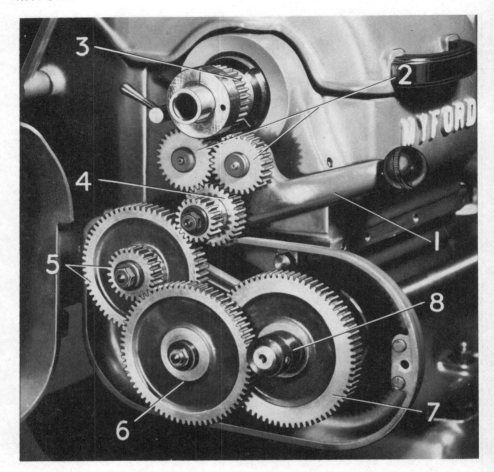

Fig. 8.7 Showing Leadscrew Drive. (1) tumbler reverse lever (2) tumbler reverse gears
(3) 25T spindle gear (4) tumbler cluster gear (5) 1st stud gears (6) 2nd stud gears
(7) leadscrew gear (8) spacer

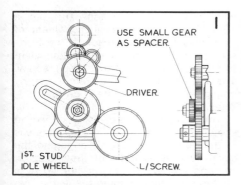

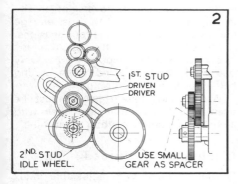

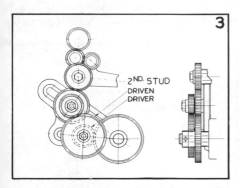

*Fig. 8.7 Showing lead screw drive*

## Calculating the Gearing

The following example illustrates the method used for calculating gear trains.

$$\text{Leadscrew} = 8\text{t.p.i.}$$
$$\text{Thread to be cut} = 40\text{t.p.i.}$$

Then $\frac{8}{40} = \frac{1}{5}$ and is the reduction required.

Multiply both figures by 20.

Then $\quad \frac{1}{5} \times \frac{20}{20} = \frac{20}{100}$.

As there is no standard 100T wheel, factorise this figure.

Then $\quad \frac{20}{100} = \frac{20}{50} \times \frac{1}{2} \quad$ and

$\frac{1}{2} = \frac{20}{40} \quad$ i.e. $\frac{20}{50} \times \frac{20}{40}$.

The gear train then becomes:

| Driver | 1st stud | 2nd stud | leadscrew |
|--------|----------|----------|-----------|
| 20 | $\frac{40}{20}$ | *idler* | 50 |

## Proving the Gear Train

Multiply the driven wheels together: divide this figure by the product of the drivers, and then multiply by the t.p.i. of the leadscrew.

From the above example:

$$\frac{40 \times 50}{20 \times 20} \times \frac{8}{1} = 40$$

which is the thread required.

## Setting the Tool

When cutting a Whitworth thread with an included angle of 55°, it is the usual practice to set over the top slide to half this angle—$27\frac{1}{2}°$—for feeding the tool into the work (Fig. 8.8). The tool then cuts mainly on its leading edge and a better finish is given to the threads. If the tool is given a few degrees of side rake at its leading edge it will cut more freely,

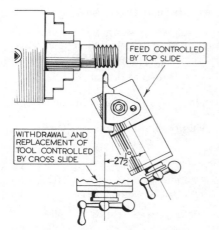

*Fig. 8.8 Setting over the top slide screw cutting*

but this edge must lie at lathe centre height throughout its length. The cutting edges of the tool are next set with the aid of a gauge (Fig. 8.9) to stand symmetrically to the work Fig. 8.10.

## The Thread Indicator (Fig. 8.10)

When cutting threads which are a multiple of the leadscrew thread, the clasp-nut can be engaged at any point on the leadscrew; but for threads of other pitches this may lead to cutting one thread on top of another. For example, one turn of the leadscrew moves the tool $\frac{1}{8}$in. but a 12t.p.i., thread requires a movement of $\frac{1}{12}$in. only between threads. If the leadscrew makes two turns, this is equivalent to three full threads of the 12t.p.i. screw. The correct thread is therefore cut by engaging every other thread on the leadscrew.

The thread indicator is designed to show when the thread of the leadscrew is in the correct position for engaging the clasp-nut. The spindle of the indicator, carrying a graduated dial, is turned by a 16-tooth pinion engaging the leadscrew. Each of the four divisions on the dial therefore represents four turns of the leadscrew, or a saddle traverse of $\frac{1}{2}$in. For cutting even-numbered threads, engage the clasp-nut at any of the four divisions.

For odd-numbered threads, use any two diametrically opposite marks. Only one mark must be used when cutting half-threads, such as $11\frac{1}{2}$t.p.i.

Where only certain marks must be used, it is advisable to indicate them with a chalk mark before starting to machine.

## Machining the Thread

For lathes fitted with adjustable index collars set the index of the top slide to zero, and move the cross slide until the tool touches the work, then set this index to zero. For the first cut a feed of some 5

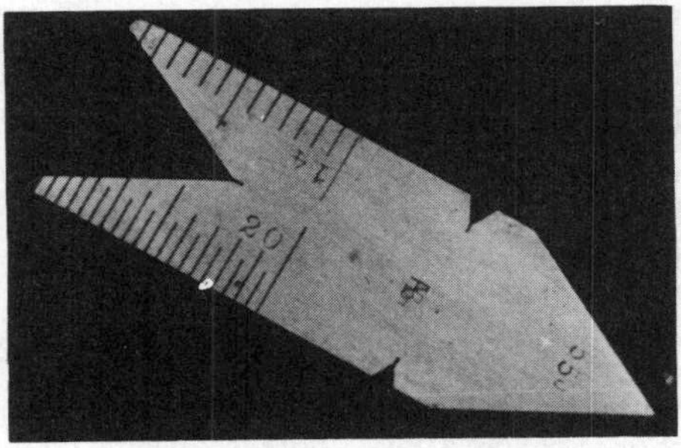

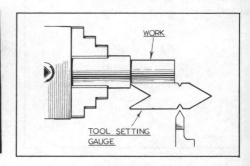

*Fig. 8.9 Thread setting gauge*

*Fig. 8.10 Thread setting gauge in use*

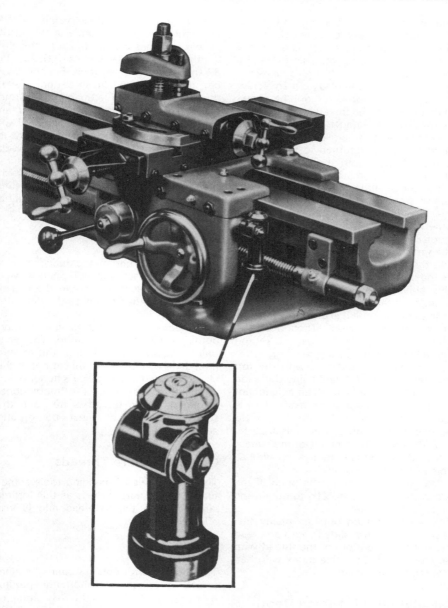

*Fig. 8.11 Thread indicator No. 1419*

thousandths of an inch is put on the tool by means of the top slide. Until experience has been gained, it is advisable to engage the backgear. This gives the operator time to stop the feed or withdraw the tool, particularly when screw cutting up to a shoulder on the work. When the end of the thread is reached, the clasp-nut is disengaged and the tool is withdrawn with the cross slide to enable the saddle to be returned to the starting position. Next, return the cross slide to the zero setting, advance the top slide for a few thousandths of an inch for the second nut, and engage the clasp-nut when the marks on the thread indicator come into line. Always maintain a continuous supply of cutting oil on the work when machining steel.

In the case of the standard ML7 lathe the index collars are fixed and so are not adjustable. It is therefore best to proceed as follows; adjust the position of the cross slide dial until it is on zero when the tool touches the work. Then note the reading of the top slide index and set the tool feed in relation to this reading.

It should be noted that with the top slide set over at $27\frac{1}{2}°$, and using this slide to control the tool in-feed, an adjustment to the reading needs to be made. This is equal to the secant of 27° 30′ ($27\frac{1}{2}°$). So the depth of the thread is multiplied by 1·1274 to give the amount of movement that needs to be made by the top slide as indicated by its index collar.

Alternatively, multiply the pitch of the thread to be cut by 0·7215 to obtain the top slide movement.

When the thread appears nearly finished, reset the top slide to zero and feed the tool to the bottom of the thread with the cross slide. The slide index will then show the depth reached.

## Calculating the Thread Depth

To calculate the full depth of a Whitworth thread, multiply the pitch value by the constant 0·64. For example, a thread of 20 per inch has a pitch of 0·05, and the depth—0·05×0·64—equals 0·032in. or 32 thousandths of an inch. For the final cut, to give a good finish to the thread, the top slide setting is unaltered and the tool is fed inwards for a thousandth of an inch, or so, from the cross slide. If an ordinary V-tool has been used, the crests of the threads can be rounded either with a die, or by means of a handchaser supported on the lathe handrest. The ends of the thread are finally chamfered by using the two side-faces of the screw-cutting tool in turn.

## Metric Threads

When screw cutting metric threads from a leadscrew of fractional inch pitch, or vice versa, on no account should the clasp-nut be disengaged owing to the difficulty of again picking up the thread; instead, the saddle is returned to the starting point by reversing the lathe. The gear trains required for cutting the metric threads in common use are set out in the chart provided in the maker's handbook.

The thread angle of the International Standard Metric thread is 60°, and the screw cutting tool must be ground accordingly.

## Cutting Square Threads

The feedscrews of machine tools sometimes have square threads as this form is stronger than the V-thread and is less affected by wear.

## Tool Forms

The tool used for cutting external square threads is formed like a short, rigid parting tool (Fig. 8.12). Where the helix angle or obliquity of the thread is small (Fig. 8.13) the tool can be formed so that its upper

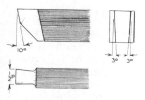

Fig. 8.12 Tool for cutting
external threads

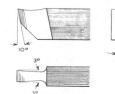

Fig. 8.13 Tool setting for
threads of small helix angle

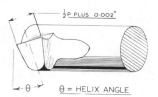

Fig. 8.14 Tool for cutting
internal square threads

surface lies in line with the long axis of the work. An increased clearance angle must be given at the leading edge to allow the tool to cut freely without rubbing. The breadth of the tool in this case is made equal to half the pitch value of the thread.

Where the helix angle is large, as in Fig. 8.15, the tool can be made stronger and will cut better if its upper surface lies at right angles to the faces of the thread. When so placed, the cutting edge of the tool must be made slightly greater in width than half the pitch value. Theoretically, the tool width becomes equal to half the pitch value multiplied by the cosine of the helix angle of the thread. The helix angle can be determined by making a scale drawing of the thread.

Tools for cutting internal square threads (Fig. 8.14) are formed in the same way, but the width is made greater than half the pitch by a thousandth of an inch or more in order to provide working clearance in the finished thread.

## Preparing the Work

In both internal and external threading, a groove is turned in the work to free the tool when it reaches the end of the thread —see Figs. 8.6(A) and (B). The width of this groove is usually made one and a half time the width of the tool. As the square-ended tool exerts considerable radial thrust, it is advisable to support the work with the travelling steady when machining long or slender shafts.

## Machining the Thread

The tool, mounted at centre height and at right-angles to the work, is fed directly inwards by means of the cross slide.

At the start, where possible the feed-screw index is set to zero to enable the thread to be machined to a depth equal to half the pitch of the screw. To avoid chatter, and to allow time for disengaging the leadscrew, the lathe should be run in backgear. Only light cuts should be taken, and a copious supply of cutting oil should be maintained when machining steel. As has been mentioned earlier, standard index dials are not adjustable. In this case, after setting the top slide round as far as it will go, proceed as described previously under the heading 'Machining the Thread'.

Internal square threads are cut in the same way, but machining is sometimes easier if the tool is mounted upside down and cuts at the back of the work. Working clearance between the nut and the roots of the threads on the shaft is allowed for by boring the nut a few thousandths of an inch more than the calculated depth, in order to provide clearance for the crests of the threads on the shaft.

## Multiple-start Threads

These may be either square or 'V' form. If the pitch of the thread is increased to provide a rapid feed motion, its depth will become correspondingly greater and the part may be unduly weakened. Quick-

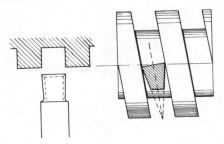

*Fig. 8.15 Tool setting for threads of large helix angle*

acting screws are therefore machined with multiple threads to give greater travel per turn—the lead—without any increase of pitch or depth. A screw having a 2-start thread will, for a single turn, travel twice the distance of the corresponding single-thread screw (Fig. 8.16). The lead has been doubled, but the thread depth and pitch remain constant, for the distance between two adjacent threads has not altered. 3- and 4-start threads are also commonly used.

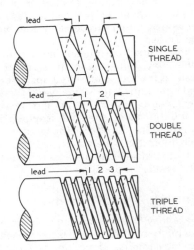

SINGLE THREAD

DOUBLE THREAD

TRIPLE THREAD

*Fig. 8.16 Comparison of single 2 and 3 start threads*

## Machining a 2-Start Thread

As the slope of the thread's helix angle increases with the lead, it may be necessary to set the tool with its upper surface at right-angles to the thread faces as in Fig. 8.14 in order to obtain adequate cutting clearance. The tool is ground to correspond with the pitch, but the wheel train is arranged to give the required lead. For a 2-start thread the lead is equal to twice the pitch.

The first thread is cut in the usual manner with reference to the thread indicator. To index the second thread, make a chalk mark on a tooth of the first driver wheel where it meshes with its driven wheel; also mark the diametrically opposite tooth on the driver. The driver wheel is now disengaged, and the mandrel is turned through 180° to allow the other marked tooth on the driver to engage with the driven wheel. The second thread is machined by closing the lead-screw clasp-nut when the thread indicator registers the original position. 3- or 4-start threads are machined in the same way, but to index the work the first driver wheel must be divisible by the number of threads cut.

## Acme Threads (Fig. 8.16)

Small Acme threads can be cut directly with a form tool of the shape shown in Fig. 8.18. When machining large threads, it is advisable first to cut a square thread a little undersize and then to finish the thread with the form tool. Clearance should then be given at both the roots and crests of the mating thread so that bearing is obtained on the thread flanks. As these threads are usually cut on long shafts, such as leadscrews, the work should be supported by means of a travelling steady. If possible, the pressure pads of the steady should be given a long bearing on the shaft, for the thread crests provide only a narrow contact surface.

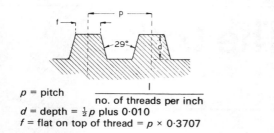

$p$ = pitch

$$d = \text{depth} = \frac{1}{2}p \text{ plus } 0\cdot010$$

$$\frac{1}{\text{no. of threads per inch}}$$

$f$ = flat on top of thread = $p \times 0\cdot3707$

*Fig. 8.17 The Acme thread*

## REMEMBER

Threading with a tap or die from the tail-stock is not as accurate as screw cutting.

Make sure that the change wheels are meshed to turn freely but without excessive backlash.

Fix the lathe carrier securely so that it cannot slip on the work.

Set the screw cutting tool at exactly centre height.

See that the tool has sufficient side clearance on the leading edge, particularly when cutting threads of coarse pitch.

To avoid mistakes, rely on the thread

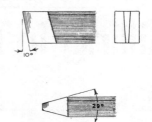

*Fig. 8.18 The tool for cutting Acme threads*

indicator for closing the clasp nut at the right moment.

Make use of the slide indices for putting on the cut and depthing the thread.

Maintain a continuous supply of cutting oil when screw cutting steel.

The crests of a Whitworth thread are rounded and should be finished with a hand chaser or cut with a form tool.

Screw threads should make accurate contact on their flanks, the fit at the roots and crests is of less importance.

When cutting multi-start threads, be careful to distinguish between the lead and the pitch of the thread.

# CHAPTER NINE

# Milling In The Lathe

THE TWO METHODS of milling in the lathe commonly employed are: (1) the work is held in the lathe chuck or supported between centres, and the cutter, mounted on a separate milling spindle, is driven from a specially fitted overhead shaft; (2) the cutter is secured to the lathe mandrel and the work is mounted on the cross slide.

The second method, which is standard Myford practice, has the advantage that the full power of the lathe is available for driving the milling cutter over a wide range of speeds.

## MILLING CUTTERS
### End-mills

These usually have four or more cutting lips formed to cut on both their end and side faces (Fig.9.1), but slotting mills with only two cutting lips (Fig. 9.2) afford better clearance for the chips and cut more freely.

To ensure true running and also to reduce the size and overhang of the mounting, end-mills are best held in a mandrel collet chuck; but the 4-jaw chuck can be employed for this purpose, and the test indicator is then used to check the true running of the teeth. When the end-mill is formed with a Morse taper shank, it can be mounted directly in the lathe mandrel taper.

In these circumstances the end of the shank should be tapped and the end-mill held in with a draw bar to avoid risk of damage to the mandrel taper.

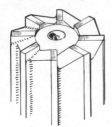

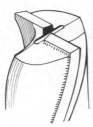

*Fig. 9.1 The end mill*    *Fig. 9.2 The slot mill*    *Fig. 9.3 Circular slot cutters*

## Circular Mills

Circular slotting cutters have teeth formed only on the periphery (Fig. 9.3) but where the teeth are also cut on the side faces (Fig. 9.4) the cutter can be used for facing and is termed a side-and-face mill.

In some cutters the teeth are cut on a bevelled face to serve for angular machining (Fig. 9.5).

Circular cutters and slitting saws, formed with a central bore, are mounted on an arbor and secured by means of a clamp nut. The arbor is held in a mandrel collet, or is centred in the 4-jaw chuck where greater driving power is needed, or a long arbor can be mounted between the lathe centres and driven by a carrier from the mandrel driveplate. Whenever, possible the arbor should be given additional support by engaging the tailstock centre.

*Fig. 9.5 Cutter with teeth cut on a bevelled face*

## Circular Saws (Fig. 9.6)

Circular saws, made of either high-speed or carbon steel, are obtainable in a wide range of thicknesses. They are used for cutting off material, slitting metal com-

*Fig 9.4 Side-and-face cutters*

Fig. 9.6 A group of circular saws

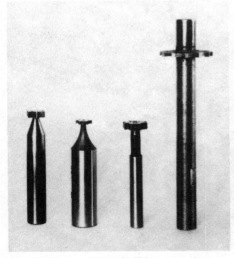

Fig. 9.7 Group of Woodruff keyway cutters

ponents, and for work such as slotting the heads of screws.

## The Woodruff Cutter (Fig. 9.7)

The Woodruff cutter is a special form of one-piece circular cutter used for machining the seats for Woodruff semi-circular keys.

## Fly Cutters

This form of milling cutter, although it cuts more slowly than a multi-tooth mill, has the advantage that it is easily made and can be readily resharpened. If the cutter bit is set at an oblique angle (Figs. 9.8 and 9.9) the tool can be used for facing, and keyways can be machined where the bit, mounted at right angles to the shank, is formed in the shape of a

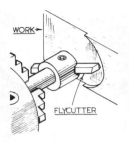
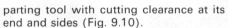

Fig. 9.8 The Fly cutter

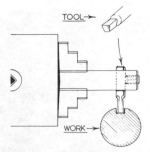

Fig. 9.10 Fly cutter for keyway cutting

parting tool with cutting clearance at its end and sides (Fig. 9.10).

The tool can be held in the self-centring chuck, as with only a single-cutting edge there is no need for the tool to be mounted exactly centrally.

*A Twin-tool Fly Cutter.* If much material needs removing a fly cutter with a pair of cutters in operation will do much to speed up the work. The component, depicted in Fig. 9.12, needed a consider-able amount of stock removal in order to produce a shoulder that could be used for bolting down purposes.

The tool itself is illustrated in Fig. 9.11. It comprises a block of mild steel some 3in. long by 1in. thick, in which a pair of ¼in. high-speed steel tool bits are set at an angle of 45°. The block is shouldered down at each end so that it will remain in location when caught in the 4-jaw chuck as seen in the illustration.

Fig. 9.9 Machining the edge of a base plate with a fly cutter

115

Fig. 9.11 A twin-tool fly cutter

Fig. 9.12 The twin-tool fly cutter in use

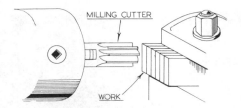

*Fig. 9.13 Work clamped to the top slide*

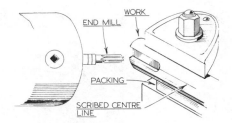

*Fig. 9.14 Setting the work to the correct height*

## MOUNTING THE WORK

### On the Top Slide

Parts clamped in the toolpost can be machined with a face cutter or an end-mill. This is a useful method of facing the ends of a batch of components to machine them to uniform length (Fig. 9. 13).

When parts mounted in this way are machined, or slotted with an end-mill, the work is set to height on packing strips by using the mandrel centre or a height gauge as a guide (Fig. 9.14).

### On the Cross Slide

The various ways of mounting work on the cross slide are described in Chapter 7; namely, by using the T-bolts for direct bolting; gripping the work in the machine vice; or bolting to an angle plate.

In addition the work may be secured to the vertical slide (Fig. 9.15) in order to obtain a feed either in the vertical direction or at any required angle.

The Myford vertical slide is made in two patterns (Fig. 9.16); the plain type, and the swivelling type in which the table can be swung or rotated to any required angle by referring to the angular scales provided (Fig. 9.17).

## MILLING WORK ON THE VERTICAL SLIDE

For most work, the slide is set squarely across the lathe bed by placing a rule or a parallel strip against the face of the chuck, and then clamping the slide base when the surface of the table is in even contact with the setting strip. If required, the table is set at an angle across the bed with the aid of a protractor, or the table can be set squarely and afterwards adjusted to the required angle by using the base scale.

### Securing the Work

Large work can often be bolted directly to the table with T-bolts. The Myford machine vice, which is designed for bolting to the table of the vertical slide, will hold the work securely and accurately square with the surface of the table. A small angle plate may be bolted to the table for mounting the work; for this purpose, Myford angle plates are supplied in three sizes, ranging in width from $1\frac{1}{2}$in. to $2\frac{1}{4}$in.

### Setting the Work with the Test Indicator

Where precise alignment of the work is required, the test indicator is mounted on a spindle gripped in the chuck, and the plunger is brought into contact with either the face or the upper edge of the part. If the cross slide is now traversed, any movement of the indicator needle will show in what direction the work, or

Fig. 9.15 Mounting the work in the vertical slide

*Fig. 9.16 Myford plain vertical slide No. 67/1*

*Fig. 9.17 Myford swivelling vertical slide No. 68/2*

*Fig. 9.18 Mounting a simple test indicator*

Fig. 9.19 Setting work with the test indicators

*Fig. 9.20 Setting work with the test indicators*

the vertical slide, has to be moved to obtain an accurate setting. This method can also be used to check the setting of both the fixed jaw and the work surface of the machine vice in order to ensure accurate machining.

## THE DIVIDING ATTACHMENT

This accessory is mounted on the lathe cross slide by securing it to either the plain or the swivelling type of vertical slide. A full description of the dividing attachment and its method of use is given under the heading of gear cutting.

When a mandrel chuck for holding the work is fitted to the spindle of the attachment, the dividing head will enable squares or hexagons or other forms to be milled on the work. If the overarm is employed to support the work, single or multiple keyways can be milled on a shaft by means of an end-mill or circular cutter held in the mandrel chuck.

## MILLING OPERATIONS
### Cutter Speed

The approximate maximum surface speeds for milling cutters are shown in the accompanying table. To find the required revolutions per minute of the lathe mandrel, divide the cutting speed given by a quarter of the cutter's diameter measured in inches. Thus, a $\frac{1}{2}$in. diameter high-speed steel end-mill can be run at 60 divided by $\frac{1}{8}$r.p.m. for machining mild steel; this equals 480r.p.m., and the

| Metals | Cutter | |
|---|---|---|
| | *High-speed Steel* ft. per min | *Carbon Steel* ft. per min |
| Mild Steel | 60 | 30 |
| Cast Iron | 50 | 25 |
| Brass | 200 | 100 |
| Aluminium and Duralumin | up to 1000 | up to 400 |

middle direct speed of the standard ML7 lathe is therefore used.

## Feed and Depth of Cut

Heavy cuts tend to heat and so blunt the cutter teeth. The machining will be done more quickly, and the work given a better finish, if light cuts are taken with a moderately fast feed.

Where the cutter is mounted to run truly, each tooth will cut in turn, and regular hand-feeding will be facilitated. The rate of feed should be kept constant, for the cutter teeth are liable to be blunted if allowed to rub against the work instead of cutting. When the automatic feed is employed, the depth of cut is adjusted to give free-cutting without chatter or other signs of overloading, such as undue heating of the work.

An ample supply of cutting oil should be maintained when machining steel.

## Centring the Work on the Cutter

When, for example, cutting a keyway in a shaft, it is essential that the cutter should

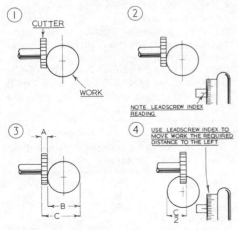

*Fig. 9.21 Centring the cutter*

be accurately located on the centre line of the work. An easy way of centring the cutter is illustrated in Fig. 9.21.

(1) Traverse the work to the left to touch the edge of one of the cutter teeth.
(2) Take the reading of the leadscrew index.
(3) Measure with the micrometer the width of the cutter—A and the diameter of the work—B. Add these together to obtain—C.
(4) Centre the cutter by using the leadscrew index to move the work to the left for a distance equal to half the value—C.
(5) Lock the lathe saddle.

This method of application, and the principle can be utilised for making most cutter settings.

## Face-milling

When milling a flat surface, an end-mill, a fly cutter, or a face-milling cutter can be used. The work, as previously illustrated, is clamped in true alignment on the lathe saddle or is secured to the vertical slide. The feed is put on from the leadscrew and the work is then traversed across the cutter.

During machining, the saddle should be locked to the lathe bed. When machining an iron casting, the surface sand is liable to blunt the cutter teeth, but if a fly cutter is used, the tool bit can be readily resharpened after the preliminary cut has been taken to remove the surface scale.

With a correctly ground and honed fly cutter, a high finish can be given to the work, but a multi-tooth cutter usually leaves some tool marks after a period of use.

## Slotting

Either an end-mill or a 2-lipped slotting mill is used for machining slots with

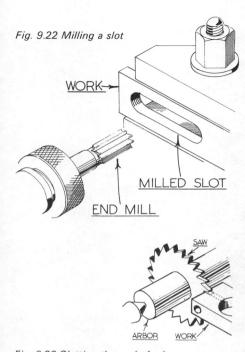

Fig. 9.22 Milling a slot

WORK

MILLED SLOT

END MILL

SAW

ARBOR    WORK

Fig. 9.23 Slotting the end of a lever

closed ends. The mill is first fed into the work for a short distance and, after the saddle has been locked, the work is traversed across the cutter.

The reading of the cross slide index at either end of the slot should be noted, so that each traversing cut to deepen the slot can be exactly repeated.

It is advisable to return the work to the starting point after each traverse, as a better finish is usually obtained by taking the cut in one direction only. The method employed for slotting the forked end of a lever with a circular milling cutter is illustrated in Fig. 9.23.

## Cutting Keyways

Short keyways with closed ends are best cut in a shaft with a 2-lipped slotting mill in the same way as machining slots.

If the work is held in the machine vice attached to the vertical slide, the cutter can readily be set on the centre line of the work by employing the method previously described. There will be less surplus metal to remove, and the cutter can be started more easily, if after mounting the work a hole is first drilled at either end of the marked-out keyway. These holes are started with a centre drill and finished with a twist drill a little under size.

Where, as in Fig. 9.25, the shaft is held in the machine vice attached to the cross slide, the keyway is cut to full depth at a single passage of the cutter. For this purpose, a fly cutter is set to the correct radius with the aid of a test indicator, in the way described in Chapter 6 for adjusting the cutter of a boring bar to machine to an exact diameter.

One advantage of using a fly cutter for this work is that the cutter bit can be ground to machine the keyway to an exact width. If the keyway is cut with a circular mill, the work is raised in the vice on a packing strip for machining the keyway to the full depth Fig. 9.26. Where the shaft lies below the cutter and the work is fed in a direction away from the operator, the cross slide gib strip should be tightened somewhat to prevent the cutter teeth from dragging the work inwards and possibly causing a jam. The cross slide feed screw should also be adjusted to remove nearly all backlash.

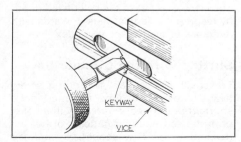

KEYWAY

VICE

Fig. 9.24 Cutting a short keyway

Fig. 9.25 Cutting a long keyway on the cross slide

## Cutting Seats for Woodruff Keys

As the special cutter has to be fed directly into the work, the machining is best carried out by securing the shaft to the vertical slide. When the cutter has been correctly centred on the shaft, both the saddle and the cross slide are locked. The keyway is cut to the calculated depth by feeding the vertical slide upwards with reference to the feed screw index.

## Slitting with the Circular Saw

For small work, such as slotting screw heads, the saw can be mounted on a short arbor gripped to run truly in a collet or in the self-centring chuck. For heavier machining, the saw should be mounted on an arbor long enough to allow the tail-stock centre to be engaged (Figs. 9.27 and 9.28). Make sure that the saw runs truly and without wobble. Do not run the saw faster than the calculated speed, especially if it is made of carbon steel.

When cutting steel, apply cutting oil continuously with a brush both to lubricate the teeth and to remove the swarf. To avoid damaging the teeth, feed the work to the saw carefully and with an even turning movement.

## REMEMBER

The milling cutter must be mounted to run truly—if necessary check with the test indicator.

When possible, support the cutter arbor with the tailstock centre.

*Fig. 9.26 Cutting a keyway with a circular mill*

Lock all slides not in actual use.

Fly cutters give a good work finish and and are easily resharpened.

Use the test indicator for aligning the work accurately.

Running the cutter too fast is liable to blunt the teeth.

Do not allow the cutter to rub on the work without cutting.

Use plenty of cutting oil when milling steel.

Light cuts and a fast feed are better than taking a heavy cut.

Too rapid or irregular feeding may damage the teeth of slitting jaws.

Use coolant on non-ferrous metals and aluminium alloys.

## Raising Block for Vertical Slides

The Raising Block is supplied complete with alignment strips to engage the T-slots in the lathe cross slide, and hexagon screws with washers to secure the block in place. The top surface of the block is provided with a T-slot that enables the Swivelling Vertical Slide Ref. No. 68/2 to be mounted and affixed by means of the central T-bolt supplied with it. When the plain Vertical Slide needs to be set on the Raising Block it can either be secured by means of hexagon head screws if the face of the slide is to be set parallel with the

*Fig. 9.27 Sawing screw slots*

Fig. 9.28 Equipment for cutting screw slots

lathe axis, or it may be held in place by standard T-slot bolts if the face of the slide needs to be aligned at right angles to the lathe axis.

The Raising Block is suitable for use on both ML7 and Super Seven lathes where it greatly extends the scope of the Myford Dividing Attachment at the same time

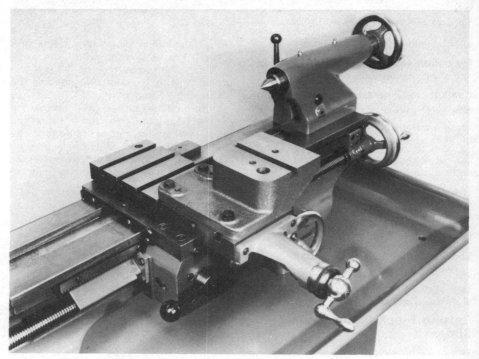

Fig. 9.29 The Myford Raising Block

greatly improving the rigidity of the set-up. The illustrations, Fig. 9.29 and Fig. 9.30 demonstrate the Raising Block in place and the Raising Block in place with the Dividing Attachment mounted. From these illustrations it will be apparent to what extent the performance of the Dividing Attachment has been improved.

For some operations it is convenient to use the Raising Block at the back of the long cross slide. This requirement was not at first appreciated by Myford. Consequently for the first 100 sets of Raising Block equipment it is not possible to make use of *both* pairs of bolting holes in the base. The reason for this discrepancy is the difference in centring between the front and rear T-slots in the cross slide.

However, as the illustration Fig. 9.31 demonstrates the author has got over the difficulty by bolting down the rear of the base while clamping down the front. Making the two clamps needed is a simple matter whilst providing a pair of hexagon screws having an extra $\frac{3}{16}$in. length should present no problem.

## Mini-Miller Reg. No. 20/170 (Figs. 9.32, 9.33, 9.34)

This attachment, which is suitable for the Series 7 and ML7 lathes, converts the lathe into a vertical milling machine. It has been designed so that it may be mounted on the lathe or removed from it rapidly, no alteration to the lathe itself being needed.

The fitment comprises a base member

*Fig. 9.30 The Raising Block with Myford Dividing Attachment mounted*

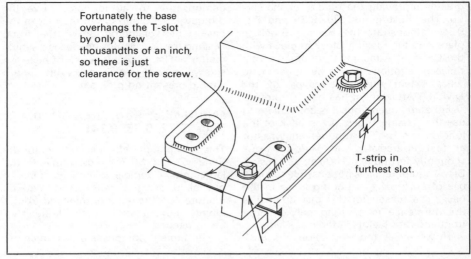

Fortunately the base overhangs the T-slot by only a few thousandths of an inch, so there is just clearance for the screw.

T-strip in furthest slot.

*Fig. 9.31 A pair of clamps as shown is used with the T-slot strip (not shown) in place. The Hexagon screws need additional $\frac{3}{16}$in of length*

which is clamped to the lathe bed and supports the vertical column, to which is attached the spindle bracket and the drive unit complete with jockey pulleys and the driven pulley with its attendant bearings.

The drive is by means of a toothed timing belt having its driving pulley mounted on ball bearings housed in the base member. The driving pulley itself makes contact with a self-aligning coupling that screws directly on to the lathe mandrel nose.

The miller spindle speed is the same as the lathe mandrel itself and, as the result of employing a toothed belt, there is no slip in the drive.

Readers will no doubt, appreciate that, with the Mini-miller being driven from the lathe mandrel, all the mandrel speeds as well as the automatic feeds are available where applicable.

In order to control lateral movement the column is keywayed while the spindle bracket is provided with a Key.

The spindle of the mini-miller is bored No. 2 Morse Taper and has the same bore as that of the lathe mandrel itself. The spindle nose details are the same as those of the lathe itself. It is carried on a pair of angular contact ball bearings, adjustable by a single screwed collar, and, in order to control the depth of cut, a feed screw is provided having 10 threads-to-the-inch. The feed screw itself has a friction-held micrometer dial, and from this the amount of down feed can be read off immediately.

## NOTES ON THE MYFORD MILLING ATTACHMENT

### Centring the Attachment

When the end-milling operation on a curved surface needs to be undertaken it is advisable to see that the spindle of the milling attachment and that of the Myford Dividing Attachment supporting the work are in alignment.

Fig. 9.32 Front view of Myford mini-miller

Fig. 9.33 The mini-miller with cover removed to show belt drive arrangements

Fig. 9.34 Coupling for use on the ML7-R lathe

The simplest way to do this, and one that is sufficiently accurate for all practical purposes is to adopt the procedure depicted in Fig. 9.35.

## Milling Curved Surfaces

One is often called upon to machine the ends of such components as locomotive

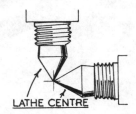

Fig. 9.35 A simple procedure for centring a milling attachment

connecting rods and the like in order to furnish a symmetrically curved surface. The job calls for an end-milling operation with the work mounted on a rotary table secured to the lathe cross slide.

As many readers will be aware rotary tables are provided with an accurate and concentrically bored hole into which a turned peg can be inserted in order to centralise the work. As will be seen in the illustration the peg, machined to a wringing fit in the eye of the component, ensures that the work will rotate concentrically as the rotary table is turned. See Fig. 9.36.

Depending on the nature of the work, an alternative method of machining a curved surface is to make use of the end of the milling cutter, making a series of longitudinal cuts along the work. If a

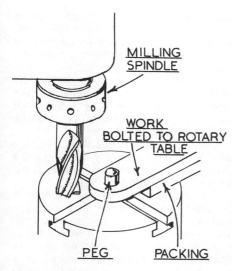

Fig. 9.36 Milling a curved surface

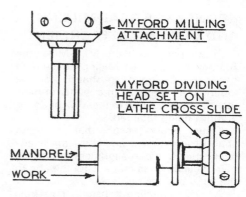

Fig. 9.37 End milling a curved surface

attachment is fitted, a thirty-second of an inch seems sufficient. One has to remember that an end-mill or slot drill $\frac{3}{32}$in. dia is not exactly a robust tool so it is better to make haste slowly.

sufficient number of these passes along the work are made, little hand work will be needed. At most a light application with a fine file will suffice. See Fig. 9.37.

When using this set-up remember that the lathe self-act can be used to traverse the work under the cutter.

## Milling a Slot in a Sleeve

An example of a component needing a slot to be milled in its periphery is the sleeve controlling the spring detent of a dividing head.

The work is set up in a self-centering chuck mounted on the lathe cross slide. In the author's workshop the chuck forms a part of the direct indexing equipment that may be used either on the drilling machines or, in this instance, in conjunction with the Myford Milling Attachment. See Fig. 9.38.

As to the cut that should be put on, using the higher mandrel speed that is available with the ML7 lathe to which the

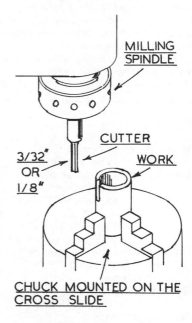

Fig. 9.38 Milling a slot in a sleeve

131

## RODNEY VERTICAL MILLING AND DRILLING ATTACHMENT

In company with the Mini-Miller the Rodney No. 20/140 Milling attachment has been designed so that it can be mounted on the lathe in a matter of minutes, no modification to the ML7 or Series 7 lathes being required.

Thrust screws ensure that the input shaft of attachment and the lathe headstock spindle are in alignment before the pair of clamp bolts that anchor the unit to the lathe bed are tightened.

A Nylon coupling transmits the whole range of lathe spindle speeds through a combination of bevel gears, vertical shaft and vee-belt to the main spindle of the attachment which turns at about $1\frac{1}{2}$ times the lathe spindle speed. In this connection the makers state that, when used on Series 7 lathes, the two fastest speeds should not be used for long periods.

The bevel gears are oil-bath lubricated and the drive shaft and vertical shaft have bearings that are sealed for life.

Provision is made for rough-setting the cutter for height by raising or lowering the spindle bracket on the column of the attachment itself. Fine settings or feeds for milling are obtained from the handwheel seen in the illustration operating a 50 to 1 worm to wormwheel reduction gear.

When used for sensitive drilling the worm is disengaged by releasing the appropriate clamp lever and the hand lever seen in the illustration can then be used to operate the down-feed.

The attachment is supplied complete with the necessary flexible coupling and a No. 2 Morse Taper adaptor with draw bar for the lathe mandrel.

The attachment main spindle nose is threaded $1\frac{1}{8}$in. $\times$ 12t.p.i. while the register diameter is $1\frac{1}{4}$in. dia. The spindle itself has an internal taper No. 2 Morse Taper. In all respects it resembles the spindles fitted to the ML7 or Series 7 lathes. Consequently any chucks or collets used with these lathes can also be used with the attachment.

The illustration also shows the Rodney Machine Vice mounted on the lathe cross slide. This vice (Ref. 20/141) has a jaw width of $2\frac{1}{4}$in. (57mm.) a jaw height of 1in. (25mm.) and fully open will admit $1\frac{15}{16}$in. (50mm. approx.).

### Specification

| | inches | mm |
|---|---|---|
| Throat depth to face of slide | $4\frac{3}{8}$ | 110 |
| to bevel box cover | $4\frac{3}{4}$ | 120 |
| Max height above cross slide | | |
| to spindle nose | 6 | 152 |
| to front of 1031 collet | $5\frac{1}{2}$ | 140 |
| to end of $\frac{1}{2}$" collet in small 'S' type | | |
| Clarkson Autolock collet chuck | $2\frac{1}{4}$ | 57 |
| to $\frac{1}{4}$" cap. 1A Jacobs drill chuck | $3\frac{1}{4}$ | 82 |
| Adjustment of spindle bracket on column | $3\frac{1}{4}$ | 82 |
| Movement (feed) of quill | 3 | 76 |
| Taper in spindle | No. 2 M.T. | |
| Spindle nose, thread | $1\frac{1}{8}$" $\times$ 12 T.P.I. | As ML7 & |
| register diameter | $1\frac{1}{4}$" | Series 7 |
| Nett weight, approx. | 60 lbs | 27 kg |

*Fig. 9.39 The Rodney vertical milling attachment*

# CHAPTER TEN

# Gear Cutting In The Lathe

## GEAR WHEELS

### Tooth Forms

THE INVOLUTE FORM of tooth is commonly used in general engineering, including the machine tool and automobile industries. As the flanks of involute teeth have a profile formed by a single curve, both the production of gear-cutters and the machining of gear wheels are greatly simplified.

The cycloidal form of tooth, having two curved surfaces, one convex and the other concave, is less used partly owing to machining difficulties.

### The Pitch Circle

When calculating the dimensions of involute gear wheels the measurements are made from the pitch circle. This circle corresponds to the diameter at the peripheries of two discs rolling together, as represented in Fig. 10.1. Where, as in Fig. 10.2, two gear wheels are correctly meshed, the two pitch circles meet exactly.

Involute gears will run together satisfactorily even if the meshing is not quite correct, but this does not apply equally to wheels with cycloidal teeth.

### Gear Centre Distances

To find the centre distance between two gear wheels meshing correctly at their pitch circles, add together the diameters of the two pitch circles and divide by two. If the pitch circles of the two gears are 3in. and 1 in.

$$\frac{3+1}{2} = \text{a centre distance of 2in.}$$

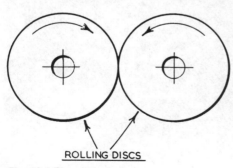

ROLLING DISCS

*Fig. 10.1 The pitch circle*

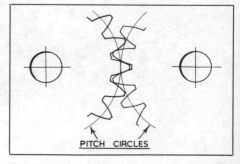

PITCH CIRCLES

*Fig. 10.2 Meshing of a pair of gear wheels*

## Tooth Pitches

The pitch of gear teeth is usually expressed as the diametral pitch, (DP) indicating the number of teeth in each inch of the wheel's diameter measured at the pitch circle.

A wheel of 16 DP and having 32 teeth, therefore, has a pitch circle 2in. in diameter.

Circular pitch indicates the distance between the centres of two adjacent teeth.

To convert diametral pitch to circular pitch, divide 3·1416, by the diametral pitch.

To convert circular pitch to diametral pitch, divide 3·1416 by the circular pitch.

To find the diametral pitch of a gear wheel, add two to the number of teeth and divide by the outside diameter.

If, therefore, the number of teeth is 30 and the outside diameter 2in., then 30+2 divided by 2in. equals 16 DP.

## Diameter of the Wheel Blank

To find the diameter of the wheel blank preparatory to cutting the gear teeth, add two to the total number of teeth and divide by the diametral pitch. If a wheel of 16 DP has 30 teeth, the outside diameter is:

$$\frac{30+2}{16}=2\text{in.}$$

For teeth of circular pitch the outside diameter of the wheel is:

$$\frac{(\text{number of teeth}+2) \times \text{circular pitch}}{3 \cdot 1416}$$

## Whole Depth of Tooth

For machining involute teeth to the correct depth, the depth of cut measured from the periphery of the blank is given by the formula:

$$\frac{2 \cdot 157}{DP}=\text{whole depth of tooth.}$$

This gives a condition of tooth meshing without backlash. To obtain clearance add to the depth of cut $\frac{0 \cdot 09}{DP}$ making the formula to give the necessary backlash:

$$\frac{2 \cdot 247}{DP}.$$

The tooth depth can also be expressed as: circular pitch multiplied by 0·6866.

## Racks

A rack corresponds to a gear of infinitely large diameter with the circumference forming a straight line. If it is to mesh with a gear of known diametral pitch, it will be necessary to calculate the spacing from one tooth to the next and this is done by dividing the diametral pitch by 3.1416.

At one time in Great Britain the included angle between the straight-sided flanks of adjacent teeth was machined to 29° as befits a pressure angle of $14\frac{1}{2}°$, but nowadays the British Standards Institution recommend a pressure angle of 20° as this provides gear teeth of increased strength particularly where small pinions are concerned. Pressure angle is that subtended by the side of the gear or rack tooth and an imaginary line at right-angles to the tooth pitch line.

## GEAR-CUTTERS (Fig. 10.3)

The teeth of circular gear-cutters are machined to cut the teeth on the gear blank to a high degree of accuracy. High-speed steel cutters can be run faster and will retain their sharpness longer than those made of carbon steel. As shown in the accompanying table, there are eight standard involute cutters for each diametral pitch.

Theoretically, a separate cutter is required for each tooth number, but in

135

*Fig. 10.3 A typical gear cutter*

### Involute Gear Cutters

No. 1 will cut wheels from 135 teeth to a rack

| | | | | | | | |
|---|---|---|---|---|---|---|---|
| No. 2 | „ | „ | „ | 55 | „ | „ | 134 Teeth |
| No. 3 | „ „ | „ | „ | 35 | „ | „ | 54 „ |
| No. 4 | „ | „ | „ | 26 | „ | „ | 34 „ |
| No. 5 | „ | „ | „ | 21 | „ | „ | 25 „ |
| No. 6 | „ | „ | „ | 17 | „ | „ | 20 „ |
| No. 7 | „ | „ | „ | 14 | „ | „ | 16 „ |
| No. 8 | „ | „ | „ | 12 | „ | „ | 13 „ |

centred to the spindle of the attachment, and the gear teeth are indexed by means of the self-contained dividing gear. As the hollow spindle, bored No. 2 Morse taper, has a threaded nose similar to that of the lathe mandrel, the lathe chucks and mandrel collet chucks can be used with the attachment; this enables turned work, while still held in the chuck, to be transferred from the lathe mandrel to the spindle of the attachment without altering the setting. To afford greater rigidity, the outer end of the work spindle is supported by an adjustable over-arm fitted with a coned centre. When in use, the attachment is secured to the Myford vertical slide, mounted on the lathe cross slide.

## The Dividing Gear

A 60-tooth worm wheel, fixed to the end of the spindle, engages a worm with a single-start thread. One turn of the worm therefore rotates the work spindle for one sixtieth of a revolution. The dividing plate is secured to the worm shaft, and the handle for turning the worm shaft is fitted with a detent that can be adjusted to engage in any of the rows of holes drilled in the dividing plate. The two dividing plates supplied with the attachment enable the work to be indexed in divisions ranging from 1° to 360° and in most numerical divisions from 1 to 100. The adjustable sector arms serve as a guide for moving the detent from one hole to another when making a succession of

practice sufficient accuracy is obtained by using a single cutter where the number of gear teeth varies over a limited range.

## GEAR CUTTING METHODS

Where the blank is mounted in a chuck on the lathe mandrel or between the lathe centres, the teeth can be machined by means of a milling attachment secured to the saddle and carrying a cutter driven from the lathe overhead gear (Fig. 10. 4).

### THE Myford Attachment
(Fig. 10.5)

With the Myford attachment, the full power of the lathe is available for driving the cutter, mounted on an arbor between the lathe centres. The gear blank is then

*Fig. 10.4 Gear cutting with a milling attachment*

*Fig. 10.5 The Myford dividing attachment*

partial turns of the worm to index the work. These two arms can be set to span any required number of holes.

## Simple Dividing

The work can be divided into the following divisions 1, 2, 3, 4, 5, 6, 10, 12, 15, 20, 30 and 60 by making one or more complete revolutions of the worm handle, and then locking the spindle by engaging the detent in the original hole in the dividing plate. In this way, hexagons can be machined by making ten full turns of the worm shaft (Fig. 10.6) and squares by turning the handle for fifteen complete turns (Fig. 10.7):

$$\frac{60 \text{ (teeth in worm wheel)}}{6 \text{ (divisions required)}}$$

=10 (turns of crank handle).

## Compound Dividing

When cutting gear wheels, the number of gear teeth may not divide exactly into the number of teeth on the worm wheel. Only a partial turn of the worm handle will then be needed for indexing the teeth, and this is made by engaging the detent in the appropriate circle of holes in the dividing plate. To index a gear wheel having 32 teeth:

$$\frac{60 \text{ (teeth in worm wheel)}}{32 \text{ (number of gear teeth)}}$$

$=1\frac{28}{32}$ (revolutions of crank handle for each tooth)

For the first tooth, engage the detent in one of the holes on the 32 hole circle. Use the numbered holes as the starting point. This avoids mistakes when using complete revolutions of the handle. To

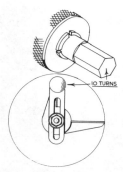

Fig. 10.6 Using the dividing attachment to cut hexagons

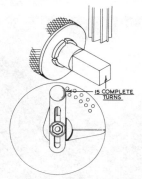

Fig. 10.7 Using the dividing attachment to cut squares

cut the second and remaining teeth, the detent is moved one revolution and 28 holes, and errors of counting are avoided by adjusting the two sector arms to span this interval.

To index a gear wheel having 25 teeth:

$$\frac{60}{25} = 2\tfrac{10}{25} \text{ turns of the crank handle for each tooth.}$$

As neither dividing plate has a circle of 25 holes, the fraction $\tfrac{10}{25}$ is converted to correspond with one of the hole circles provided:

$$\frac{10}{25} = \frac{2}{5} \text{ and } \frac{2 \times 9}{\underline{\quad}} = \frac{18}{\underline{\quad}}$$

The number of turns of the crank for indexing each tooth then becomes $2\tfrac{18}{45}$. The 45 hole circle is therefore used, and the sector arms are adjusted to span 19 holes.

The device illustrated in Fig. 10.8 was made by the author many years ago to simplify the dividing of work held in the chuck or mounted between centres. It consists of a division plate provided with sector arms and a detent, and has a worm that will engage a change wheel mounted on an extension to the lathe mandrel. Since the change wheel mounted may be selected to suit the work in hand the

dividing operation is much simplified.

A simplified method of making use of a change wheel for dividing purposes is depicted in Fig. 10.9. The wheel is again mounted on a mandrel extension and can be engaged by the screw detent seen attached to the vertical arm affixed to the end of the lathe bed. The wheel itself is marked off as appropriate, for example if a gear with 20 teeth has to be cut then each successive third tooth space needs to be marked and the detent engaged with them.

## Mounting the Cutter

The gear-cutter must be rigidly mounted and accurately centred. If the cutter wobbles, the tooth spaces will be machined over-width and the teeth themselves will be thinned. When the cutter runs out of truth, only some of the teeth will cut, and machining will be slowed. Lack of rigidity in the cutter mounting will result in poorly-finished teeth.

Mounting the cutter on the Myford arbor between the lathe centres will ensure true-running and rigidity. Where necessary, the rigidity of the arbor can be increased by using the fixed steady. The cutter is mounted so that the work is fed against the run of the cutter teeth.

*Fig. 10.8 The mandrel dividing attachment*

## Mounting the Work

The gear blank should be firmly pressed on to a ground, taper arbor and the arbor is then held at one end in a collet chuck, with the other end supported by the over-arm centre (Fig. 10.10). To ensure that the blank is correctly centred, it should first be turned to size on the arbor mounted between the lathe centres.

## Centring the Cutter

The cutter must be accurately centred on the gear blank in order to machine the teeth exactly radially. One method of centring the cutter Fig. 10.11 is to apply a try-square to the two sides of the work in turn, and to adjust the position of the lathe saddle until the distance between the work and the side face of the cutter is

140

Fig. 10.9 Wheel mounted on the mandrel extension

Fig. 10.10 Using the over-arm

equal on the two sides. These measurements are made with either a taper gauge or the inside calipers.

## Setting the Depth of Cut
(Fig. 10.12)

After the cutter has been centred, a feeler-gauge is laid on the work and the blank is raised until contact is made. To cut the teeth to the full depth, the work is raised, by reference to the feed-screw index, for a distance equal to $\frac{2 \cdot 157}{DP}$in., plus the thickness of the feeler-gauge.

If the diametral pitch is 20, and the feeler-gauge 4 thousandths of an inch in thickness, then $\frac{2 \cdot 157}{20} + 0 \cdot 004$in. $= 0 \cdot 112$in. which is the whole depth of the tooth.

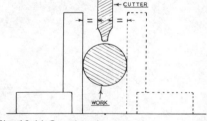

Fig. 10.11 Centring the cutter

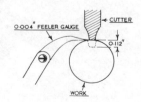

Fig. 10.12 Setting the depth of cut

## MACHINING THE GEAR TEETH

### Cutter Speeds

A table of speeds for both high-speed steel and carbon steel cutters, when machining various metals, is given in the previous chapter. These speeds are suitable for gear cutting with a moderate rate of feed and depth cut.

### Rate of Feed

The rate of feed will depend partly on the depth of cut taken and on the machinability of the material. A slow, even rate of hand feeding should be maintained in order to avoid chatter and to leave a high surface finish on the gear teeth.

### Depth of Cut

Gear teeth of fine pitch can be machined to full depth with a single passage of the cutter. Coarse teeth may have to be machined in two or more stages, and it is then advisable to cut all the teeth a few thousandths of an inch short of the full depth; this is followed by taking a light finishing cut all over the teeth in turn. When machining steel gear blanks, a plentiful supply of cutting oil should be maintained.

### MACHINING RACKS IN THE LATHE (Fig. 10.13)

As a rack corresponds to a gear-wheel of infinitely large diameter with its teeth

*Fig. 10.13 Machining a rack in the lathe*

lying on a straight line, the pitch of the rack teeth is equal to the circular pitch of the equivalent gear-wheel. The pitch is obtained by applying the formula:

$$\text{Pitch of rack} = \frac{3 \cdot 1416}{\text{DP of gear-wheel}}.$$

The pitch of a rack to mesh with a gear-wheel of 20 DP is therefore:

$$\frac{3 \cdot 1416}{20} = 0 \cdot 157 \text{in}.$$

and the rack is traversed for this distance to space the individual teeth during machining. The depth of the rack teeth is equal to the depth of the gear wheel teeth, which is $\frac{2 \cdot 247}{DP}$ and for a gear wheel of 20 DP in order to give working clearance this equals 0·112in.

To cut the rack teeth, a No. 1 cutter is mounted on an arbor between the lathe centres and the work is gripped in the machine vice, secured to the cross slide with the jaws aligned parallel with the lathe axis. As no adjustment for height is provided, the work is set up in the vice so that the rack teeth are machined to the full depth at a single passage of the cutter. To gain height, it may be necessary to raise the vice itself on parallel packings. With the work resting evenly on the floor of the vice, the distance between the work surface and the cutter teeth is measured with a feeler-gauge or a taper-gauge. Packing strips are then used to raise the work for this distance, plus the full depth of the rack teeth. The teeth are spaced by referring to the leadscrew index, and the saddle is locked while each tooth is being machined.

## REMEMBER

The teeth of the gear-cutters must be kept sharp to do accurate machining.

Make sure that the sector arms of the dividing gear are set to span the correct number of holes.

The cutter must be rigidly and centrally mounted.

Make sure that the wheel blank is firmly mounted on its arbor.

The wheel blank will be centrally mounted if turned to size on its arbor.

It is important to centre the cutter accurately on the gear blank.

Several cuts may be needed to machine coarse teeth to the full depth. It is advisable to take a finishing cut over all the teeth in turn.

If the cutter is run too fast, its cutting edges may be blunted.

When machining racks, the work must be aligned parallel with the lathe axis.

Keep the saddle locked while cutting the gear teeth.

PLATE No. 1 CIRCLES
91:77:49:45:38:34:32
PLATE No. 2 CIRCLES
47:46:43:42:41:37:31:29

# MYFORD
# DIVIDING
# ATTACHMENT

PLATE No. 3 CIRCLES
97:83:73:67:61:27
PLATE No. 4 CIRCLES
89:79:71:66:59:53

## WORM AND WHEEL RATIO:— 60/1
Plates 3 and 4 are supplied as extra

| No. of divisions | Index circle | No. of turns of Index crank | No. of divisions | Index circle | No. of turns of Index crank | No. of divisions | Index circle | No. of turns of Index crank |
|---|---|---|---|---|---|---|---|---|
| 1 | ANY | 60 | 31 | 31 | $1\frac{29}{31}$ | 61 | 61 | $\frac{60}{61}$ |
| 2 | ANY | 30 | 32 | 32 | $1\frac{28}{32}$ | 62 | 31 | $\frac{30}{31}$ |
| 3 | ANY | 20 | 33 | 77 | $1\frac{63}{77}$ | 63 | 42 | $\frac{40}{42}$ |
| 4 | ANY | 15 | 34 | 34 | $1\frac{26}{34}$ | 64 | 32 | $\frac{30}{32}$ |
| 5 | ANY | 12 | 35 | 49 | $1\frac{35}{49}$ | 65 | 91 | $\frac{84}{91}$ |
| 6 | ANY | 10 | 36 | 45 | $1\frac{30}{45}$ | 66 | 77 | $\frac{70}{77}$ |
| 7 | 49 | $8\frac{28}{49}$ | 37 | 37 | $1\frac{23}{37}$ | 67 | 67 | $\frac{60}{67}$ |
| 8 | 32 | $7\frac{16}{32}$ | 38 | 38 | $1\frac{22}{38}$ | 68 | 34 | $\frac{30}{34}$ |
| 9 | 45 | $6\frac{30}{45}$ | 39 | 91 | $1\frac{49}{91}$ | 69 | 46 | $\frac{40}{46}$ |
| 10 | ANY | 6 | 40 | 32 | $1\frac{16}{32}$ | 70 | 49 | $\frac{42}{49}$ |
| 11 | 77 | $5\frac{35}{77}$ | 41 | 41 | $1\frac{19}{41}$ | 71 | 71 | $\frac{60}{71}$ |
| 12 | ANY | 5 | 42 | 49 | $1\frac{21}{49}$ | 72 | 42 | $\frac{35}{42}$ |
| 13 | 91 | $4\frac{56}{91}$ | 43 | 43 | $1\frac{17}{43}$ | 73 | 73 | $\frac{60}{73}$ |
| 14 | 49 | $4\frac{14}{49}$ | 44 | 77 | $1\frac{28}{77}$ | 74 | 37 | $\frac{30}{37}$ |
| 15 | ANY | 4 | 45 | 45 | $1\frac{15}{45}$ | 75 | 45 | $\frac{36}{45}$ |
| 16 | 32 | $3\frac{24}{32}$ | 46 | 46 | $1\frac{14}{46}$ | 76 | 38 | $\frac{30}{38}$ |
| 17 | 34 | $3\frac{18}{34}$ | 47 | 47 | $1\frac{13}{47}$ | 77 | 77 | $\frac{60}{77}$ |
| 18 | 45 | $3\frac{15}{45}$ | 48 | 32 | $1\frac{8}{32}$ | 78 | 91 | $\frac{70}{91}$ |
| 19 | 38 | $3\frac{6}{38}$ | 49 | 49 | $1\frac{11}{49}$ | 79 | 79 | $\frac{60}{79}$ |
| 20 | ANY | 3 | 50 | 45 | $1\frac{9}{45}$ | 80 | 32 | $\frac{24}{32}$ |
| 21 | 49 | $2\frac{42}{49}$ | 51 | 34 | $1\frac{6}{34}$ | 81 | 27 | $\frac{20}{27}$ |
| 22 | 77 | $2\frac{56}{77}$ | 52 | 91 | $1\frac{14}{91}$ | 82 | 41 | $\frac{30}{41}$ |
| 23 | 46 | $2\frac{28}{46}$ | 53 | 53 | $1\frac{7}{53}$ | 83 | 83 | $\frac{60}{83}$ |
| 24 | 32 | $2\frac{16}{32}$ | 54 | 45 | $1\frac{5}{45}$ | 84 | 49 | $\frac{35}{49}$ |
| 25 | 45 | $2\frac{18}{45}$ | 55 | 77 | $1\frac{7}{77}$ | 85 | 34 | $\frac{24}{34}$ |
| 26 | 91 | $2\frac{28}{91}$ | 56 | 42 | $1\frac{3}{42}$ | 86 | 43 | $\frac{30}{43}$ |
| 27 | 45 | $2\frac{10}{45}$ | 57 | 38 | $1\frac{2}{38}$ | 87 | 29 | $\frac{20}{29}$ |
| 28 | 42 | $2\frac{6}{42}$ | 58 | 29 | $1\frac{1}{29}$ | 88 | 66 | $\frac{45}{66}$ |
| 29 | 29 | $2\frac{2}{29}$ | 59 | 59 | $1\frac{1}{59}$ | 89 | 89 | $\frac{60}{89}$ |
| 30 | ANY | 2 | 60 | ANY | 1 | 90 | 45 | $\frac{30}{45}$ |

For angular dividing use 42 circle   $1° = \frac{7}{42}$

| No. of divisions | Index circle | No. of turns of Index crank | No. of divisions | Index circle | No. of turns of Index crank | No. of divisions | Index circle | No. of turns of Index crank |
|---|---|---|---|---|---|---|---|---|
| 91 | 91 | $\frac{60}{91}$ | 128 | | $\frac{15}{32}$ | 165 | | $\frac{28}{77}$ |
| 92 | 46 | $\frac{30}{46}$ | 129 | | $\frac{20}{43}$ | 166 | | $\frac{30}{83}$ |
| 93 | 31 | $\frac{20}{31}$ | 130 | | $\frac{42}{91}$ | 167 | | |
| 94 | 47 | $\frac{30}{47}$ | 131 | | | 168 | | $\frac{15}{42}$ |
| 95 | 38 | $\frac{24}{38}$ | 132 | | | 169 | | |
| 96 | 32 | $\frac{20}{32}$ | 133 | | | 170 | | $\frac{12}{34}$ |
| 97 | 97 | $\frac{60}{97}$ | 134 | | $\frac{30}{67}$ | 171 | 57 | $\frac{20}{57}$ |
| 98 | 49 | $\frac{30}{49}$ | 135 | | $\frac{20}{45}$ | 172 | | $\frac{15}{43}$ |
| 99 | 66 | $\frac{40}{66}$ | 136 | | $\frac{15}{34}$ | 173 | | |
| 100 | 45 | $\frac{27}{45}$ | 137 | | | 174 | | $\frac{10}{29}$ |
| 101 | | | 138 | | $\frac{20}{46}$ | 175 | 35 | $\frac{12}{35}$ |
| 102 | | $\frac{20}{34}$ | 139 | | | 176 | 44 | $\frac{15}{44}$ |
| 103 | | | 140 | | $\frac{18}{42}$ | 177 | | $\frac{20}{59}$ |
| 104 | 26 | $\frac{15}{26}$ | 141 | | $\frac{20}{47}$ | 178 | | $\frac{30}{89}$ |
| 105 | | $\frac{24}{42}$ | 142 | | $\frac{30}{71}$ | 179 | | |
| 106 | | $\frac{30}{53}$ | 143 | | | 180 | | $\frac{15}{45}$ |
| 107 | | | 144 | 12 | $\frac{5}{12}$ | 181 | | |
| 108 | | $\frac{25}{45}$ | 145 | | $\frac{12}{29}$ | 182 | | $\frac{30}{91}$ |
| 109 | | | 146 | | $\frac{30}{73}$ | 183 | | $\frac{20}{61}$ |
| 110 | | $\frac{42}{77}$ | 147 | | $\frac{20}{49}$ | 184 | | $\frac{15}{46}$ |
| 111 | | $\frac{20}{37}$ | 148 | | $\frac{15}{37}$ | 185 | | $\frac{12}{37}$ |
| 112 | 28 | $\frac{15}{28}$ | 149 | | | 186 | | $\frac{10}{31}$ |
| 113 | | | 150 | | $\frac{18}{45}$ | 187 | | |
| 114 | | $\frac{20}{38}$ | 151 | | | 188 | | $\frac{15}{47}$ |
| 115 | | $\frac{24}{46}$ | 152 | | $\frac{15}{38}$ | 189 | 63 | $\frac{20}{63}$ |
| 116 | | $\frac{15}{29}$ | 153 | 51 | $\frac{20}{51}$ | 190 | | $\frac{12}{38}$ |
| 117 | 39 | $\frac{20}{39}$ | 154 | | $\frac{30}{77}$ | 191 | | |
| 118 | | $\frac{30}{59}$ | 155 | | $\frac{12}{31}$ | 192 | | $\frac{10}{32}$ |
| 119 | | | 156 | | $\frac{35}{91}$ | 193 | | |
| 120 | | $\frac{16}{32}$ | 157 | | | 194 | | $\frac{30}{97}$ |
| 121 | | | 158 | | $\frac{30}{79}$ | 195 | | $\frac{28}{91}$ |
| 122 | | $\frac{30}{61}$ | 159 | | $\frac{20}{53}$ | 196 | | $\frac{15}{49}$ |
| 123 | | $\frac{20}{41}$ | 160 | | $\frac{12}{32}$ | 197 | | |
| 124 | | $\frac{15}{31}$ | 161 | | | 198 | | $\frac{20}{66}$ |
| 125 | 25 | $\frac{12}{25}$ | 162 | | $\frac{10}{27}$ | 199 | | |
| 126 | | $\frac{20}{42}$ | 163 | | | 200 | 10 | $\frac{3}{10}$ |
| 127 | | | 164 | | $\frac{15}{41}$ | | | |

For angular dividing use 42 circle $1° = \frac{7}{42}$

# CHAPTER ELEVEN

# Taper Turning

STRAIGHT-SIDED TAPERS are usually de-noted either by the value of the included angle or by the difference between the large and small diameters. When the linear value is given, this is stated either as the increase of diameter over a unit of length, such as $\frac{1}{4}$in. to the foot, or this degree can be expressed as 1 in 48.

The accompanying reference tables give the linear measurements of angular tapers and also the converse values. There are three methods (in common use) for turning tapers:

    (1) Swivelling the topslide;
    (2) Setting over the tailstock centre;
    (3) Employing a taper turning attach-ment.

## Swivelling the Topslide

When the value of the taper is given in degrees, the top slide is rotated for half this amount by referring to the scale engraved on the base casting. Where the amount of taper is expressed in parts of an inch to the foot, the corresponding value in degrees can be ascertained from the conversion table.

## Machining the Taper

The tool must be mounted with its cutting point at exactly centre height, otherwise a straight-sided taper will not be formed. The correct setting of the tool will be

| Tapers | | | |
|---|---|---|---|
| Taper per foot | Included angle deg. / min. | | Included angle deg. | Taper per foot |
| $\frac{1}{8}$in. | 0 | 36 | 1 | 0·209in. |
| $\frac{3}{16}$in. | 0 | 54 | 2 | 0·419in. |
| $\frac{1}{4}$in. | 1 | 11 | 3 | 0·628in. |
| $\frac{5}{16}$in. | 1 | 29 | 4 | 0·838in. |
| $\frac{3}{8}$in. | 1 | 47 | 5 | 1·048in. |
| $\frac{7}{16}$in. | 2 | 5 | 6 | 1·258in. |
| $\frac{1}{2}$in. | 2 | 23 | 7 | 1·458in. |
| $\frac{9}{16}$in. | 2 | 41 | 8 | 1·678in. |
| $\frac{5}{8}$in. | 2 | 59 | 9 | 1·889in. |
| $\frac{11}{16}$in. | 3 | 17 | 10 | 2·099in. |
| $\frac{3}{4}$in. | 3 | 35 | 11 | 2·310in. |
| $\frac{13}{16}$in. | 3 | 52 | 12 | 2·522in. |
| $\frac{7}{8}$in. | 4 | 10 | 13 | 2·734in. |
| $\frac{15}{16}$in. | 4 | 28 | 14 | 2·946in. |
| 1 in. | 4 | 46 | 15 | 3·159in. |

facilitated, and the machining will be more accurate, if the tool has a narrow cutting edge. Whenever possible, the tailstock centre should be used to support the work. To obtain a good finish on the work, run the lathe at high speed and feed the top slide with a regular turning movement.

## External Tapers

Where a male taper is being machined to match a female taper, as when making an arbor for a drill chuck, the fit is tested by thinly smearing the work with marking paste and then engaging it in the female taper with a twisting motion. The transfer marks will show if any alteration of the top slide setting is necessary. Some workers remove the high places by applying a fine Swiss file to the rotating work, but accurate machining is preferable.

## Internal Tapers

When machining matching external and internal tapers, a correct fit will not be obtained by using the same setting of the top slide in both instances. This is because the direction of the cutting thrust becomes reversed, and any play in the lathe slides and mandrel bearings is taken up in opposite directions. If the internal taper is machined with the tool mounted upside down and cutting at the back of the work (Fig. 11.1) the thrust will remain in the same direction as before and a more accurate fit should be obtained.

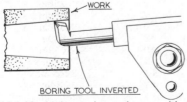

Fig. 11.1 Machining an internal taper with tool inverted

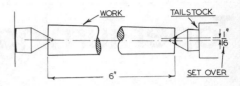

Fig. 11.2 Diagram to show tailstock set over

## Setting over the Tailstock

When the tailstock is set over and the work is mounted between centres, the lathe centres are thrown out of line. The tailstock centre does not then bear evenly in the work and irregular wear of the work centre may follow. This method of taper turning should, therefore, be employed only for machining tapers of small angularity. To determine the distance to set over the tailstock, an angular value is first converted to inches per foot of taper. The set over is equal to half the amount of the taper in inches multiplied by the length of the work measured in feet. If therefore, as in Fig. 11.2, the taper is $\frac{1}{4}$in. per foot and the length of the work is 6in. the tailstock is set towards the operator for $\frac{1}{16}$in.

During machining, the tailstock centre should be kept well lubricated and must be adjusted from time to time to take up wear in the work centre.

## The Taper Turning Attachment (Fig. 11.3)

The Myford attachment is bolted on to a machined surface at the back of the lathe bed, and four positions are available for machining work over the full distance between the lathe centres.

After removal of the cross slide feed screw, the cross slide is connected to the slide of the attachment by means of an adjustable link. This secondary slide moves on a pivoted slideway which has an angular travel of 10° on either side of

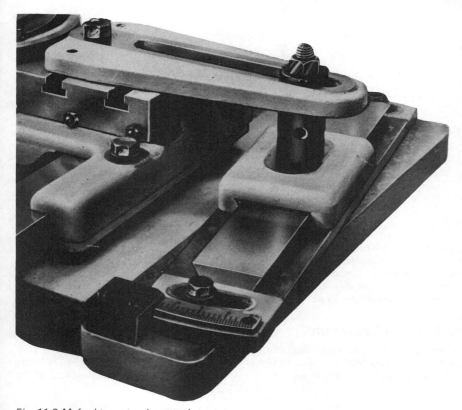

*Fig. 11.3 Myford taper turning attachment*

the parallel or zero position. When, therefore, the lathe saddle is moved along the bed, the cross slide is guided by the angular setting of the slideway. In this way, tapers up to 6in. in length can be machined, with the graduated slideway set to half the included angle of taper required. To enable the tool to be fed to the work, the top slide is rotated in a direction to the maximum swivel of the top slide, i.e. 63° to the lathe axis. The attachment has the advantage that, with it the automatic saddle traverse can be employed; this makes for accurate machining and a good work finish.

## Knurling

Two types of knurling, the straight and the diamond pattern (Fig. 11.4) are commonly used on collars and other fittings to provide a finger hold.

The corresponding knurling wheels, for impressing the pattern on the work, are made of hardened steel and run on pivots in a knurling holder.

Diamond knurling is formed by employing two wheels with their teeth set at opposite angles. With the simple type of holder fitted with a pivoted head (Fig. 11.5) the pressure applied by feeding the

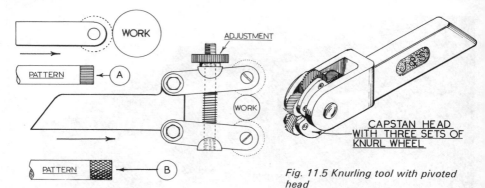

Fig. 11.4 The two types of knurling tool

Fig. 11.5 Knurling tool with pivoted head

tool directly inwards throws a heavy load on the lathe mandrel bearings. In the improved form of holder (Fig. 11.6) in which the wheels are mounted on pivoted arms, the work is compressed equally between the two wheels and the lathe bearings are relieved of strain.

## The Knurling Operation

After the part has been machined to run truly, bring the knurling wheels into light contact with the work. Move the knurls to the right, clear of the work and then close the wheels for some 10 thousandths of an inch or, as the case may be, feed the plain type of tool inwards by this amount. Engage the backgear and feed the tool by hand for a short distance along the work. Stop the lathe and examine the impression formed on the work. If the knurling shows that the two wheels are not in step, close the wheels a little on the work and start the lathe again.

As soon as the proper pattern is being cut, engage the low, direct speed of the

Fig. 11.6 Straddle wheel knurling tool

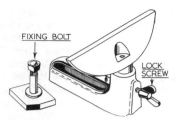

Fig. 11.7 The hand rest

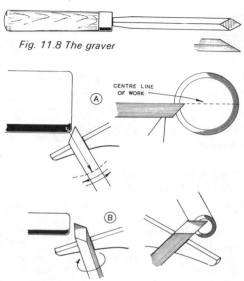

Fig. 11.8 The graver

Fig. 11.9 Using the graver

lathe and feed the tool carefully along the work by hand. Continue until the knurling is cleanly cut and the diamong-shaped impressions are left with sharp points.

If possible coolant should be used during the operation. Failing this apply oil to the work with a brush and cleanse the knurled surface by wire brushing before making a final pass across the work with the knurl wheels. The swarf produced during the knurling operation takes the form of a fine metal dust. If this is allowed to remain on the work surface the finished knurling can never be sharp.

For light knurling on mild steel a single passage over the work should be sufficient to give a satisfactory finish. Repeated cuts are liable to roll chips into the work surface and spoil the finish.

## Turning with Hand Tools

A great variety of work can be carried out in the lathe with hand tools when these are supported on the hand rest (Fig. 11.7). Brass parts with flat or curved surfaces can, in this way, readily be turned with a high finish. For small work, the graver is commonly used (Fig. 11.8). This tool is made from a length of square, tool steel, and its cutting edges are formed by grinding and afterwards honing a single oblique flat surface at the tip.

In Fig. 11.9 the methods used by the author when turning with the hand graver are depicted diagrammatically. At

(A) the tool approach for brass is shown. As will be seen when rounding the corner of the work the cutting edge of the graver is set on the centre line and the tool itself swung backwards and forwards on the hand rest using as a fulcrum centre the imaginary point indicated on the diagram.

With steel components, on the other hand, the opposite edge of the graver is used and this is applied well above the centre line, the tool as a whole being rotated axially as shown by the arrow in diagram (B).

For heavier turning, the tools shown in Fig. 11.10 are generally used; these are formed with either a rounded tip (A) or with a straight or an oblique cutting edge (B). As with the graver, these tools are tilted in relation to the work until the best cutting position is found. The hand rest should always be set as close as possible to the work and, to give proper control, the tool should be fitted with a long handle.

151

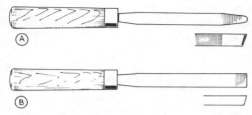

*Fig. 11.10 Turning tools for heavy work: A and B.*

## THE MYFORD SAWING ATTACHMENT (Fig. 11.11)

Circular saws, mounted on an arbor between the lathe centres, can be used for cutting off material and slitting sheet metal. A pin screwed into the arbor serves for driving the saw from the mandrel catchplate. The saw table is readily adjustable for height, and an adjustable guide fence is provided for controlling the width of the material cut by the saw.

A 5in. diameter high-speed steel saw can be used for cutting steel when driven by the middle speed of the backgear, but for a carbon steel saw the lowest speed of the backgear should be engaged. When sawing steel, use a brush to supply cutting oil to the saw teeth.

The speeds given can be doubled for sawing brass or aluminium alloys.

## The Chuck Stop (Fig. 11.12)

It is sometimes necessary to chuck thin components, washers or distance pieces for example, so that they may be machined in one way or another. The difficulty, here, is to ensure that the work stands upright or it will wobble when the lathe is set in motion. This is the purpose of the chuck stop illustrated in the dia-

*Fig. 11.11 The Myford sawing attachment*

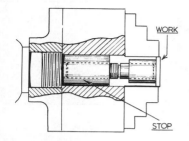

*Fig. 11.12 The chuck stop*

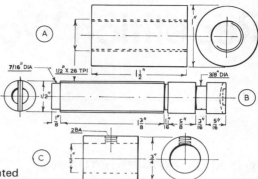

*Fig. 11.13 Detail of the chuck stop*

gram Fig. 11.12, where it is seen mounted inside the chuck. The device comprises three parts, the body (A), the spindle (B) and the sleeve (C) details of all three being given in Fig. 11.13.

The body abuts against the end of the lathe mandrel, so by adjusting the stand-out of the spindle, and fitting the sleeve if the work is of large diameter or has a hole greater than ½in. diameter, the part to be machined can be set to run true.

Although this is not depicted in the illustration it is advisable to adopt the procedure described in an earlier chapter and provide a sleeve the same diameter as the work. This can be placed in the back of the chuck jaws to prevent them tipping when they are closed on the work.

For drilling and boring operations it is necessary to back off the stop spindle so that the tools can have free passage. To this end the spindle has a screw-driver slot enabling it to be turned back and then returned to its original place after the machining has been completed.

153

# CHAPTER TWELVE

# Repetition Work

## THE MYFORD 4-TOOL TURRET

THIS ATTACHMENT can be fitted to the lathe top slide in place of the standard tool clamp.

Repetition work is simplified, as once the four tools carried in the turret have been accurately set, they can, in turn, be quickly brought into the operating position and are then positively located.

A rigid, ratchet stop-mechanism, housed within the turret body, enables the individual tools to be accurately located at any of the eight stations provided; the turret is then firmly secured by tightening the clamp handle. The

*Fig. 12.1 The 4-tool turret*

mechanism is fully protected against the entry of swarf, and chips cannot lodge under the base, as the turret is not lifted when being turned into position.

The 4-tool turret illustrated is a standard ML7 accessory fitted to the author's 4in. Myford lathe, now out of production.

## Machining Screws

As an example of simple repetition work, the 4-tool turret can be used for machining a batch of countersink-head screws:

(1) Grip a length of rod in the self-centring chuck or in a mandrel collet chuck.

(2) Set the chamfering tool against the end of the work, with the leadscrew and cross slide indices at zero.

(3) Chamfer the end of the rod by traversing the saddle, and note the reading of the leadscrew index.

(4) Set a knife tool to turn the shank diameter. Note the reading of the cross slide index, and also the leadscrew index reading at the end of the cut.

(5) Set a second chamfering tool to touch the shank, and note the leadscrew index reading after chamfering the screw head.

(6) Thread the screw, using the tailstock die holder.

(7) Mount the parting tool and note the leadscrew index reading when parting off the screw to length.

(8) Return the saddle and cross slide to their original positions, with indices at zero, and use the tool as a distance stop for resetting the rod in the chuck.

If no 4-tool turret is available, but there is a back toolpost on the lathe, it is still possible to machine a range of single components as the following series of diagrams will show. It will be necessary, however, to provide an improvised saddle stop consisting of a piece of metal strip some $\frac{1}{2}$in. thick secured to the face of the lathe bed using, for preference, the special clamp bolt taken from the fixed steady. But note that, if the self-act or automatic carriage traverse is engaged, it should be disengaged well before the carriage comes into contact with the improvised stop or the clasp nut may be damaged. The carriage traverse is then completed by hand using the traverse wheel on the apron.

The amount of in-feed for the tool is read off on the cross slide index, and the tool itself is used as a stop when sliding the material through the chuck after successive components have been machined. The actual length of the component will determine the amount of stock that needs to be set against the face of the tool. This is dependent on the distance between the face of the carriage and the improvised stop on the lathe bed, a measurement that is best made with a pair of inside callipers. A second stop can then be set on the opposite side of the carriage to ensure that this distance is always maintained.

The diagram Fig. 12.2 shows the sequence of operations in making one of a batch of cheese head screws. The turn-

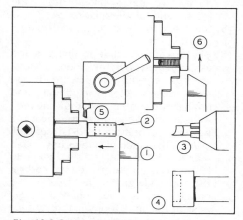

*Fig. 12.2 Sequence of operations for Machining screws*

ing tools needed are a right-hand knife tool set on the top slide, which should have its index set to zero before operations start, and a parting-off tool set in the rear toolpost. The sequence of operations then is:

(1) Turn stock to screw head diameter for a length sufficient to provide for the full length of the screw plus 0·030in. for facing the head at a later operation. On completion of the operation secure the front bed stop. Note the reading of the cross slide index.

(2) Back off top slide for a distance equal to the width of the screw head plus 0·030in. Use the top slide index to make the necessary measurement and note the reading. Turn the screw body to diameter and note the reading of the cross slide index.

(3) Round end of screw with form cutter set in the tailstock chuck.

(4) Thread screw using the tailstock die holder with saddle in contact with the front bed stop. When using the tailstock die holder backgear should be used and the mandrel speed reduced to that available from the lowest and middle gear ratios.

(5) Set back toolpost to part off screw and part off.

(6) Set forward top slide to first position as indicated by the index. Move carriage against the left-hand bed stop, release stock in chuck and bring it into contact with the knife tool. All will then be in order to repeat the sequence of operations just described.

After the batch of screws have been machined face off screw heads to length. Use the front bed stop and set the top slide using the face of the chuck jaws as a reference. A single pass of the knife tool will then suffice to face the head of the screw to length.

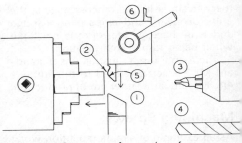

Fig. 12.3 Sequence of operations for machining washers

## Making Washers

The sequence of operations for making washers is depicted in the diagram Fig. 12.3. The process is much the same as that previously indicated but in this instance the back toolpost needs to be able to accommodate a pair of tools; one for parting off, the other a combination tool capable of both facing and chamfering. The sequence of machining operations, therefore, is:

(1) Turn stock to correct diameter;
(2) Face end of work piece;
(3) Centre drill;
(4) Drill;
(5) Chamfer;
(6) Turn back toolpost capstan to bring parting tool into place and part off.

Note that if a sufficient length of stock is turned down during operation (1) the knife tool can still be used as a material stop in the manner described previously, whilst setting the parting tool at the correct distance in advance of the knife tool will ensure that washers are machined to the correct thickness. The carriage must be locked and a bed stop put in place to maintain correct location.

## Making Nuts

The third process that is illustrated is the making of nuts (Fig. 12.4). The tooling is

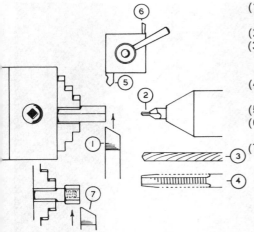

(1) Set hexagon stock in self-centring chuck and face end of work;
(2) Centre drill work;
(3) Drill work tapping size for a depth that will enable four or five nuts to be made;
(4) Set tap in tailstock chuck and tap work;
(5) Chamfer nut;
(6) Bring parting tool into play and part off nut;
(7) If it is important that all nuts produced should be the same length, set each on a threaded arbor and face off underside of nut. The carriage should be locked, and the cut put on the top slide. Once the correct length has been established the facing of succeeding nuts is controlled by the cross slide.

*Fig. 12.4 Sequence of operations for machining nuts*

similar to that required for making washers in that a back toolpost with a pair of tools is required in addition to the knife tool which, here, is only required for a facing operation and to act as a material stop.

The sequence of operations is as follows:

## Back Toolpost Tools

The tools that need to be mounted in the back toolpost are illustrated in Fig. 12.5. At (A) the combined facing and chamfering tool for turret type post is depicted. It will be seen that there are two chamfering faces right- and left-hand, and a rounded cutting edge on the left to be

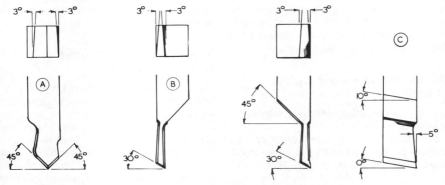

*Fig. 12.5 Back toolpost tools needed for machining screws, washers and nuts:*
*(A) Chamfering tool  (B) parting tool  (C) combined chamfering and parting tool*

157

*Fig. 12.6 Lever operated collet chuck*

used for facing operations. The parting tool (B) follows normal practice with the addition of a 30° angular point to ensure clean parting off.

The parting tool illustrated at (C) is intended for mounting in a non-reversible back toolpost. Again, the tool is normal; but it has additionally a 45° cutting face that can be used for chamfering.

## The Lever Operated Collet Chuck

This Myford attachment has a maximum holding capacity of ⅝in.

For rapid repetition work, parts can be gripped or removed from the chuck by a movement of the operating lever, and without having to stop the machine.

The body of the attachment is screwed to the lathe mandrel nose. The thrust when

closing the collet is taken against a ball thrust race.

The collets are of dead length pattern and are supplied in a wide range of sizes.

To show the constructional details, a sectional view of the attachment is given in Fig. 12.7.

## The Cross Slide Turret Attachment

This attachment is machined to bolt to the lathe cross slide, and is designed for rapid repetition work. The revolving turret has six stations and a like number of housings for mounting the tools. A wide range of tools can be fitted to the turret head, including box tools and quick-opening die-heads. The turret is released by means of a convenient clamping collar bearing on the upper surface of the turret body.

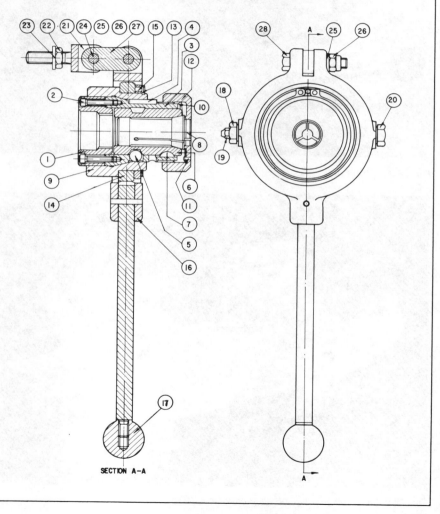

Fig. 12.7 Lever operated collet chuck section drawing. (1) backplate (2) cap head screw body sec'g (3) body (4) key—body (5) ball (6) sleeve (7) woodruff key (8) collet (9) closing ring (10) spring (11) rivet-spring sec'g (12) nose cap (13) circlip (14) thrust ring (15) thrust ring and pin assembly (16) lever assembly (17) knob (18) pivot pin (19) oil nipple (20) pivot pin (21) eye bolt—headstock (22) hexagonal lock nut (23) washer (24) hexagonal head bolt (25) washer (26) Simmonds nut (27) pivot link (28) hexagonal head bolt

SECTION A-A

Fig. 12.8 Saddle turret

Fig. 12.9 Lever operated cut-off slide number 20/088

*Fig. 12.10 Multi-stop*

## The Cut-Off Slide

The illustration shows a Myford ML7 lathe fully equipped for repetition work. In addition to the lever operated collet chuck and the saddle turret, a cut-off slide is fitted to enable a greater range of machining operations to be undertaken. The cut-off slide carries both front and rear toolposts, each mounting a single tool designed either for form turning or for parting off the finished work-piece.

## Cut-off Slide

The Cut-off slide No. 1458 has now been withdrawn from production. The only slide now available is the lever-operated slide No. 20/088. See Fig. 12.9.

In this connection the readers' attention is drawn to Myfords publication No. 755. This lists, with relevant line drawings all the additional equipment available for Myford Series 7 lathes. The publication referred to has the advantage of greater clarity in presenting the various items for selection.

## The Multi-stop

This fitting, attached to the back of the lathe bed, is used in conjunction with the saddle turret for rapid repetition machining. The purpose of the attachment is to limit the forward travel of the saddle for the exact distance required to operate each of the six tools fitted to the revolving turret. As shown, there are six adjustable stop-screws. These control the forward movement of the saddle by coming into contact with the stop-bar secured to the body of the attachment. To avoid complication, the stops are moved manually, to conform with the turret stations, and do not come into position automatically as the turret is rotated.

## The Lever-Feed Tailstock

The hand wheel housing of the standard

## MYFORD

Myford tailstock is machined to enable the lever-feed mechanism to be fitted without alteration.

The attachment is designed to afford ample leverage for drilling, and the adjustable stop mechanism ensures uniformly accurate depthing when repetition drilling is undertaken. The sensitive feed obtained with the attachment is a great advantage where small drills or centre drills are used.

# CHAPTER THIRTEEN

# Additional Fitments & Operations

THERE ARE A NUMBER of lathe operations that may be classified as unusual. In some instances they need special equipment, in others, however, modification to existing fitments will suffice, or some simple tooling will solve the problem.

## Cutting Rubber Rings from Tubing

The procedure to be described was developed in order to produce a number of special rings from standard rubber tubing. Anyone who has attempted this work freehand, with only a penknife to help him, will appreciate that it is impossible to produce a presentable ring by this means, let alone a whole uniform series of them. However, employing the simple tool depicted in Fig. 13.1 and mounting the rubber tubing on a mandrel held in the lathe chuck, rings of uniform section, and with perfect finish, may be produced rapidly. The tool shown was improvised from a length of square mild steel to which a discarded safety razor blade had been clamped by a fitting borrowed from some other equipment (Fig. 13.2).

In use, as illustrated in Fig. 13.3, the tool is set under the tool post with the razor blade upright and truly at right-angles to the work. A short length of

*Fig. 13.1 Tool for cutting rubber rings*

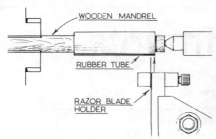

*Fig. 13.2 Using the washer cutter*

rubber tube of the required size is mounted on a wooden mandrel set in the self-centring chuck and supported by the tail-stock. The tool itself is then fed into the rotating work with liquid soap detergent applied as a lubricant.

## Mandrel Handles

Tapping or threading work held in the chuck is often better carried out if the mandrel can be turned by hand. This may be done in two ways, either by fitting an adaptor directly to the mandrel so that a handle can be attached to it, or by fixing the handle to the large countershaft wheel as seen in Fig. 13.3. The details of the fitting and the modifications to the wheel are given in Figs. 13.4. and 13.5. However, a handle directly applied to the mandrel itself is the most convenient arrangement, and the mandrel extension described in Chapter 9 the simplest mounting for it. The handle illustrated in Fig. 13.6 is a die-cast component having a counterbalancing weight integral with it. It is held in place in the same way as the change wheels for which the mandrel extension adaptor was originally made. It is unlikely that a handle of the same form could be obtained today, but this is of little moment since one of built up con-struction, and made from mild steel, will serve equally well. Indeed, by this means one can devise a handle with variable leverage that can be adjusted to suit the

*Fig. 13.3 The mandrel handle*

work in hand. It will be obvious, for example that the leverage needed to form a $\frac{3}{8}$in. whit. thread on work held in the chuck is likely to be much greater than

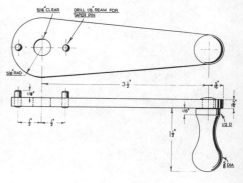

*Fig. 13.4 Detail of the mandrel handle*

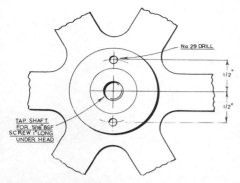

*Fig. 13.5 Details of the wheel modifications*

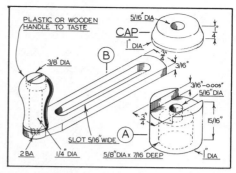

*Fig. 13.7 Mandrel handle for the ML7*

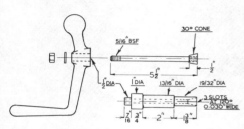

*Fig. 13.6 Handle fitted directly to the mandrel*

the work. To this end the slide is deprived of its complete feedscrew assembly which is replaced by the bracket and cross head illustrated in Fig. 13.9. A connecting rod is then attached to the crosshead and also to a lever anchored to the far end of the lathe bed, as seen in Fig. 13.10. Movement can then be imparted to the top slide, with adjustable leverage if thought desirable, and with the slide itself set over at an angle if and when this is necessary. A number of applications for the process

will be needed when dieing down some 6BA studs. As seen in Fig. 13.7, the parts needed are few consisting as they do of the hub (A) machined to accept the lever (B) which is secured by the expander bolt forming part of the mandrel extension assembly. The design is similar to that used by the author for handles on other machines in the workshop.

## Shaping in the ML7 Lathe

The process of shaping in the lathe is one in which the work is held stationary in the chuck where it can be indexed if necessary. An elementary example is the cutting of a keyway to full depth (Fig. 13.8).

A better proposition, however, is to lock the carriage and let the top slide do

*Fig. 13.8 Shaping a keyway*

Fig. 13.9 Top slide fitted with cross head

Fig. 13.10 Lever and connecting rod for the shaping unit

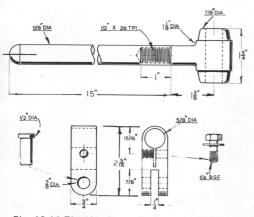

Fig. 13.11 The shaping unit: the operating lever

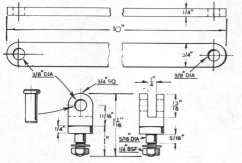

Fig. 13.12 The shaping unit: the connecting rod

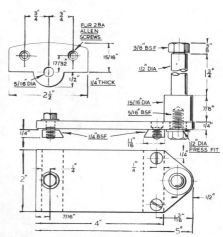

Fig. 13.13 The shaping unit: original anchorage for the operating lever together with top slide anchor plate

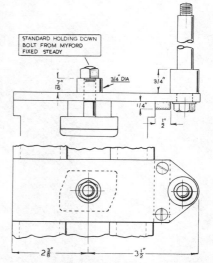

Fig. 13.14 Modified lever anchorage for the ML7 lathe

will no doubt suggest themselves. The most advanced work ever undertaken by the author was the cutting of the internal teeth in the ring gear of an epicyclic reduction box. For this purpose the work was suitably indexed and the cross slide provided with a stop to ensure that all tooth spaces were cut to a uniform depth.

## Slotting in the Lathe

Many years ago, when contemplating the machining of horn blocks for a loco-motive, the author improvised some elementary slotting equipment for the purpose. This comprised the lathe top slide mounted on end and driven from the mandrel by a connecting rod and disc

Fig. 13.15 Extemporised slotting attachment

*Fig. 13.16 Slotting attachment for the ML7*

crank attached to the mandrel nose as depicted in Fig. 13.15.

Later the equipment depicted in Fig. 13.16, was built up by the author and fitted to an ML7 lathe. The mechanism, which can be clearly seen in the illustration, comprises a variable stroke disc crank and means of setting the slide in relation to the work itself.

The disc crank is formed from the lathe driverplate by attaching to it a pair of quadrants machined to form a T-slotted unit in which the crankpin can be adjusted for stroke and locked when the stroke required has been set.

The various parts of the slotting attach-ment are illustrated in Fig. 13.17. They are as follows: (A) is the topslide which is mounted on the base unit (B). The base itself is located by the tenon passing between the shears of the lathe bed and is held in place by the clamp bolt (C) engaging the underside of the shears.

As has been said the disc crank (D) is a modified driverplate enabling an adjust-able crankpin (E) to be mounted. The connecting rod (F) engages a small end assembly (G) that can be adjusted for position in the cross head (H) fixed to the topslide after the removal of its feed screw. The attachment, within its capacity there-fore, can be adjusted to suit the work in

*Fig. 13.17 Parts of the slotting attachment*

*Fig. 13.17a Slotting attachment*

hand, even to the tool slide being set over at an angle.

Since the photograph which forms the basis of Fig. 13.17 was taken a strut has been added to up-rate the rigidity of the device. This strut is affixed to the top of the main frame and is secured to the head-stock casting by a stud that also forms an extension to the mandrel lubricator seating as depicted in Fig. 13.17.

In addition, in order to strengthen the Link H which takes the drive from the connecting Rod F to the top slide A, a pair of thrust blocks have been fitted to the underside of the Link itself. These abut the under side of the top slide and in doing so, reduce the bending movement imposed by the Connecting Rod on the Link. The arrangement is illustrated in Fig. 13.17a.

171

# CHAPTER FOURTEEN

# Maintenance

THE USEFUL LIFE of any machine depends very much on how well it is maintained. The lathe is no exception to this for it is one of the machine tools that operate under somewhat adverse conditions. For this reason the user should try to maintain his lathe in the best condition possible.

## Lubrication

The makers have furnished the Series 7 range of lathes with a very comprehensive lubrication system and have coupled this with a chart that is included in the handbook. This should enable the operator to recognise the many points that need lubricating and provide him with information on the correct type of lubricant to be employed.

It is not proposed to detail all the points that need attention, but rather to call to the reader's notice one or two particular components or assemblies needing special care. These are items, for the most part, that the author in his experience with industrial practice, has found to be neglected or, because of the programme set out for the works maintenance staff, do not receive sufficient lubrication.

Perhaps the most obvious example is the *headstock pulley*. This has a sleeve bearing needing regular oiling. The makers recommend that it should receive frequent attention from the oil gun whenever the backgear is used. If the gear is engaged and operating for some

hours at a time then, clearly, lubrication should be carried out every two hours or so. Both the ML7 and Super 7 have oil nipples fitted to the headstock pulley enabling the oil gun to be used readily. The location of the nipples on the ML7 and Super 7 are illustrated in the lubrication charts at the end of this book.

## The Tumbler Reverse Gear System

This system is often in operation for much of the time when the lathe is being run; but here again recourse to the oil gun seems all too often infrequent seeing that the gears themselves turn at a high speed and so need to be well lubricated. In the ML7 and Super 7 the gears have no bushing and run directly on their respective pins. In addition the sleeve gear itself, located on the tumbler reverse stud has both a plain and roller bearing incorporated in it as depicted in the illustration Fig. 14.1. Adequate lubrication and the removal of unwanted swarf from around the parts will do much to lengthen the life of the gear system.

A word to the wise at this point. If for any reason the tail end of a lathe spindle does not project through the change wheel cover, ingress of swarf into the change wheel assembly as a whole, and resulting from a boring operation for example, can be prevented if a piece of tightly rolled rag is pushed into the bore of

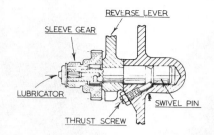

*Fig. 14.1 Details of the sleeve gear Super 7*

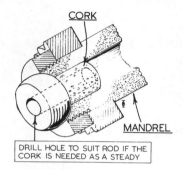

DRILL HOLE TO SUIT ROD IF THE CORK IS NEEDED AS A STEADY

*Fig. 14.2 Using a cork to keep back swarf*

the headstock spindle for an inch or so to stop the swarf working along inside the spindle.

Alternatively, a cork can be inserted into the outer end of the mandrel to achieve the same result. This method, depicted in the sketch Fig. 14.2 can, if the cork is drilled to suit, also be used to support thin rods that would otherwise rattle around during any turning operation that was being performed on them. The plastic-headed corks now much used by wine bottlers serve very well for the purpose. Lubrication of the change wheel studs is also important. As has been described elsewhere the change wheels themselves are mounted on keyed bushes that run on the studs attached to the change wheel quadrant. These should be oiled frequently.

## Swarf Trays

Tied up with the whole subject of maintenance is the prevention, so far as possible, of swarf produced by the turning operation from falling directly on the surface of the lathe bed. Cast iron dust and mild steel turnings may not have an immediate harmful effect on the carriage slideway but they do cumulative damage if not inhibited; moreover, when modern stainless or high-tensile steels are the subject of a turning operation the resulting chippings are often work-hardened and will then score the surface of the lathe bed and slides.

The makers provide felt wipers to the leading edge of the saddle. These will do much to isolate any possible damage, but it is only prudent to take steps that will reduce the amount of swarf falling on the bed surface itself.

Much may be done in this direction by fitting trays to the leading and trailing edges of the cross slide or by supporting them on the saddle itself in the manner depicted by the illustration Fig. 14.3 and Fig. 14.4. The tray shown is secured by a cap screw engaging a tapped hole in the saddle itself, and is provided with a gauze filter to permit coolant to run back to the lathe tray. The dimensions of the tray illustrated are given in Fig. 14.5.

## Care of Chucks

Chucks need to be cleaned and lubricated regularly if they are to provide the best possible service. They are not difficult to dismantle, indeed in the case of the 4-jaw independent variety this only amounts to withdrawing the chuck jaws and their securing screws. For the self-centring chuck the makers provide ample instruction, and this should be followed closely.

The mechanism of a self-centring chuck is such that ingress of swarf or metal dust is relatively easy. Initially the unwanted material is deposited on the

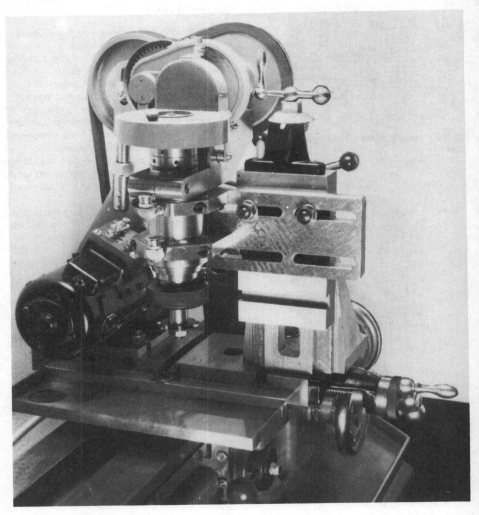

*Fig. 14.3 Location of swarf trays*

scroll and on the corresponding threads at the back of the chuck jaws. In time however, the finer particles of metal may find their way into the back of the scroll and on to the gears that turn it. Cleaning will then involve completely stripping the chuck according to the maker's instructions. Before removing the chuck from its backplate for this purpose however, remember to mark both backplate and chuck body so that both can be re-instated in their original relative positions when re-assembling.

When being dismantled for any pur-

*Fig. 14.4 Location of swarf trays*

pose, Jacobs drill chucks need special care. Used in the tailstock they do not suffer as much from swarf as do mandrel chucks, but they need a particular procedure to be used when stripping. For the most part this is only necessary if replacement parts have to be fitted, so

*Fig. 14.5 Details of the swarf tray*

washing in petrol or paraffin followed by immersion in a thin machine oil will usually be sufficient treatment.

## Cleaning Chuck Backplate Threads

Even when steps are taken to prevent swarf entering the body of the chuck by plugging its throat with a piece of rag, it sometimes happens that pieces of metal get trapped in the threads of the chuck backplate. This may occur as the chuck is withdrawn from the mandrel nose, or if it is placed backplate downwards, as a preliminary to being cleaned before putting away. If compressed air is available a good blast will usually remove un-

175

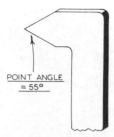

*Fig. 14.6 Tool for cleaning backplate threads*

wanted swarf. Occasionally a piece of metal remains stubbornly in the threads; in this event the tool depicted in Fig. 14.6 will remove it.

The illustration should explain itself. The tool is best made from a piece of $\frac{1}{8}$in. thick mild steel filed to the shape shown and left soft. It is worked round the backplate threads it will effectively dislodge anything trapped in them.

## Adjustment of Slides

If a lathe is to operate efficiently it is vital that the slides, on which much of its accuracy rests, are properly adjusted. The makers in their handbooks give detailed instructions for making these adjustments so there is no need to repeat them here. A word may be said, however, about the quality of the adjustment to be carried out. In the case of the saddle this should always move freely, but without shake, or the accuracy and finish of the turned work will suffer. The same remarks apply to the cross slide. This too should work freely. Very often one finds that the adjustment has been set far too tight, it is then virtually impossible to carry out any turning to close limits because of the difficulty of setting the feedscrew itself.

Unless the top slide is being used for a taper turning operation it should be set firmly. The top slide is the mount for the

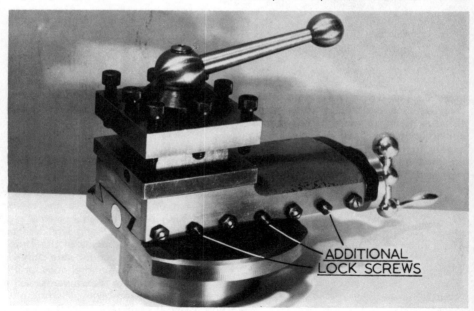

ADDITIONAL
LOCK SCREWS

*Fig. 14.7 Fitting additional lock screws to the top slide*

turning tool and is, for the most part, only required to be moved a short distance in order to put on the cut.

When turning a taper, however, set the top slide to move freely or the operation will be attended by finger fatigue long before the work has been completed. The fitting of some extra adjusting screws will help here (Fig. 14.7). They can be used to cause the slide to move firmly when required, and released when freedom of movement is needed. In this way the normal slide setting will be unaffected.

## Cleaning

It is very important, to keep the lathe as clean as possible and to remove any swarf that has been produced once turning operations have finished for the day. When the tool is not in use it should be kept covered to keep out any dust, remembering that dust is a by-product of workshop activity and that when mixed with oil forms a somewhat abrasive compound.

A properly fitting cover such as that obtainable from the makers will do much to reduce dust gaining direct access to the lathe. In default old bed sheets, or lengths of discarded upholstery material will serve. When using such covering,

however, it must be remembered that it is likely to attract moisture, so it is well to cover the machine with polythene sheeting before putting on the outer covering. In this way the possibility of rust forming on bright metal parts will be prevented, though it is not, of course, the answer to the condensation nuisance always present in workshops that do not have continuous heating. From the author's experience the solution to this problem, that has taken him some fifty years to resolve, is to install the oil-fired central-heating boiler in the shop itself. In this way all products of combustion, and these include water vapour, are discharged to atmosphere by way of the flue pipe. In addition, the air changes at floor level, resulting from the boilers' operating, coupled with the uniform general heating seem to inhibit any dampness there might possibly be.

Failing the solution outlined above the use of vapour phase inhibition paper spread over the machines will do much to reduce the nuisance.

On the subject of corrosion or staining, if unseasoned oak is being turned in the lathe get rid of the wood dust at once. Oak contains tannic acid which stains rapidly so oil the lathe bed and slides before and after the turning operation.

# CHAPTER FIFTEEN

# A Two-Tool Back Toolpost

SOME YEARS AGO the author with a colleague, under the pen-name 'Duplex', published details of a back toolpost carrying a pair of tools in a reversible capstan head. This fitment was suitable for the Myford ML7 lathe and also for the $3\frac{1}{2}$in. Drummond lathe which was, at the time of publication, still being made by Myford Limited.

For this reason, and because there are still many examples of the Drummond lathe in existence, it has been thought well to reproduce here the details of the toolpost in its original form and to add some information on certain additional fitments made for it.

As many will be aware, when the tool is used in the inverted position at the back

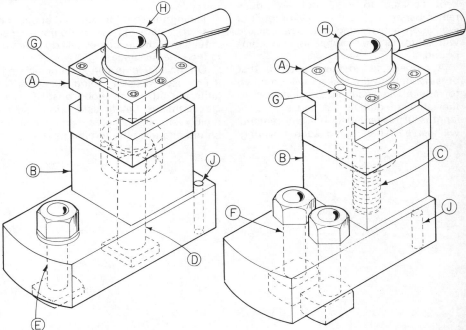

Fig. 15.1 Toolpost Type 'M'                    Fig. 15.2 Toolpost Type 'D'

of the lathe, parting off is greatly simplified and, in addition, heavy chamfering cuts can be taken with much less tendency to chatter.

In practice, it is found that a gap of $1\frac{1}{2}$in. between the points of the tools in the front and back toolposts is sufficient for comfortable working, but if at any time more room is needed here, either the turret of the back toolpost can be turned into its sideways position to get the tools out of the way, or the attachment as a whole can be removed by merely slackening its two securing bolts.

It is advisable, therefore, at the outset to make sure that the length of the cross slide is sufficient to afford ample working space between the two sets of tools.

The 2-station toolpost was designed in the first instance to carry a parting and a chamfering tool for turning steel, but those who habitually work in both brass and steel can either mount two parting tools suitable for machining these metals or, by the provision of an extra turret, the set of tools can be quickly changed at will for turning either material.

Although no claim is made that the methods adopted are necessarily the best or the quickest, it will, nevertheless, be found that they are designed to ensure a reasonable degree of accuracy in the finished product, as nothing is left to guess-work and the machining can be checked at every stage.

A set of working drawings is included which gives the necessary dimensions of the components used in the two patterns of toolposts suitable for lathes of different design (Figs. 15.1 and 15.2).

It will be observed that the difference lies in the position of the holding-down bolts, which are located to conform with the design of the cross slide and, at the same time, to space the back toolpost at a sufficient working distance from the front post.

The fitting of a long central bolt, is, perhaps, on the whole, preferable and should be used where the T-slots run in a direction across the cross slide, but the alternative form of attachment has been found entirely satisfactory in practice.

The tool housings are machined to take $\frac{1}{4}$in. square tools which are best made of short lengths of ground high-speed steel such as the well-known Eclipse brand. The breadth of the parting tool should be between $\frac{1}{16}$in. and $\frac{1}{8}$in., and the most generally useful tool forms are illustrated in Fig. 15.3.

The angle of the chamfering tool can be made either 45° or 40°, for the latter is the standard angle generally used for chamfering nuts, bolts and washers.

This tool, if formed as shown in Fig.

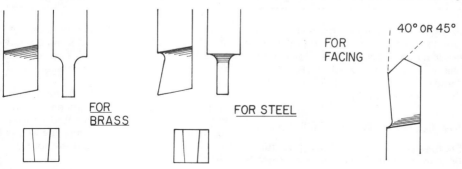

FOR BRASS

FOR STEEL

FOR FACING

40° OR 45°

*Fig. 15.3 Parting tools for brass and steel*

*Fig. 15.4 Chamfering tool*

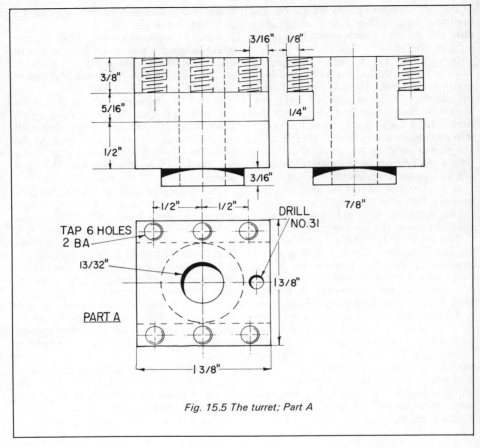

3/16"  1/8"

3/8"

5/16"  1/4"

1/2"

3/16"

1/2" — 1/2"

7/8"

DRILL
NO.31

TAP 6 HOLES
2 BA

13/32"

1 3/8"

PART A

1 3/8"

*Fig. 15.5 The turret; Part A*

15.4 can be employed for taking facing cuts to save having to bring the front toolpost into operation when, for example, making a number of washers. Each tool is clamped in place by three 2-BA Allen screws ⅜in. in length.

## The Turret.   A (Fig. 15.5)

It is best to start by machining the turret, for then the exact tool height can readily be adjusted later when machining the upper surface of the base casting.

The turret, when finally in position, should overhang the base casting so that no ledge is left, on which chips can collect to interfere with the proper seating of the turret.

The turret is held in the 4-jaw chuck and all its surfaces are machined in the lathe. If a tool with a cemented carbide tip is used, all the turning operations described can be carried out without the aid of the backgear.

The casting is removed from the chuck and its upper surface is marked-out with

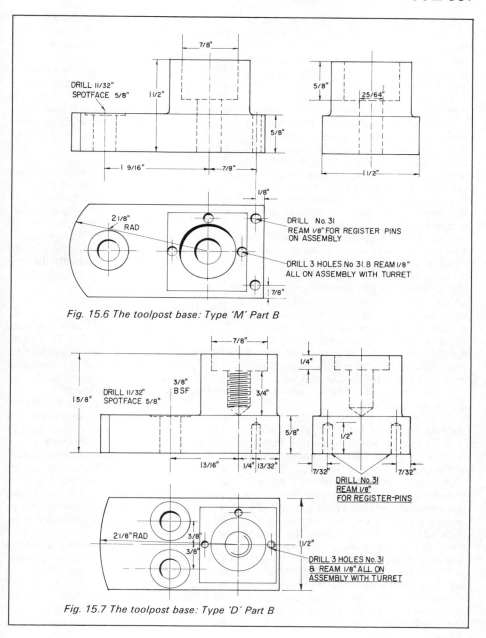

Fig. 15.6 The toolpost base: Type 'M' Part B

Fig. 15.7 The toolpost base: Type 'D' Part B

the jenny calipers to indicate the centres of the six 2-BA tool clamping screws. After they have been centre-punched, these marks are drilled with a small centre-drill to locate the No. 23 tapping size drill which follows.

To prevent raising the surface of the metal when tapping, the tapping holes are opened out with a $\frac{3}{16}$in. drill to a depth of some $\frac{1}{32}$in. The holes are then tapped 2 BA, and any burrs are removed from the upper surface of the casting with a scraper or fine file. At this stage the position of the hole for the register pin is also marked out, and when the centre has been centre-drilled, a No. 31 drill is put right through the casting.

The centre of the lower surface of the casting is marked-out with the jenny calipers and this point is then drilled with a centre-drill.

The turret is again secured in the 4-jaw chuck and the centre mark is set to run truly be means of a centre-finder supported by the back centre. If a centre-finder is not available, an $\frac{1}{8}$in. diameter hole should be drilled at the centre mark prior to mounting the casting in the chuck, and a peg is fitted in the drill hole. This peg can then be set to run truly with the aid of the test indicator.

The register spigot is turned to a diameter of $\frac{7}{8}$in. and to a length of $\frac{3}{16}$in.

A central hole is drilled from the tailstock and bored $\frac{13}{32}$in. to provide clearance for the clamping bolt.

A circular milling cutter or a square-ended fly cutter is mounted between the lathe centres, and the casting is bolted to an angle plate set at right-angles to the back edge of the cross-slide. The casting rests on a packing-piece to keep it level and also to set the correct depth of cut.

The bottom and sides of the tool slot are then machined while the work is fed against the run of the cutter, and not in the reverse direction, in order to prevent the tool from grabbing.

The slot is formed $\frac{1}{4}$in. deep and $\frac{5}{16}$in. wide to provide for height adjustment when later the tool is mounted in the turret.

During machining, the saddle positions are noted on the leadscrew index so that, when the casting is turned over, the second tool slot can be machined in a similar manner to the same dimensions.

As an alternative method, the tool slots can be machined by taking one or more cuts with an end-mill.

For this purpose, the casting is clamped to the lathe cross slide and its height is set by means of a packing piece, or, to afford a ready means of height adjustment, it can be secured in the machine vice attached to the vertical milling slide.

The turret should be accurately aligned against a rule held in contact with the face of the chuck.

## The Base.   B.

In the drawings, bases of two types are shown: that marked -M- (Fig. 15.6) with the long central fixing-bolt is suitable for the Myford ML7 lathe, and that indicated by -D- (Fig. 15.7) is made to fit the Myford Drummond-type lathe.

For the sake of simplicity, these letters will be used hereafter in the text whenever it is necessary to describe any difference in the machining of the two types.

In the first place, as in all mechanical work of this kind, reference or datum surfaces, as they are termed, must be machined, from which the remaining working surfaces and dimensions can be set out and checked as the machining proceeds.

The base casting is, therefore, mounted in the 4-jaw chuck with its pillar approximately central, and the underside of the base is faced flat. The radius at the end of the base is also turned at the same setting.

The three remaining sides of the foot are faced in the same way, and if the

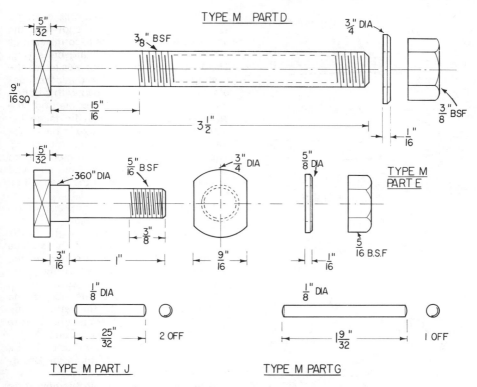

*Fig. 15.8 Details of fixing bolts: Parts D and E and register pins parts G and J. type 'M' toolpost*

casting has been carefully set in the chuck, these should then lie at right-angles to one another.

The casting is replaced in the chuck with its base in contact with the chuck face or jaws, and the upper surface of the pillar is faced flat. The centre of the upper surface of the pillar is then marked out and centre-punched as illustrated above.

Stand the casting on the surface plate and adjust it on a packing-piece with the aid of a square so that the underside of the base stands upright. Set the scriber of the surface gauge to the centre marked on the upper surface of the pillar and

scribe a line across the under surface of the base.

To mark out the centre-line of the short fixing-bolts, reset the scriber to the distance above the previous centre-line as shown in the working drawings of either the M or D pattern base. Mark out the centre-line of the base register-pins in the same way (Fig. 15.8).

Turn the casting on its side and, as before, adjust the base to stand at right-angles to the surface plate. Set the scriber point to the centre-mark on the upper surface of the pillar and scribe the hori-zontal centre-line along the base.

183

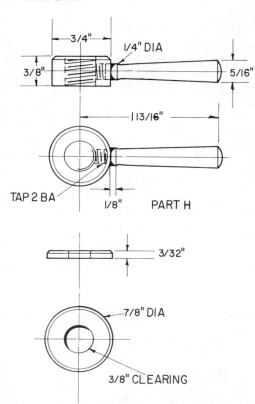

*Fig. 15.9 The clamping nut and washer types 'M' and 'D'*

Lightly punch-mark the intersections of the vertical and horizontal centre-lines, and from these points mark out the centres of the fixing-bolts and register-pins with the dividers, in accordance with the dimensions given in the drawing for either the M or D type base.

Grip the casting in the machine vice, base uppermost, and drill the register-pin holes with a No. 31 drill for a depth of $\frac{1}{2}$in. in the D type and right through the base in the M type.

Drill the fixing-bolt hole or holes with a $\frac{3}{16}$in. diameter drill.

With a $\frac{5}{8}$in. diameter pin drill, having a $\frac{3}{16}$in. diameter guide peg, spot-face the upper surface of the base to form seatings for the washers of the fixing-bolts (Fig. 15.9). If a pin drill is not available, the casting can be clamped to the lathe face-plate and the seatings faced with a boring tool, or, as an alternative method, the whole bolting surface can be faced flat when the casting is mounted in the chuck for working out and centre-punching. The bolt holes are then drilled out to $\frac{11}{32}$in., and any burrs formed are removed from the under surface of the base with a scraper.

Lastly, centre-drill the centre mark on the upper surface of the pillar.

To mark-out the overall height on the base casting, the scriber of the surface gauge is set to the height shown in the drawing; that is to say, when the upper edge of the tool slot lies, as it should, $\frac{1}{4}$in. above the lathe centre height, the scriber is set equal to the lathe centre height, X, measured from the surface of the cross slide, less the distance Y.

The distance X was found to be $2\frac{1}{16}$in. in the ML7 lathe and $2\frac{3}{16}$in. in the Drummond type Myford lathe.

A line is then scribed at this height on all four sides of the base pillar to act as the machining dimension line.

For the next operation the casting is mounted in the 4-jaw chuck as above, and the centre-drill mark is centred. In the M type a central hole $\frac{25}{64}$in. in diameter is drilled right through the casting for the passage of the long fixing bolt, but should there be any difficulty in drilling this hole straight, it should be bored to the finished diameter. In the D type base the tapping size hole to receive the central stud is drilled with a $\frac{21}{64}$in. diameter drill to a depth of $\frac{3}{4}$in. beyond the height dimension line scribed on the pillar. The upper end of the pillar is next faced down to the scribed height dimension line.

The drill hole is then bored out to form

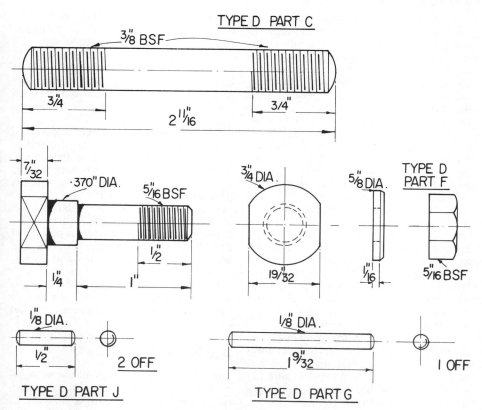

Fig. 15.10 Details of stud Part C and fixing bolts Part F together with register pins Parts G and J. For Type 'D' toolpost

an accurate fit for the register spigot of the turret and to the depth shown in the drawings of the two types of base. The drill hole in the D-type base is threaded $\frac{3}{8}$in.×20t.p.i., and to ensure that the tap enters squarely it may be started in the hole while supported in the tailstock drill chuck.

The central stud (C) is made in accordance with Fig. 15.10 and is then firmly screwed in place.

For the M type base the long central bolt (D) is turned in the lathe from a length of $\frac{3}{4}$in. diameter round mild steel,

and its shank is threaded $\frac{3}{8}$in.×20t.p.i. to receive the lower securing and upper clamping nuts. At the same time, the single fixing bolt (E) for the M type base can be machined, or in the case of the D type base two bolts (F) will be required.

As will be seen these T-bolts have flats formed on their heads to engage the T-slots in the cross-slide. It is important for accurate fitting that these flats should be equidistant from the shank of the bolt; this is best ensured by working to micrometer measurements, as illustrated in the drawing, when filing the heads to shape.

185

To fit the register-pin used to locate the turret at its two stations, the turret is clamped in place on the pillar with a $\frac{3}{8}$in. BSF nut and then adjusted to lie evenly on a packing-strip while resting on the surface plate. After the nut has been securely tightened, the assembly is transferred to the drilling machine where a No. 31 drill, entered in the hole previously drilled in the turret, is fed into the pillar to a depth of $\frac{1}{2}$in. The turret is then turned through an angle of 180° and reset on the surface plate to bring the second tool slot into position for drilling its register hole in the pillar.

In the same way, a third hole is drilled in the pillar at right-angles to these holes so that the turret can, if required, be clamped with its tools turned to the side in order to afford greater working spece.

The register-pin (G), made from a length of silver steel, is fitted to the turret after the hole to receive it has been opened out from below with an $\frac{1}{8}$in. reamer to afford a light press fit.

The three holes in the pillar are then carefully enlarged with the reamer until the pin fixed in the turret enters freely but without shake. The two register-pins (J) are fitted in the base in the same way with the aid of the reamer.

The clamping nut (H) is faced, turned and chamfered; it is then drilled $\frac{21}{64}$in. and also tapped from the tailstock with the tap supported in the drill chuck.

After it has been parted off, the nut can be faced on its underside by mounting it on a stub of screwed rod held in the chuck.

At this operation the tool is fed across the work to scribe a light centre-line on its face, and this line is then continued along the edge of the nut in a similar manner.

A centre-punch mark is made at the centre of the line scribed on the edge of the nut. The nut is then clamped in the machine vice with the cross-centre line set vertically with the aid of a square. After the punch mark has been enlarged with a centre drill, a No. 22 drill is fed in to meet the bore, and the drill hole is opened out at its mouth to $\frac{1}{4}$in. diameter to accommodate the shoulder turned on the handle. Finally, the hole is tapped 2BA.

The handle is formed from a length of $\frac{5}{16}$in. diameter steel rod. After the end of the rod has been reduced in diameter to 0·184in. and threaded 2BA with the aid of the tailstock die-holder, the tapered portion is turned with the top slide set over for about 1°. When the handle has been parted off to length, it should be lightly gripped by the threaded portion in the chuck of the drilling machine and then finished with a fine file and emery-cloth.

To afford a rigid fixing, the handle is screwed firmly in place with the shouldered portion engaging the recess formed in the nut.

## Finishing

The turret can be left in its machined state, or, if preferred, its exposed surfaces can be finished by filing with a fine file to remove the tool marks.

An easier method of producing a pleasing finish is to ply the scraper with diagonally crossing cuts until a uniform frosted appearance is obtained.

Surplus metal where the base overhangs the cross slide can be removed with the hacksaw. The edges of the base should be given a good finish by draw-filing with a fine file and then smoothing the surfaces with a strip of oiled emery-cloth backed by a file.

To give a good appearance, the un-machined surfaces should be painted, preferably with a cellulose paint, as this does not stain with oil.

# CHAPTER SIXTEEN

# Attachments For The Back Toolpost

PARTING, OR CUTTING-OFF TOOLS, of the Eclipse brand for example, are supplied in sizes and in a form that can readily be clamped in the turret head of the back toolpost, these tools, which are illustrated in Fig. 16.1, are made of a special grade of high-speed steel and are supplied in two forms; that shown in Fig. 16.1(A) has its flat side surfaces sloping away from the cutting edge in order to provide the requisite clearance, whereas, for this purpose, the blade depicted in Fig. 16.1(B) has its flanks hollow ground. The latter form of tool has been selected for use with the back toolpost, as in the smallest size the blade measures only $\frac{1}{16}$in. in thickness and $\frac{1}{2}$in. in depth.

As a result of tests, and in the interests of simplicity, the turret is machined to locate the tool horizontally and with its cutting edge set at exactly centre height. When sharpening the tool, it should be ground on the end face only in order to maintain the front clearance. A tool in this form has been found suitable for machining non-ferrous metals as well as steel.

The standard length of blade of $4\frac{1}{2}$in.

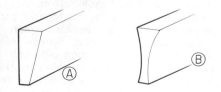

*Fig. 16.1 The two forms of Eclipse blades*

is unnecessarily long for use in the back toolpost, and it may be divided into two by means of a cutting-off wheel mounted on the grinding head.

A general view of the back toolpost, equipped with the parting tool described, is shown in Fig. 16.2 and the constructional details of the turret are illustrated in Fig. 16.3. It will be apparent that it is now akin to the ordinary English pattern tool holder fitted to the top slide of the lathe.

The base portion (A) is recessed to accommodate the parting tool which is secured in place by means of the clamping plate (B). The two Allen screws (C) act as clamping screws in connection with the two levelling or fulcrum screws (D), so that, when the tool is gripped, the upper surface of the clamp plate lies horizontally in order to afford a level bearing surface for the clamping nut (E). This mode of construction ensures that the tool is retained in place and its setting preserved even when the turret is removed from its base.

To ensure accurate location of the tool, the register-pegs in the base of the toolpost align the attachment as a whole, and the turret itself is located on the base portion by means of a register-pin which, as in the case of the standard form of turret previously described, automatically maintains the tool at right-angles to the lathe axis.

As the tool is wedge shaped in cross-section, two grub screws, shown in Fig.

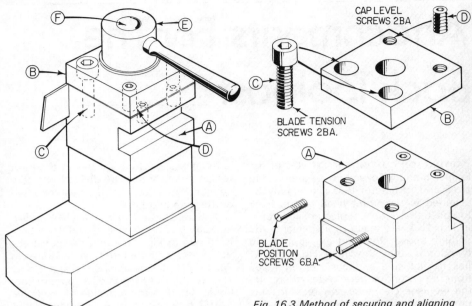

*Fig. 16.2 The complete parting tool
attachment*

*Fig. 16.3 Method of securing and aligning
the parting tool with the clamping and
levelling screws*

16.3, are fitted to the face of the tool slot for the purpose of maintaining the tool in an exactly vertical position when it is clamped in place. In order that the turret may be used for repetition work and for carrying out more than a single machining operation, it is also equipped with a second tool, as in the original type of turret. If, as previously recommended, a combined chamfering and facing tool is fitted in this position, the back toolpost will alone be capable of machining parts, such as nuts and washers, without the ordinary front toolpost having to be brought into action.

## Construction

The constructional details and dimensions of the individual parts are shown in the working drawings Fig. 16.4.

It will at once be apparent that, as the overall height of the turret has been increased by $\frac{3}{16}$in. to accommodate the deeper parting tool, a longer central clamping bolt or stud must be fitted to afford a firm hold for the turret clamping nut.

The dimensions of both the clamping bolt for the 'M' type toolpost for use with the Myford ML7 lathe, and the stud for the 'D' or Myford-Drummond pattern post are given in the drawings Fig. 16.5. No alteration of the handled clamp nut (E) is required, the dimensions for this part are those given in the previous chapter.

The base (A) is most conveniently made from an iron casting although a piece of mild steel can be used for the ; urpose. The machining operations for facing the surfaces, turning the register spigot, and forming the bore for the

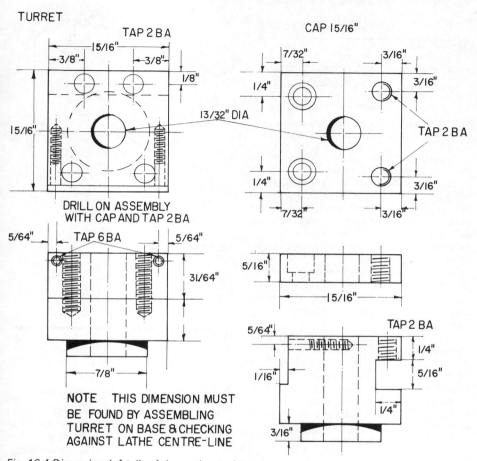

Fig. 16.4 Dimensional details of the parting tool turret

passage of the central bolt are identical with those previously detailed for making the ordinary 2-tool turret.

The flat surface and shoulder against which the parting tool abuts can be machined with an end-mill or fly cutter when the turret is clamped at the correct height on the boring table, or the turret can be held in the machine vice attached to the vertical slide in order to facilitate the height setting operation.

The clamping plate (B) should be made of mild-steel, as it is comparatively thin and has to bear a bending stress; it may be secured in the 4-jaw chuck and both the upper and lower surfaces faced parallel and flat, or, if preferred, the work can be carried out by filing and scraping.

The hole for the passage of the central bolt is then drilled and bored. The centres for the clamping screws (C) and the levelling screws (D) are marked out, centre

189

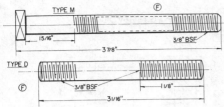

Fig. 16.5 Long central bolt and stud securing the parting tool to either 'M' or 'D' type base

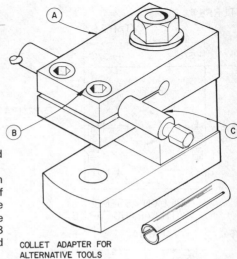

COLLET ADAPTER FOR
ALTERNATIVE TOOLS

Fig. 16.6 General view of the attachment fitted with boring bar

Fig. 16.7 The Eclipse boring bar tool

punched, centre drilled and finally drilled through with a No. 23 drill.

The clamping plate is now secured in position on the turret base by means of the central bolt, and the tapping-size holes for the clamping screws (C) are drilled in the turret base with a No. 23 drill guided by the holes previously drilled in the clamping plate.

The clamping plate is then removed for tapping the holes for the screws (D) 2BA and the holes to receive the clamping screws (C) are opened out to the clearing size with a No. 12 drill.

The enlarged heads of the clamping screws are let into the clamping plate by drilling to a depth of $\frac{5}{32}$in. with a $\frac{5}{16}$in. diameter drill and then counterboring to a total depth of $\frac{3}{16}$in. with a $\frac{5}{16}$in. end-mill, in order to form a flat seating for the screw and to allow its head to lie flush with the surface of the clamping plate.

The holes in the turret to receive the blade-positioning screws are first drilled to the tapping size with a No. 43 drill; they are then enlarged for part of their length with a No. 34 clearing size drill before finally tapped 6BA as represented in the drawing.

To complete the work on the turret, the holes for the clamping screws (C) are tapped 2 BA, and the register-pin is fitted to locate the tool slots truly at right-angles to the lathe axis; in addition, the holes to receive the two clamping screws for the chamfering tool are drilled and tapped in accordance with the drawing.

## A Turret For the Boring Tool

When boring operations are undertaken, it may save much time and trouble if a complete boring unit is available for immediate use, instead of having to mount a boring tool in the lathe front tool holder or turret and adjust it to the correct height with packing strips. This interchangeable turret is illustrated in Fig. 16.6, and it will be seen that the turret, itself (A) is split so that the short boring-bar (C) can be secured in place by tightening the clamping screws (B). Moreover, the turret is designed to carry the small boring tools of Eclipse make, shown in Fig. 16.7, which have round section shanks ranging from $\frac{3}{16}$in. to $\frac{3}{8}$in. in diameter, but to enable the smaller sizes of these tools to be held, split collet adapters are required of the pattern illustrated at the foot of the general arrangement drawing (Fig. 16.6). At first sight it might be thought that the centre line of the boring-bar, or of the shank of the tool, should be at the same height as the lathe centres but it has been considered advisable to mount the bar *below* centre height in order to ensure that the upper surface of the boring tool lies on the lathe centre-line.

A hexagon nut is used to secure the turret instead of the handled finger-nut fitted, to the previous pattern for as the turret in this case is not located by means of a register-pin, and as in addition, it is more liable when in use to be rotated by the projecting boring tool, the more secure hold obtainable by a nut is an advantage.

## Construction

Although the turret can be machined from mild steel bar, it is unlikely that a sufficiently large piece of this material will generally be available, so usually an iron casting will be preferred.

In the first place, the casting is gripped in the 4-jaw chuck and the upper and rear surfaces are faced flat and right-angles to one another to form datum surfaces when marking out the part.

The two sides of the casting and also the front face are machined in a similar manner to reduce the part to width and length as shown in the working drawings (Fig. 16.8).

The centre-line of the $\frac{7}{8}$in. diameter register which fits into the toolpost base is marked out on the lower surface while the casting stands on its rear surface on the surface plate; and when the part is in position the centre-line of the two clamping screws is also marked out, but on the upper surface.

Next, with the casting lying on its upper machined face, a line is scribed with the

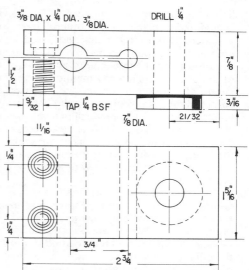

*Fig. 16.8 Dimensions of the boring tool turret*

surface gauge round all its sides to denote the finished thickness of the post, and $\frac{3}{16}$in. above this the dimension line is scribed to indicate the position of the lower face of the register. The back-to-front centre-line is scribed across the register with the casting standing on its side, and the point of intersection of the two centre-lines on the register is punch-marked and then centre drilled.

The turret can now be mounted in the 4-jaw chuck with the centre in the register set to run true with the end of the centre-finder or wobbler supported by the tailstock centre; the hole for the passage of the central clamping bolt is then drilled and bored to size. The under surface of the casting is now faced back to the scribed dimension lines indicating its thickness, and at the same time the register is also faced and then turned to the correct diameter to fit closely into the toolpost base.

To determine the position of the centre-line of the bore to carry the tool, the turret is clamped in place on the toolpost base, attached to the lathe cross slide, and a pointed tool gripped in the chuck is used to scribe a line at centre height on the side of the casting. As already mentioned, the centre of the bore is located $\frac{1}{16}$in. below centre height; so to mark out the centre-line for the tool, the jenny callipers are set to this dimension. The vertical cross centre-line of the bore is marked out with the jenny callipers from the front face of the casting in accordance with the working drawings.

The bore is then machined on this centre either by mounting the casting in the 4-jaw chuck and using the same procedure as when boring the turret register, or the work can be carried out in the drilling machine, but in either case the bore should be finished to size by means of a reamer.

The cross centre-lines for the $\frac{1}{4}$in. BSF clamping screws Fig. 16.6(B) are marked out with the jenny callipers from the sides of the casting, and these centres are then drilled to the tapping size with a No 4 drill prior to being opened out to $\frac{9}{32}$in. for a depth of $\frac{7}{16}$in. to provide adequate clearance for the shanks of the screws when the turret is closed to grip the boring tool. Likewise, the recesses for the heads of the Allen screws are formed to a depth of $\frac{1}{4}$in. with a $\frac{13}{32}$in. diameter drill, and a flat seating for the underside of the head is machined with an end-mill or counterbore.

It now remains to slit the casting to enable the clamping screws, when tightened, to close the turret and so grip the boring tool securely. In addition a cross hole is drilled at the end of the slit to allow the clamping screws to close the casting on the bar more easily and so relieve them of unneeded strain.

The casting, while lying on its upper surface on the surface plate, is marked out on all three sides with the surface gauge to denote the centre-line of the slit which passes through the bore centre; the vertical centre-line of the cross hole at the end of the slit is then marked out, and this hole is drilled right through the casting with a $\frac{1}{4}$in. diameter drill.

The ideal method of forming the slit to obtain a good appearance is to employ a circular slitting saw mounted on an arbor between the lathe centres; the turret, meanwhile, can either be gripped in the lathe tool holder or bolted to an angle-plate attached to the cross-slide. In either case it may be found advisable to support the overhanging end of the casting on a packing-piece or a small screw-jack.

During the machining operation it will be found that, when the saw teeth reach the holes drilled to receive the clamp screws, they will tend to grab and may be broken in so doing; so to prevent this, the backlash in the cross slide feedscrew should be reduced as much as possible, and at the same time the locking screws fitted to the slide should be partially tightened to impart some degrees of stiffness to the feed.

If a suitable milling saw is not available, the hand hacksaw can be used to cut the slit, but great care must be taken to maintain a perfectly straight and even cut, or the appearance of the work will be marred. It will probably be found helpful if a guide line is scribed on either side of the centre line to enable the direction of the cut to be more readily sighted as the work proceeds.

As already mentioned, the turret is secured by means of a standard $\frac{3}{8}$in. BSF nut and washer, and as the standard central clamping bolt or stud fitted to the base is of sufficient length to serve in the present instance no additional parts are required to complete the turret and its mounting.

The tool collets, illustrated in Fig. 16.9 can be made at a single sitting in the lathe. The dimension (B) has to be made to suit

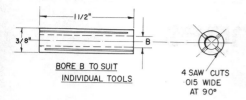

BORE B TO SUIT
INDIVIDUAL TOOLS

4 SAW CUTS
·015 WIDE
AT 90°

*Fig. 16.9 Details of the tool collets*

the particular size of Eclipse boring tool it is intended to accommodate. This may involve drilling and reaming, or drilling only if this will provide a close enough fit over the shank of the tool.

The 0·015m wide saw cuts are test made with a milling attachment mounted on the cross slide and with the work indexed in the manner described in Chapter 10. After this operation the collet is parted off the parent material.

It should be noted that when making the saw cuts while two of them can be cut end on with the milling attachment traversed by the leadscrew, the other two will need to be plunge cut and then, if needed, elongated by traversing the attachment from left to right. Note that, when plunge cutting, the saddle should be locked to avoid the possibility of the cutter taking charge as it is fed into the work.

# CHAPTER SEVENTEEN

# Design Changes

## Design Changes in the ML7 and the Super 7 Lathes

AT THE TIME OF WRITING a series of design changes to the lathes is being carried out and will take effect in four phases. These are set out in the following chart together with the serial numbers of the first machine embodying the modification listed.

In addition, quick change gearboxes fitted to Super 7 lathes phases 2, 3 and 4 and all subsequent machines will not require the packing strip No. 230 in the parts list.

ML7 lathes phases 2, 3 and 4 and all subsequent machines will be fitted with a $\frac{3}{4}$in. diameter leadscrew to conform with the Super 7 apron now being employed with the ML7 at this stage.

It should be noted, however, that quick change gearboxes supplied as accessories for fitment to existing lathes, and those to phase 1, ML7, will still require the $\frac{5}{8}$in. diameter leadscrew A4183. In the case of

| Phase | ML7 | Super 7 |
|-------|-----|---------|
| 1 | Lathe bed now ground on rear face of rear shear to provide guidance across outside of the bed. K107657A | Does not apply |
| 2 | Super 7 apron now used with 4 instead of 5 securing screws M5 (metric) wedgelock adjustings screws for cross slide gib strip K108718B. | Super 7 and ML7 beds SK108891B made interchangeable, securing screws for apron reduced from 5 to 4 wedgelock adjusting screws for C/S. |
| 3 | New bed casting Long-bed KSL108728C Standard K110296C | New bed casting Long-bed SKL109039C Standard SK110311C |
| 4 | New saddle casting K111728 | New saddle casting Long-bed SK111838D |

*Fig. 17.1 Auto cross traverse (1) new apron (2) new cross slide end bracket (3) push-pull knob (4) pin*

the Super 7 lathe all machines prior to phase 2 will need the above-mentioned packing strip.

## Super 7 Auto Cross Traverse

Myford Ltd. have recently introduced a modification to the Super 7 Lathe that enables the cross slide to be traversed under power. This provision has meant, inevitably, that a number of changes have had to be made to certain major components of the lathe.

The mechanism ·for the traverse is driven directly from the lead screw which now has an axial keyway to accommodate a key fitted to the running gear that engages a corresponding pinion on the cross slide feed screw. In this way power is transmitted from the lead screw

to the feed screw, the gearing being such that the powered cross traverse will be 0·9472 times any longitudinal feed that may have been selected.

Of the major components, in addition to a new bed casting, it has been necessary to introduce a new apron seen in Fig. 17.1 at (1) and a revised cross slide end bracket illustrated in Fig. 17.1 at (2).

The automatic traverse is controlled by the push-pull knob (3) seen in the same illustration. The knob is pulled to engage the powered feed and pushed to disengage it. As a safeguard a pin (4) is set in the cross slide projecting downward so that it will engage the knob when the feed is inwards. This arrangement will then act as a safety device should the cross feed be allowed to over-run.

Since it is likely that the automatic cross

195

*Fig. 17.2 Plug insert to replace the seating for the topslide*

feed will be used in conditions with the topside unit removed, a plug is being provided to fill in the seating for the topslide and so protect the feedscrew gear once the slide has been taken off. This plug may be seen in Fig. 17.2.

## Hoybide Tools

The tungsten carbide tools described on pages **58** and **86** have had their availability modified. Tools with a 90° approach are available Right Hand only. Right Hand or Left Hand inserts may be used in either 90° or 45° holders. For a Left Hand Knife Tool use the 45° holder set at an angle with a Left Hand insert.

## Fitting Chucks

The service offered by Myford for fitting chucks has been discontinued in favour of supplying chucks having a threaded body only. However, the range of backplates enabling the customer to fit his own chucks is still available, and Myford can also supply chucks that customers may fit to the backplates themselves.

## Fitting New Chuck Jaws

It is now established that the chuck manufacturers themselves do not wish to undertake this work any longer, since, when examined, chucks as a whole are basically found to be beyond economical repair.

Replacement jaws can be supplied, however for customers to fit themselves but without any guarantee of accuracy when they have been fitted.

## Cutting Square Threads (see page 108)

Mention has been made of the use of square threads for screws fitted to machine tools for feed purposes.

Modern practice dictates however, that for the most part the Acme Thread should replace the Square Thread.

## Design Changes

For a number of applications Myford have used *large head* cap screws which the screw manufacturers are now deliberately pricing off the market.

In most instances the corresponding metric screws have heads of a size that are between the standard and the large head of the original Imperial screws.

Therefore commencing with ML7 lathe Serial No. K125240 and Super 7 SK124461 the headstock is secured with screws threaded M8×1·25. For the gearbox and the apron M6×1 are used.

The studs for the Tri-leva have, of course, also had to be altered.

# CHAPTER EIGHTEEN

# Formulae For Gearing

CIRCULAR PITCH

Circular pitch is the distance from the centre of one tooth to the centre of the next tooth, measured along the pitch circle.

| To get | Having | Rule |
|---|---|---|
| The circular pitch | The diametral pitch | Divide 3·1416 by the diametral pitch |
| The circular pitch | The pitch diameter and number of teeth | Divide pitch diameter by the product of 0·3183 and number of teeth |
| The circular pitch | The outside diameter and number of teeth | Divide outside diameter by by the product of 0·3183 and number of teeth plus 2 |
| Pitch diameter | Number of teeth and the circular pitch | The continued product of the number of teeth, the circular pitch and 0·3183 |
| Pitch diameter | The number of teeth and the outside diameter | Divide the product of number of teeth and outside diameter by number of teeth plus 2 |
| Pitch diameter | The outside diameter and circular pitch | Subtract from the outside diameter the product of the circular pitch and 0·6366 |
| Pitch diameter | Addendum and the number of teeth | Multiply the number of teeth by the addendum |
| Outside diameter | Number of teeth and the circular pitch | The continued product of the number of teeth plus 2, the circular pitch and 0·3183 |
| Outside diameter | The pitch diameter and circular pitch | Add to the pitch diameter the product of the circular pitch and 0·6366 |

# MYFORD

## CIRCULAR PITCH — *Continued*

| To get | Having | Rule |
|---|---|---|
| Outside diameter | The number of teeth and the addendum | Multiply addendum by number of teeth plus 2 |
| Number of teeth | The pitch diameter and circular pitch | Divide the product of pitch diameter and 3·1416 by the circular pitch |
| Thickness of tooth | The circular pitch | One-half the circular pitch |
| Addendum | The circular pitch | Multiply the circular pitch by 0·3183 or $s = D'/N$ |
| Dedendum | The circular pitch | Multiply the circular pitch by 0·3683 |
| Working depth | The circular pitch | Multiply the circular pitch by 0·6366 |
| Whole depth | The circular pitch | Multiply the circular pitch by 0·6866 |
| Clearance | The circular pitch | Multiply the circular pitch by 0·05 |
| Clearance | Thickness of tooth | One-tenth the thickness of tooth at pitch line |

## DIAMETRAL PITCH
Diametral pitch is the number of teeth to each inch of the pitch diameter

| To get | Having | Rule |
|---|---|---|
| The diametral pitch | The circular pitch | Divide 3·1416 by the circular pitch |
| The diametral pitch | The pitch diameter and number of teeth | Divide number of teeth by pitch diameter |
| The diametral pitch | The outside diameter and number of teeth | Divide number of teeth plus 2 by outside diameter |
| Pitch diameter | The number of teeth and diametral pitch | Divide number of teeth by the diametral pitch |
| Pitch diameter | The number of teeth and outside diameter | Divide the product of outside diameter and number of teeth by number of teeth by number of teeth plus 2 |

DIAMETRAL PITCH – *Continued*

| To get | Having | Rule |
|--------|--------|------|
| Pitch diameter | The outside diameter and diametral pitch | Subtract from the outside diameter the quotient of 2 divided by the diametral pitch |
| Pitch diameter | Addendum and number of teeth | Multiply addendum by the number of teeth |
| Outside diameter | The number of teeth and diametral pitch | Divide number of teeth plus 2 by the diametral pitch |
| Outside diameter | The pitch diameter and diametral pitch | Add to the pitch diameter the quotient of 2 divided by the diametral pitch |
| Outside diameter | The pitch diameter and number of teeth | Divide the number of teeth plus 2 by the quotient of the number of teeth divided by the pitch diameter |
| Outside diameter | The number of teeth and addendum | Multiply the number of teeth plus 2 by addendum |
| Number of teeth | The pitch diameter and diametral pitch | Multiply pitch diameter by the diametral pitch |
| Number of teeth | The outside diameter and diametral pitch | Multiply outside diameter by the diametral pitch and subtract 2 |
| Thickness of tooth | The diametral pitch | Divide 1·5708 by the diametral pitch |
| Addendum | The diametral pitch | Divide 1 by the diametral pitch or $s = D'/N$ |
| Dedendum | The diametral pitch | Divide 1·157 by the diametral pitch |
| Working depth | The diametral pitch | Divide 2 by the diametral pitch |
| Whole depth | The diametral pitch | Divide 2·157 by the diametral pitch |
| Clearance | The diametral pitch | Divide 0·157 by the diametral pitch |
| Clearance | Thickness of tooth | Divide thickness of tooth at pitch line by 10 |

# CHAPTER NINETEEN

# Tables For Threads

## Table 1     STANDARD WHITWORTH THREADS (BSW)

| Diameter in | Threads per in. | Depth of thread in | Clearing size drill | Clearance thousandths in. | Tapping size drill | % depth of engage-ment |
|---|---|---|---|---|---|---|
| $\frac{1}{16}$/0·0625 | 60 | 0·0107 | 52 | 1 | 57 | 92 |
|  |  |  |  |  | 56 | 75 |
| $\frac{3}{32}$/0·0937 | 48 | 0·0133 | 2·4mm | 0·7 | 50 | 88 |
|  |  |  | 41 | 2·2 | 49 | 77 |
| $\frac{1}{8}$/0·1250 | 40 | 0·0160 | 3·2mm | 1 | $\frac{3}{32}$ | 97 |
|  |  |  | 3·25mm | 3 | 41 | 91 |
|  |  |  | 30 | 3·5 | 40 | 84 |
|  |  |  |  |  | 39 | 80 |
| $\frac{5}{32}$/0·1562 | 32 | 0·0200 | 22 | 0·8 | 31 | 90 |
|  |  |  | 21 | 2·8 | $\frac{1}{8}$ | 78 |
| $\frac{3}{16}$/0·1875 | 24 | 0·0267 | 12 | 1·5 | 28 | 88 |
|  |  |  | 11 | 3·5 | 27 | 81 |
|  |  |  |  |  | 26 | 76 |
| $\frac{7}{32}$/0·2187 | 24 | 0·0267 | 5·6mm | 1·7 | 18 | 92 |
|  |  |  | 2 | 2·2 | 17 | 86 |
|  |  |  | 5·7mm | 5·6 | 16 | 78 |
| $\frac{1}{4}$/0·2500 | 20 | 0·0320 | 6·4mm | 2 | 10 | 88 |
|  |  |  | 6·5mm | 6 | 9 | 84 |
|  |  |  | F | 7 | 8 | 80 |
|  |  |  |  |  | 7 | 76 |
| $\frac{9}{32}$/0·2812 | 20 | 0·0320 | 7·2mm | 2·3 | 2 | 94 |
|  |  |  | L | 8·8 | 1 | 83 |
| $\frac{5}{16}$/0·3125 | 18 | 0·0356 | 8mm | 2·5 | D | 93 |
|  |  |  | O | 3·5 | $\frac{1}{4}$ | 88 |
|  |  |  |  |  | F | 78 |

**Table 1** – *Continued*

| Diameter in | Threads per in. | Depth of thread in | Clearing size drill | Clearance thousandths in. | Tapping size drill | % depth of engagement |
|---|---|---|---|---|---|---|
| $\frac{3}{8}$/0·3750 | 16 | 0·0400 | V | 2 | N | 91 |
| | | | 9·7mm | 6·9 | $\frac{5}{16}$ | 78 |
| $\frac{7}{16}$/0·4375 | 14 | 0·0457 | 11·2mm | 3·4 | 9mm | 91 |
| | | | 11·3mm | 7·4 | T | 87 |
| | | | | | 23/64 | 85 |
| | | | | | U | 76 |
| $\frac{1}{2}$/0·5000 | 12 | 0·0534 | 12·75mm | 2 | Y | 90 |
| | | | 12·8mm | 3·9 | $\frac{13}{32}$ | 88 |
| | | | 12·9mm | 7·9 | Z | 81 |
| $\frac{9}{16}$/0·5625 | 12 | 0·0534 | 14·5mm | 7·4 | $\frac{15}{32}$ | 88 |
| | | | $\frac{37}{64}$ | 15·6 | 12mm | 84 |
| $\frac{5}{8}$/0·6250 | 11 | 0·0582 | 16mm | 4·9 | $\frac{33}{64}$ | 94 |
| | | | $\frac{41}{64}$ | 15·6 | $\frac{17}{32}$ | 80 |
| $\frac{11}{16}$/0·6875 | 11 | 0·0582 | 17·5mm | 1·5 | $\frac{37}{64}$ | 94 |
| | | | 17·75mm | 11·3 | 15mm | 83 |
| | | | $\frac{45}{64}$ | 15·6 | $\frac{19}{32}$ | 80 |
| $\frac{3}{4}$/0·7500 | 10 | 0·0640 | 19·25mm | 7·9 | 16mm | 94 |
| | | | $\frac{49}{64}$ | 15·6 | $\frac{41}{64}$ | 86 |
| $\frac{7}{8}$/0·8750 | 9 | 0·0711 | 22·5mm | 10·8 | 19mm | 89 |
| | | | $\frac{57}{64}$ | 15·6 | $\frac{3}{4}$ | 88 |
| 1/1·000 | 8 | 0·0800 | 25·5mm | 3·9 | 21·5mm | 96 |
| | | | $1\frac{1}{64}$ | 15·6 | $\frac{55}{64}$ | 88 |
| | | | | | 22mm | 84 |

## Table 2  BRITISH STANDARD FINE THREADS (BSF)

| Diameter in | Threads per in. | Depth of thread in | Clearing size drill | Clearance thousandths in. | Tapping size drill | % depth of engagement |
|---|---|---|---|---|---|---|
| $\frac{3}{16}$/0·1875 | 32 | 0·0200 | 12 | 1·5 | 25 | 95 |
| | | | 11 | 3·5 | 24 | 89 |
| | | | | | 23 | 84 |
| | | | | | $\frac{5}{32}$ | 78 |
| $\frac{7}{32}$/0·2188 | 28 | 0·0228 | 5·6mm | 1·7 | 16 | 91 |
| | | | 2 | 2·2 | 15 | 85 |
| | | | 5·7mm | 5·6 | 14 | 80 |
| $\frac{1}{4}$/0·2500 | 26 | 0·0246 | 6·4mm | 2 | $\frac{13}{64}$ | 95 |
| | | | 6·5mm | 6 | 6 | 93 |
| | | | F | 7 | 5 | 90 |
| | | | | | 4 | 83 |
| | | | | | 3 | 75 |
| $\frac{9}{32}$/0·2812 | 26 | 0·0246 | 7·2mm | 2·3 | $\frac{15}{64}$ | 95 |
| | | | L | 8·8 | 6mm | 91 |
| | | | | | B | 88 |
| | | | | | C | 80 |
| $\frac{5}{16}$/0·3125 | 22 | 0·0291 | 8mm | 2·5 | F | 95 |
| | | | O | 3·5 | G | 88 |
| | | | | | $\frac{17}{64}$ | 80 |
| $\frac{3}{8}$/0·3750 | 20 | 0·0320 | V | 2 | 8mm | 94 |
| | | | 9·7mm | 6·9 | O | 92 |
| | | | | | P | 81 |
| $\frac{7}{16}$/0·4375 | 18 | 0·0356 | 11·2mm | 3·4 | U | 98 |
| | | | 11·3mm | 7·4 | $\frac{3}{8}$ | 88 |
| | | | | | V | 85 |
| $\frac{1}{2}$/0·5000 | 16 | 0·0400 | 12·75mm | 2 | $\frac{27}{64}$ | 98 |
| | | | 12·8mm | 3·9 | 11mm | 84 |
| | | | 12·9mm | 7·9 | $\frac{7}{16}$ | 78 |
| $\frac{9}{16}$/0·5625 | 16 | 0·0400 | 14·5mm | 7·4 | $\frac{31}{64}$ | 98 |
| | | | $\frac{37}{64}$ | 15·6 | 12·5mm | 88 |
| | | | | | $\frac{1}{2}$ | 78 |
| $\frac{5}{8}$/0·6250 | 14 | 0·0457 | 16mm | 4·9 | $\frac{35}{64}$ | 85 |
| | | | $\frac{41}{64}$ | 15·6 | 14mm | 81 |
| $\frac{11}{16}$/0·6875 | 14 | 0·0457 | 17·5mm | 1·5 | $\frac{39}{64}$ | 85 |
| | | | 17·75mm | 11·3 | | |
| | | | $\frac{45}{64}$ | 15·6 | | |

| Diameter in | Threads per in. | Depth of thread in. | Clearing size drill | Clearance thousandths in. | Tapping size drill | % depth of engage- ment |
|---|---|---|---|---|---|---|
| $\frac{3}{4}$/0·7500 | 12 | 0·0534 | 19·25mm | 7·9 | 16·5mm | 94 |
| | | | $\frac{49}{64}$ | 15·6 | $\frac{21}{32}$ | 88 |
| | | | | | 17mm | 75 |
| $1\frac{3}{6}$/0·8125 | 12 | 0·0534 | 20·75mm | 4·4 | 18mm | 97 |
| | | | 21mm | 14·3 | $\frac{23}{32}$ | 88 |
| | | | $\frac{53}{64}$ | 15·6 | 18·5mm | 79 |
| $\frac{7}{8}$/0·8750 | 11 | 0·0582 | 22·5mm | 10·8 | $\frac{49}{64}$ | 94 |
| | | | $\frac{57}{64}$ | 15·6 | 19·5mm | 92 |
| | | | | | $\frac{25}{32}$ | 80 |
| 1/1·000 | 10 | 0·0640 | 25·5mm | 3·9 | $\frac{7}{8}$ | 98 |
| | | | $1\frac{1}{64}$ | 15·6 | 22·5mm | 89 |
| | | | | | $\frac{57}{64}$ | 86 |

**Table 3**  **BRITISH STANDARD BRASS THREAD**

Threads 26in. throughout.  Depth of thread 0·0246in.

| Diameter in. | Clearing size drill | Clearance thousandths in. | Tapping size drill | % depth of engagement |
|---|---|---|---|---|
| $\frac{1}{8}$/0·1250 | 3·2mm | 1 | $\frac{5}{64}$ | 95 |
|  | 3·25mm | 3 | 47 | 94 |
|  | 30 | 3·5 | 46 | 89 |
|  |  |  | 45 | 87 |
| $\frac{3}{16}$/0·1875 | 12 | 1·5 | $\frac{9}{64}$ | 95 |
|  | 11 | 3·5 | 27 | 88 |
| $\frac{1}{4}$/0·2500 | 6·4mm | 2 | $\frac{13}{64}$ | 95 |
|  | 6·5mm | 6 | 6 | 93 |
|  | F | 7 | 5 | 90 |
|  |  |  | 4 | 83 |
| $\frac{5}{16}$/0·3125 | 8mm | 2·5 | $\frac{17}{64}$ | 95 |
|  | O | 3·5 | H | 94 |
|  |  |  | 1 | 82 |
| $\frac{3}{8}$/0·3750 | V | 2 | $\frac{21}{64}$ | 95 |
|  | 9·7mm | 6·9 | Q | 88 |
|  |  |  | 8·5mm | 82 |
| $\frac{7}{16}$/0·4375 | 11·2mm | 3·4 | $\frac{25}{64}$ | 95 |
|  | 11·3mm | 7·4 | 10mm | 89 |
|  |  |  | X | 83 |
| $\frac{1}{2}$/0·5000 | 12·75mm | 2 | $\frac{29}{64}$ | 95 |
|  | 12·8mm | 3·9 | 11·6mm | 88 |
|  | 12·9mm | 7·9 |  |  |
| $\frac{5}{8}$/0·6250 | 16mm | 4·9 | $\frac{37}{64}$ | 95 |
|  | $\frac{41}{64}$ | 15·6 | 14·75mm | 90 |
| $\frac{3}{4}$/0·7500 | 19·25mm | 7·9 | $\frac{45}{64}$ | 95 |
|  | $\frac{49}{64}$ | 15·6 | 18mm | 84 |
| $\frac{7}{8}$/0·8750 | 22·5mm | 10·8 | $\frac{53}{64}$ | 95 |
|  | $\frac{57}{64}$ | 15·6 |  |  |
| 1/1·0000 | $1\frac{1}{64}$ | 15·6 | $\frac{61}{64}$ | 95 |
|  |  |  | 24·25mm | 92 |

Table 4          BRITISH STANDARD PARALLEL PIPE THREAD (BSP)

| Size in. | Outside diameter | Threads per in. | Depth of thread in. | Clearing size drill | Clearance thousandths in. | Tapping size drill | % depth of engagement |
|---|---|---|---|---|---|---|---|
| $\frac{1}{8}$ | 0·3830 | 28 | 0·0230 | 9·75mm<br>W<br>$\frac{25}{64}$ | 1<br>3<br>7·6 | R<br>$\frac{11}{32}$<br>S | 96<br>86<br>76 |
| $\frac{1}{4}$ | 0·5180 | 19 | 0·0335 | 13·25mm<br>$\frac{17}{32}$ | 3·6<br>13·2 | $\frac{29}{64}$<br>11·7mm | 96<br>85 |
| $\frac{3}{8}$ | 0·6560 | 19 | 0·0335 | 16·75mm<br>17mm<br>$\frac{43}{64}$ | 3·4<br>13·3<br>15·9 | 15mm<br>$\frac{19}{32}$<br>15·25mm | 97<br>92<br>83 |
| $\frac{1}{2}$ | 0·8250 | 14 | 0·0455 | 21mm<br>$\frac{53}{64}$<br>21·25mm | 1·8<br>3·1<br>11·6 | $\frac{47}{64}$<br>19mm<br>$\frac{3}{4}$ | 99<br>94<br>82 |
| $\frac{5}{8}$ | 0·9020 | 14 | 0·455 | 23mm<br>$\frac{29}{32}$<br>23·25mm | 3·5<br>4·2<br>13·4 | $\frac{13}{16}$<br>21mm<br>$\frac{53}{64}$ | 98<br>82<br>81 |

Table 5 — MODEL ENGINEER STANDARD (ME) AND SPECIAL FINE THREADS

| ME diam. in. | Special fine diam. in. | Threads per in. | Depth of thread in. | Clearing size drill | Clearance thousandths in. | Tapping size drill | % depth of engagement |
|---|---|---|---|---|---|---|---|
| 1/8/0·1250 | | 40 | 0·0160 | 3·2mm | 1 | 3/32 | 97 |
| | | | | 3·25mm | 3 | 41 | 91 |
| | 1/8 | 60 | 0·0107 | 30 | 3·5 | 40 | 84 |
| | | | | 30 | 3·5 | 37 | 98 |
| | | | | | | 36 | 87 |
| 5/32/0·1562 | | 40 | 0·0160 | 22 | 0·8 | 1/8 | 97 |
| | | | | 21 | 2·8 | 30 | 86 |
| | 5/32 | 60 | 0·0107 | 21 | 2·8 | 29 | 95 |
| | | | | | | 3·5mm | 86 |
| 3/16/0·1875 | | 40 | 0·0160 | 12 | 1·5 | 5/32 | 97 |
| | | | | 11 | 3·5 | 22 | 93 |
| | 3/16 | 60 | 0·0107 | 11 | 3·5 | 21 | 86 |
| | | | | | | 18 | 89 |
| 7/32/0·2187 | | 40 | 0·0160 | 5·6mm | 1·7 | 3/16 | 97 |
| | | | | 2 | 2·2 | 12 | 93 |
| | | | | 5·7mm | 5·6 | 11 | 86 |

**Table 5**—*Continued*

| ME diam. in. | Special fine diam. in. | Threads per in. | Depth of thread in. | Clearing size drill | Clearance thousandths in. | Tapping size drill | % depth of engagement |
|---|---|---|---|---|---|---|---|
| ¼/0·2500 | ¼ | 32 | 0·0200 | 6·4mm | 2 | 3 | 93 |
| | | | | 6·5mm | 6 | 5·5mm | 84 |
| | | 40 | 0·0160 | F | 7 | 7/32 | 97 |
| | | | | F | 7 | 2 | 91 |
| | ¼ | 60 | 0·0107 | | | 5·8mm | 100 |
| | | | | F | 7 | 5·9mm | 83 |
| | 9/32/0·2812 | 32 | 0·200 | 7·2mm | 2·3 | C | 98 |
| | | | | L | 8·8 | 6·2mm | 93 |
| | | | | | | D | 88 |
| | 9/32 | 40 | 0·0160 | L | 8·8 | ¼ | 97 |
| | | | | | | 6·4mm | 91 |
| | | | | | | 6·5mm | 80 |
| 5/16/0·3125 | | 32 | 0·0200 | 8mm | 2·5 | 7mm | 92 |
| | | | | O | 3·5 | J | 89 |
| | | | | | | K | 79 |
| | 5/16 | 40 | 0·0160 | O | 3·5 | 9/32 | 97 |
| | | | | | | 7·2mm | 81 |
| | 5/16 | 60 | 0·0107 | O | 3·5 | 7·5mm | 99 |
| | | | | | | M | 83 |

**Table 5** – *Continued*

| ME diam. in. | Special fine diam. in. | Threads per in. | Depth of thread in. | Clearing size drill | Clearance thousandths in | Tapping size drill | % depth of engagement |
|---|---|---|---|---|---|---|---|
| $\frac{3}{8}$/0·3750 | $\frac{3}{8}$ | 24 | 0·0267 | V | 2 | P | 98 |
| | | | | | | $\frac{21}{64}$ | 88 |
| | | 32 | 0·0200 | 9·7mm | 6·9 | R | 90 |
| | | | | | | $\frac{11}{32}$ | 78 |
| | $\frac{3}{8}$ | 40 | 0·0160 | 9·7mm | 6·9 | $\frac{11}{32}$ | 97 |
| | | | | | | S | 84 |
| | $\frac{3}{8}$ | 60 | 0·0107 | 9·7mm | 6·9 | 9mm | 99 |
| | | | | | | T | 80 |
| $\frac{7}{16}$/0·4375 | $\frac{7}{16}$ | 26 | 0·0246 | 11·2mm | 3·4 | $\frac{25}{64}$ | 95 |
| | | | | | | 10mm | 89 |
| | | | | | | X | 83 |
| | | 32 | 0·0200 | 11·2mm | 3·4 | 10·2mm | 90 |
| | | | | | | 10·25mm | 85 |
| | | | | | | Y | 84 |
| | $\frac{7}{16}$ | 40 | 0·0160 | 11·2mm | 3·4 | $\frac{13}{32}$ | 97 |
| | | | | | | 10·4mm | 88 |
| $\frac{1}{2}$/0·5000 | | 26 | 0·0246 | 12·75mm | 2 | $\frac{29}{64}$ | 95 |
| | | | | 12·8mm | 3·9 | 11·6mm | 88 |
| | $\frac{1}{2}$ | 32 | 0·0200 | 12·9mm | 7·9 | 11·75mm | 94 |
| | | | | 12·9mm | 7·9 | 11·8mm | 89 |
| | $\frac{1}{2}$ | 40 | 0·0160 | 12·9mm | 7·9 | $\frac{15}{32}$ | 97 |
| | | | | | | 12mm | 86 |

Table 6

## BRITISH ASSOCIATION THREAD (BA)

| No. | Diam. in. | Pitch mm | Threads per in. approx. | Depth of thread in. | Clearing size drill | Clearance thousandths in. | Tapping size drill | % depth of engagement |
|---|---|---|---|---|---|---|---|---|
| 0 | 0·2362 | 1·00 | 25·4 | 0·0236 | B<br>6·1mm<br>C | 1·8<br>4<br>5·8 | 11<br>10<br>9<br>8 | 96<br>90<br>85<br>78 |
| 1 | 0·2087 | 0·90 | 28·2 | 0·0213 | 4<br>5·4mm<br>3 | 0·3<br>3·9<br>4·3 | 18<br>17<br>16 | 92<br>84<br>74 |
| 2 | 0·1850 | 0·81 | 31·4 | 0·0191 | 4·75mm<br>$\frac{3}{16}$<br>12 | 2<br>2·5<br>4 | 25<br>24<br>23<br>$\frac{5}{32}$ | 93<br>86<br>81<br>75 |
| 3 | 0·1614 | 0·73 | 34·8 | 0·0172 | 4·15mm<br>4·2mm<br>19 | 2<br>4<br>4·6 | 30<br>3·4mm<br>29 | 95<br>79<br>73 |
| 4 | 0·1417 | 0·66 | 38·5 | 0·0156 | 3·65mm<br>27<br>26 | 2<br>2·3<br>5·3 | 33<br>32<br>3mm | 92<br>83<br>76 |
| 5 | 0·1260 | 0·59 | 43 | 0·0139 | 3·25mm<br>30 | 2<br>2·5 | 39<br>38<br>37 | 95<br>88<br>79 |

Table 6 – Continued

| No. | Diam. in. | Pitch mm. | Threads per in. approx. | Depth of thread in. | Clearing size drill | Clearance thousandths in. | Tapping size drill | % depth of engagement |
|---|---|---|---|---|---|---|---|---|
| 6 | 0·1102 | 0·53 | 47·9 | 0·0125 | 34<br>33 | 0·8<br>2·8 | 44<br>43<br>2·3mm | 96<br>84<br>78 |
| 7 | 0·0984 | 0·48 | 52·9 | 0·0112 | 39<br>38 | 1·1<br>3·1 | $\frac{5}{64}$<br>47<br>46 | 89<br>87<br>76 |
| 8 | 0·0866 | 0·43 | 59·1 | 0·0102 | 2·25mm<br>43 | 2<br>2·4 | 51<br>50<br>1·8mm | 96<br>81<br>78 |
| 9 | 0·0748 | 0·39 | 65·1 | 0·0092 | 48 | 1·2 | 1·5mm<br>53 | 85<br>83 |
| 10 | 0·0669 | 0·35 | 72·6 | 0·0083 | 51<br>50 | 0·1<br>3·1 | 55<br>1·35mm | 90<br>83 |
| 11 | 0·0591 | 0·31 | 81·9 | 0·0073 | 53<br>1·55mm | 0/4<br>1·9 | 56<br>$\frac{3}{64}$ | 84<br>82 |
| 12 | 0·511 | 0·28 | 90·9 | 0·0066 | 55<br>1·35mm | 0·9<br>2 | 62<br>61<br>1mm<br>60 | 99<br>93<br>90<br>86 |

Table 7      **METRIC SCREW THREADS—INTERNATIONAL SYSTEM (SI)**

| Diameter mm | Diameter in. | Pitch mm | Depth of thread mm | Depth of thread in. | Clearing size drill | Tapping size drill | % depth of engagement |
|---|---|---|---|---|---|---|---|
| 6 | 0·2362 | 1 | 0·700 | 0·0275 | B | 10<br>9<br>5mm | 95<br>90<br>88 |
| 7 | 0·2756 | 1 | 0·700 | 0·0275 | J | A<br>$\frac{15}{64}$<br>6mm | 93<br>92<br>88 |
| 8 | 0·3150 | 1·25 | 0·875 | 0·0344 | P | G<br>$\frac{17}{64}$<br>H | 96<br>88<br>87 |
| 9 | 0·3458 | 1·25 | 0·875 | 0·0344 | T | N | 93 |
| 10 | 0·3937 | 1·5 | 1·050 | 0·0413 | X | $\frac{21}{64}$<br>Q<br>8·5mm | 98<br>92<br>88 |
| 11 | 0·4331 | 1·5 | 1·050 | 0·0431 | $\frac{7}{16}$ | U<br>9·5mm<br>$\frac{3}{8}$ | 97<br>88<br>86 |
| 12 | 0·4724 | 1·75 | 1·225 | 0·0482 | 12·1mm | X<br>Y | 96<br>87 |

**Table 7** – *Continued*

| Diameter mm | in. | Pitch mm | Depth of thread mm | in. | Clearing size drill | Tapping size drill | % depth of engagement |
|---|---|---|---|---|---|---|---|
| 14 | 0·5512 | 2·0 | 1·400 | 0·0551 | 14·25mm | $\frac{15}{32}$ <br> 12mm | 92 <br> 88 |
| 16 | 0·6299 | 2·0 | 1·400 | 0·0551 | $\frac{41}{64}$ | $\frac{35}{64}$ <br> 14mm | 93 <br> 88 |
| 18 | 0·7087 | 2·5 | 1·750 | 0·0689 | $\frac{23}{32}$ | $\frac{39}{64}$ <br> 15·5mm | 89 <br> 88 |
| 20 | 0·7874 | 2·5 | 1·750 | 0·0689 | $\frac{51}{64}$ | $\frac{11}{16}$ <br> 17·5mm | 89 <br> 88 |
| 22 | 0·8661 | 2·5 | 1·750 | 0·0689 | 22·25mm | $\frac{49}{64}$ <br> 19·5mm | 90 <br> 88 |
| 24 | 0·9449 | 3·0 | 2·100 | 0·0826 | 24·25 | $\frac{13}{16}$ <br> 21mm <br> $\frac{53}{64}$ | 99 <br> 88 <br> 87 |
| 27 | 1·0630 | 3·0 | 2·100 | 0·0826 | 1·5/64 | $\frac{15}{16}$ <br> 24mm | 93 <br> 88 |
| 30 | 1·1811 | 3·5 | 2·450 | 0·0964 | 1·3/32 | 1·1/32 <br> 26·5mm | 96 <br> 88 |

**Table 8**  **TWIST DRILLS**

| Inch or gauge | mm | Decimal inch | Inch or gauge | mm | Decimal Inch |
|---|---|---|---|---|---|
| 80 | | 0·0135 | $\frac{1}{32}$ | | 0·0312 |
| | 0·35 | 0·0138 | | 0·8 | 0·0315 |
| 79 | | 0·0145 | 67 | | 0·0320 |
| | 0·375 | 0·0148 | | 0·825 | 0·0325 |
| $\frac{1}{64}$ | | 0·0156 | 66 | | 0·0330 |
| | 0·4 | 0·0157 | | 0·85 | 0·0335 |
| 78 | | 0·0160 | | 0·875 | 0·0344 |
| | 0·425 | 0·0167 | 65 | | 0·0350 |
| | 0·45 | 0·0177 | | 0·9 | 0·0354 |
| 77 | | 0·0180 | 64 | | 0·0360 |
| | 0·475 | 0·0187 | | 0·925 | 0·0364 |
| | 0·5 | 0·0197 | 63 | | 0·0370 |
| 76 | | 0·0200 | | 0·95 | 0·0374 |
| | 0·525 | 0·0207 | 62 | | 0·0380 |
| 75 | | 0·0210 | | 0·975 | 0·0384 |
| | 0·55 | 0·0216 | 61 | | 0·0390 |
| 74 | | 0·0225 | | 1·00 | 0·0394 |
| | 0·575 | 0·0226 | 60 | | 0·0400 |
| | 0·6 | 0·0236 | 59 | | 0·0410 |
| 73 | | 0·0240 | | 1·05 | 0·0413 |
| | 0·625 | 0·0246 | 58 | | 0·0420 |
| 72 | | 0·0250 | 57 | | 0·0430 |
| | 0·65 | 0·0256 | | 1·1 | 0·0433 |
| 71 | | 0·0260 | | 1·15 | 0·0453 |
| | 0·675 | 0·0266 | 56 | | 0·0465 |
| | 0·7 | 0·0276 | $\frac{3}{64}$ | | 0·0469 |
| 70 | | 0·0280 | | 1·2 | 0·0472 |
| | 0·725 | 0·0285 | | 1·25 | 0·0492 |
| 69 | | 0·0292 | | 1·3 | 0·0512 |
| | 0·75 | 0·0295 | 55 | | 0·0520 |
| | 0·775 | 0·0305 | | 1·35 | 0·0531 |
| 68 | | 0·0310 | | | |

**Table 8**–*Continued*

| Inch or gauge | mm | Decimal Inch | Inch or gauge | mm | Decimal Inch |
|---|---|---|---|---|---|
| 54 | | 0·0550 | 42 | | 0·0935 |
| | 1·4 | 0·0551 | $\frac{3}{32}$ | | 0·0938 |
| | 1·45 | 0·0571 | | 2·4 | 0·0945 |
| | 1·5 | 0·0590 | | | |
| 53 | | 0·0595 | 41 | | 0·0960 |
| | 1·55 | 0·0610 | | 2·45 | 0·0964 |
| $\frac{1}{16}$ | | 0·0625 | 40 | | 0·0980 |
| | 1·6 | 0·0630 | | 2·5 | 0·0984 |
| 52 | | 0·0635 | 39 | | 0·0995 |
| | 1·65 | 0·0650 | | 2·55 | 0·1004 |
| | 1·7 | 0·0669 | 38 | | 0·1015 |
| 51 | | 0·0670 | | 2·6 | 0·1024 |
| | 1·75 | 0·0689 | 37 | | 0·1040 |
| 50 | | 0·0700 | | 2·65 | 0·1043 |
| | 1·8 | 0·0709 | | 2·7 | 0·1063 |
| | 1·85 | 0·0728 | 36 | | 0·1065 |
| 49 | | 0·0730 | | 2·75 | 0·1083 |
| | 1·9 | 0·0748 | $\frac{7}{64}$ | | 0·1094 |
| 48 | | 0·0760 | 35 | | 0·1100 |
| | 1·95 | 0·0768 | | 2·8 | 0·1102 |
| $\frac{5}{64}$ | | 0·0781 | 34 | | 0·1110 |
| 47 | | 0·0785 | | 2·85 | 0·1122 |
| | 2·00 | 0·0787 | 33 | | 0·1130 |
| | 2·05 | 0·0807 | | 2·9 | 0·1142 |
| 46 | | 0·0810 | 32 | | 0·1160 |
| 45 | | 0·0820 | | 2·95 | 0·1161 |
| | 2·1 | 0·0827 | | 3·00 | 0·1181 |
| | 2·15 | 0·0846 | 31 | | 0·1200 |
| 44 | | 0·0860 | | 3·05 | 0·1201 |
| | 2·2 | 0·0866 | | 3·1 | 0·1220 |
| | 2·25 | 0·0886 | | 3·15 | 0·1240 |
| 43 | | 0·0890 | $\frac{1}{8}$ | | 0·1250 |
| | 2·3 | 0·0906 | | 3·2 | 0·1260 |
| | 2·35 | 0·0925 | | 3·25 | 0·1280 |

| Inch or Gauge | mm | Decimal Inch | Inch or Gauge | mm | Decimal Inch |
|---|---|---|---|---|---|
| 30 | | 0·1285 | 19 | | 0·1660 |
| | 3·3 | 0·1299 | | 4·25 | 0·1673 |
| | 3·35 | 0·1319 | | 4·3 | 0·1693 |
| | 3·4 | 0·1339 | | | |
| | 3·45 | 0·1358 | 18 | | 0·1695 |
| | | | | 4·35 | 0·1713 |
| 29 | | 0·1360 | | | |
| | 3·5 | 0·1378 | $\frac{11}{64}$ | | 0·1719 |
| | 3·55 | 0·1398 | | | |
| | | | 17 | | 0·1730 |
| 28 | | 0·1405 | | 4·4 | 0·1732 |
| | | | | 4·45 | 0·1752 |
| $\frac{9}{64}$ | | 0·1406 | | | |
| | 3·6 | 0·1417 | 16 | | 0·1770 |
| | 3·65 | 0·1437 | | 4·5 | 0·1772 |
| | | | | 4·55 | 0·1791 |
| 27 | | 0·1440 | | | |
| | 3·7 | 0·1457 | 15 | | 0·1800 |
| | | | | 4·6 | 0·1811 |
| 26 | | 0·1470 | | | |
| | 3·75 | 0·1476 | 14 | | 0·1820 |
| | | | | 4·65 | 0·1831 |
| 25 | | 0·1495 | | | |
| | 3·8 | 0·1496 | 13 | 4·7 | 0·1850 |
| | 3·85 | 0·1516 | | 4·75 | 0·1870 |
| | | | | | |
| 24 | | 0·1520 | $\frac{3}{16}$ | | 0·1875 |
| | 3·9 | 0·1535 | | | |
| | | | 12 | 4·8 | 0·1890 |
| 23 | | 0·1540 | | 4·85 | 0·1909 |
| | 3·95 | 0·1555 | | | |
| | | | 11 | | 0·1910 |
| $\frac{5}{32}$ | | 0·1562 | | 4·9 | 0·1929 |
| | | | | | |
| 22 | | 0·1570 | 10 | | 0·1935 |
| | 4·00 | 0·1575 | | 4·95 | 0·1949 |
| | | | | | |
| 21 | | 0·1590 | 9 | | 0·1960 |
| | 4·05 | 0·1594 | | 5·00 | 0·1968 |
| | | | | | |
| 20 | | 0·1610 | 8 | | 0·1990 |
| | 4·1 | 0·1614 | | 5·1 | 0·2008 |
| | 4·15 | 0·1634 | | | |
| | 4·2 | 0·1654 | 7 | | 0·2010 |

**Table 8**—*Continued*

| Inch or Gauge | mm | Decimal Inch | Inch or Gauge | mm | Decimal Inch |
|---|---|---|---|---|---|
| $\frac{13}{64}$ | | 0·2031 | F | | 0·2570 |
| | | | | 6·6 | 0·2598 |
| 6 | | 0·2040 | G | | 0·2610 |
| | 5·2 | 0·2047 | | 6·7 | 0·2638 |
| 5 | | 0·2055 | | | |
| | 5·25 | 0·2067 | $\frac{17}{64}$ | | 0·2656 |
| | 5·3 | 0·2087 | | 6·75 | 0·2657 |
| 4 | | 0·2090 | H | | 0·2660 |
| | 5·4 | 0·2126 | | 6·8 | 0·2677 |
| 3 | | 0·2130 | | 6·9 | 0·2716 |
| | 5·5 | 0·2165 | I | | 0·2720 |
| $\frac{7}{32}$ | | 0·2188 | | 7·00 | 0·2756 |
| | 5·6 | 0·2205 | J | | 0·2770 |
| 2 | | 0·2210 | | 7·1 | 0·2795 |
| | 5·7 | 0·2244 | K | | 0·2810 |
| | 5·75 | 0·2264 | $\frac{9}{32}$ | | 0·2812 |
| 1 | | 0·2280 | | 7·2 | 0·2835 |
| | 5·8 | 0·2283 | | 7·25 | 0·2854 |
| | 5·9 | 0·2323 | | 7·3 | 0·2874 |
| A | | 0·2340 | L | | 0·2900 |
| $\frac{15}{64}$ | | 0·2344 | | 7·4 | 0·2913 |
| | 6·00 | 0·2362 | M | | 0·2950 |
| B | | 0·2380 | | 7·5 | 0·2953 |
| | 6·1 | 0·2402 | $\frac{19}{64}$ | | 0·2969 |
| C | | 0·2420 | | 7·6 | 0·2992 |
| | 6·2 | 0·2441 | N | | 0·3020 |
| D | | 0·2460 | | 7·7 | 0·3031 |
| | 6·25 | 0·2461 | | 7·75 | 0·3051 |
| | 6·3 | 0·2480 | | 7·8 | 0·3071 |
| E/$\frac{1}{4}$ | | 0·2500 | | 7·9 | 0·3110 |
| | 6·4 | 0·2520 | $\frac{5}{16}$ | | 0·3125 |
| | 6·5 | 0·2559 | | 8·00 | 0·3150 |

| Inch or Gauge | mm | Decimal Inch | | Inch or Gauge | mm | Decimal Inch |
|---|---|---|---|---|---|---|
| O | | 0·3160 | | W | | 0·3860 |
| | 8·1 | 0·3189 | | | 9·9 | 0·3898 |
| | 8·2 | 0·3228 | | | | |
| | | | | $\frac{25}{64}$ | | 0·3906 |
| P | | 0·3230 | | | 10·00 | 0·3937 |
| | 8·25 | 0·3248 | | | | |
| | 8·3 | 0·3268 | | X | | 0·3970 |
| | | | | | 10·1 | 0·3976 |
| $\frac{21}{64}$ | | 0·3281 | | | 10·2 | 0·4016 |
| | 8·4 | 0·3307 | | | 10·25 | 0·4035 |
| | | | | | | |
| Q | | 0·3320 | | Y | | 0·4040 |
| | 8·5 | 0·3346 | | | 10·3 | 0·4055 |
| | 8·6 | 0·3386 | | | | |
| | | | | | | |
| R | | 0·3390 | | $\frac{13}{32}$ | | 0·4062 |
| | 8·7 | 0·3425 | | | 10·4 | 0·4094 |
| | | | | | | |
| $\frac{11}{32}$ | | 0·3438 | | Z | | 0·4130 |
| | 8·75 | 0·3445 | | | 10·5 | 0·4134 |
| | 8·8 | 0·3465 | | | 10·6 | 0·4173 |
| | | | | | 10·7 | 0·4213 |
| S | | 0·3480 | | | | |
| | 8·9 | 0·3504 | | $\frac{27}{64}$ | | 0·4219 |
| | 9·00 | 0·3543 | | | 10·75 | 0·4232 |
| | | | | | 10·8 | 0·4252 |
| T | | 0·3580 | | | 10·9 | 0·4291 |
| | 9·1 | 0·3583 | | | 11·00 | 0·4331 |
| | | | | | 11·1 | 0·4370 |
| $\frac{23}{64}$ | | 0·3594 | | | | |
| | 9·2 | 0·3622 | | $\frac{7}{16}$ | | 0·4375 |
| | 9·25 | 0·3642 | | | 11·2 | 0·4409 |
| | 9·3 | 0·3661 | | | 11·25 | 0·4429 |
| | | | | | 11·3 | 0·4449 |
| U | | 0·3680 | | | 11·4 | 0·4488 |
| | 9·4 | 0·3701 | | | 11·5 | 0·4528 |
| | 9·5 | 0·3740 | | | | |
| | | | | $\frac{29}{64}$ | | 0·4531 |
| $\frac{3}{8}$ | | 0·3750 | | | 11·6 | 0·4567 |
| | | | | | 11·7 | 0·4606 |
| V | | 0·3770 | | | 11·75 | 0·4626 |
| | 9·6 | 0·3780 | | | 11·8 | 0·4646 |
| | 9·7 | 0·3819 | | | 11·9 | 0·4685 |
| | 9·75 | 0·3839 | | | | |
| | 9·8 | 0·3858 | | | | |

**Table 8**—*Continued*

| Inch or Gauge | mm | Decimal Inch | Inch | mm | Decimal Inch |
|---|---|---|---|---|---|
| $\frac{15}{32}$ | | 0·4688 | $\frac{41}{64}$ | | 0·6406 |
| | 12·00 | 0·4724 | | 16·5 | 0·6496 |
| | 12·1 | 0·4764 | $\frac{21}{32}$ | | 0·6562 |
| | 12·2 | 0·4803 | | 16·75 | 0·6594 |
| | 12·25 | 0·4823 | | 17·00 | 0·6693 |
| | 12·3 | 0·4842 | | | |
| $\frac{31}{64}$ | | 0·4844 | $\frac{43}{64}$ | | 0·6719 |
| | 12·4 | 0·4882 | | 17·25 | 0·6791 |
| | 12·5 | 0·4921 | $\frac{11}{16}$ | | 0·6875 |
| | 12·6 | 0·4961 | | 17·5 | 0·6890 |
| $\frac{1}{2}$ | 12·7 | 0·5000 | | 17·75 | 0·6988 |
| | 12·75 | 0·5020 | $\frac{45}{64}$ | | 0·7031 |
| | 12·8 | 0·5039 | | 18·00 | 0·7087 |
| | 12·9 | 0·5079 | | 18·25 | 0·7185 |
| | 13·00 | 0·5118 | | | |
| $\frac{33}{64}$ | | 0·5156 | $\frac{23}{32}$ | | 0·7188 |
| | 13·25 | 0·5216 | | 18·5 | 0·7284 |
| $\frac{17}{32}$ | | 0·5312 | $\frac{47}{64}$ | | 0·7344 |
| | 13·5 | 0·5315 | | 18·75 | 0·7382 |
| | 13·75 | 0·5413 | | 19·00 | 0·7480 |
| $\frac{35}{64}$ | | 0·5469 | $\frac{3}{4}$ | | 0·7500 |
| | 14·00 | 0·5512 | | 19·25 | 0·7579 |
| | 14·25 | 0·5610 | $\frac{49}{64}$ | | 0·7656 |
| $\frac{9}{16}$ | | 0·5625 | | 19·5 | 0·7677 |
| | 14·5 | 0·5709 | | 19·75 | 0·7776 |
| $\frac{37}{64}$ | | 0·5781 | $\frac{25}{32}$ | | 0·7812 |
| | 14·75 | 0·5807 | | 20·00 | 0·7874 |
| | 15·00 | 0·5906 | $\frac{51}{64}$ | | 0·7969 |
| $\frac{19}{32}$ | | 0·5938 | | 20·25 | 0·7972 |
| | 15·25 | 0·6004 | | 20·5 | 0·8071 |
| $\frac{39}{64}$ | | 0·6094 | $\frac{13}{16}$ | | 0·8125 |
| | 15·5 | 0·6102 | | 20·75 | 0·8169 |
| | 15·75 | 0·6201 | | 21·00 | 0·8268 |
| $\frac{5}{8}$ | | 0·6250 | $\frac{53}{64}$ | | 0·8281 |
| | 16·00 | 0·6299 | | 21·25 | 0·8366 |
| | 16·25 | 0·6398 | | | |

| Inch or Gauge | mm | Decimal Inch | | Inch or Gauge | mm | Decimal Inch |
|---|---|---|---|---|---|---|
| $\frac{27}{32}$ | | 0·8438 | | $\frac{59}{64}$ | | 0·9219 |
| | 21·5 | 0·8465 | | | 23·5 | 0·9252 |
| | 2·751 | 0·8563 | | | 23·75 | 0·9350 |
| $\frac{55}{64}$ | | 0·8594 | | $\frac{15}{16}$ | | 0·9375 |
| | 22·00 | 0·8661 | | | 24·00 | 0·9449 |
| $\frac{7}{8}$ | | 0·8750 | | $\frac{61}{64}$ | | 0·9531 |
| | 22·25 | 0·8760 | | | 24·25 | 0·9547 |
| | 22·5 | 0·8858 | | | 24·5 | 0·9646 |
| $\frac{57}{64}$ | | 0·8906 | | $\frac{31}{32}$ | | 0·9688 |
| | 22·75 | 0·8957 | | | 24·75 | 0·9744 |
| | 23·00 | 0·9055 | | | 25·00 | 0·9842 |
| $\frac{29}{32}$ | | 0·9062 | | $\frac{63}{64}$ | | 0·9844 |
| | 23·25 | 0·9154 | | 1 | | 1·0000 |

**Table 9**      **COMBINATION CENTRE DRILLS**

| Size | Diam. of body in. | Diam. of drill in. | Size | Diam. of body in. | Diam. of drill in. |
|---|---|---|---|---|---|
| A | $\frac{3}{10}$ | $\frac{3}{32}/\frac{1}{8}$ | 1 | $\frac{1}{2}$ | $\frac{7}{32}$ |
| B | $\frac{3}{10}$ | $\frac{1}{8}$ | 2 | $\frac{1}{2}$ | $\frac{9}{32}$ |
| C | $\frac{3}{10}$ | $\frac{3}{32}$ | 3 | $\frac{1}{2}$ | $\frac{11}{32}$ |
| D | $\frac{15}{64}$ | $\frac{5}{64}$ | 4 | $\frac{1}{2}$ | $\frac{13}{32}$ |
| E | $\frac{13}{64}$ | $\frac{1}{16}$ | 5 | $\frac{5}{8}$ | $\frac{7}{32}$ |
| F.1 | $\frac{7}{16}$ | $\frac{5}{32}$ | 6 | $\frac{5}{8}$ | $\frac{9}{32}$ |
| F.2 | $\frac{7}{16}$ | $\frac{3}{16}$ | 7 | $\frac{5}{8}$ | $\frac{11}{32}$ |
| H | $\frac{5}{32}$ | $\frac{3}{64}$ | 8 | $\frac{5}{8}$ | $\frac{13}{32}$ |
| L | $\frac{13}{64}$ | $\frac{1}{16}$/No. 45 | 9 | $\frac{3}{4}$ | $\frac{1}{4}$ |
| R | $\frac{7}{16}$ | $\frac{5}{32}/\frac{3}{16}$ | 10 | $\frac{3}{4}$ | $\frac{5}{16}$ |
| S | $\frac{1}{8}$ | No. 57 | | | |

## Table 9–*Continued*  BRITISH STANDARD CENTRE DRILLS

| Size | Diam. of body in. | Diam. of drill in. | Size in. | Diam. of body in. | Diam. of drill in. |
|------|------|------|------|------|------|
| BS 1 | $\frac{1}{8}$ | $\frac{3}{64}$ | BS 5 | $\frac{7}{16}$ | $\frac{3}{16}$ |
| BS 2 | $\frac{3}{16}$ | $\frac{1}{16}$ | BS 6 | $\frac{5}{8}$ | $\frac{1}{4}$ |
| BS 3 | $\frac{1}{4}$ | $\frac{3}{32}$ | BS 7 | $\frac{3}{4}$ | $\frac{5}{16}$ |
| BS 4 | $\frac{5}{16}$ | $\frac{1}{8}$ | | | |

## Table 10

| UNIFIED COARSE THREAD (U.N.C.) | | |
|------|------|------|
| Nominal Size of Tap | Tapping Drill Size (mm) | Clearance Drill Size (mm) |
| 1 | 1·55 | 1·95 |
| 2 | 1·85 | 2·30 |
| 3 | 2·10 | 2·65 |
| 4 | 2·35 | 2·95 |
| 5 | 2·65 | 3·30 |
| 6 | 2·85 | 3·60 |
| 8 | 3·50 | 4·30 |
| 10 | 3·90 | 4·90 |
| 12 | 4·50 | 5·60 |
| 1/4" | 5·10 | 6·50 |
| 5/16" | 6·60 | 8·10 |
| 3/8" | 8·00 | 9·70 |
| 7/16" | 9·40 | 11·30 |
| 1/2" | 10·80 | 13·00 |
| 9/16" | 12·20 | 14·50 |
| 5/8" | 13·50 | 16·25 |
| 3/4" | 16·50 | 19·25 |
| 7/8" | 19·50 | 22·50 |
| 1" | 22·25 | 25·75 |
| 1,1/8" | 25·00 | 29·00 |
| 1,1/4" | 28·00 | 32·00 |
| 1,3/8" | 30·75 | 35·50 |
| 1,1/2" | 34·00 | 38·50 |
| 1,3/4" | 39·50 | 45·00 |
| 2" | 45·00 | 51·00 |

## Table 11  UNIFIED FINE THREAD (UNF)

| Nominal Size of Tap | Tapping Drill Size (mm) | Clearance Drill Size (mm) |
|---|---|---|
| 0 | 1·25 | 1·60 |
| 1 | 1·55 | 1·95 |
| 2 | 1·90 | 2·30 |
| 3 | 2·15 | 2·65 |
| 4 | 2·40 | 2·95 |
| 5 | 2·70 | 3·30 |
| 6 | 2·95 | 3·60 |
| 8 | 3·50 | 4·30 |
| 10 | 4·10 | 4·90 |
| 12 | 4·70 | 5·60 |

## Table 12  UNIFIED FINE THREAD (UNF)

| Nominal Size of Tap | Tapping Drill Size (mm) | Clearance Drill Size (mm) |
|---|---|---|
| 1/4″ | 5·50 | 6·50 |
| 5/16″ | 6·90 | 8·10 |
| 3/8″ | 8·50 | 9·70 |
| 7/16″ | 9·90 | 11·30 |
| 1/2″ | 11·50 | 13·00 |
| 9/16″ | 12·90 | 14·50 |
| 5/8″ | 14·50 | 16·25 |
| 3/4″ | 17·50 | 19·25 |
| 7/8″ | 20·40 | 22·50 |
| 1″ | 23·25 | 25·75 |
| 1,1/8″ | 26·50 | 29·00 |
| 1,1/4″ | 29·50 | 32·00 |
| 1,3/8″ | 32·75 | 35·50 |
| 1,1/2″ | 36·00 | 38·50 |

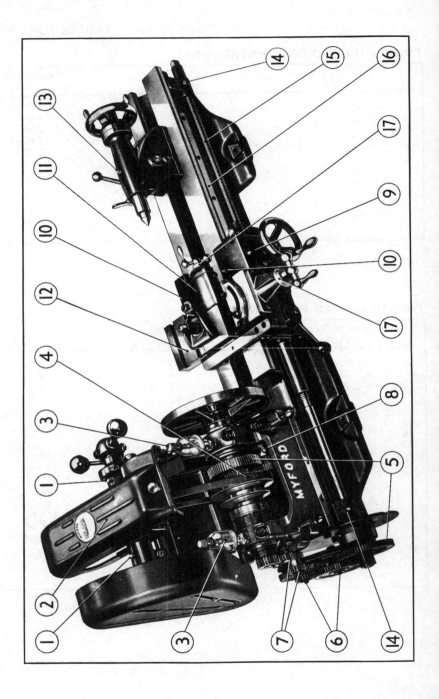

222

## Myford ML7 Lubrication Chart

*Use Esso Nuto H32 except where otherwise stated*

### Lubricate at regular intervals

(1) Countershaft. Use the oil gun on both nipples (3) Headstock bearings. Check the oil level of Sight Feed Lubricators, and replenish when necessary (4) Headstock Pulley. Lubricate with oil gun frequently whenever the reduction gear is used via the oil nipple at the large end of the pulley *(5) Backgears and Changegear over teeth. A small amount of oil (viscosity SAE 30) will effectively lubricate the gear teeth (6) Changewheel Studs. Oil frequently *(7) Tumbler gears. These fast running components should be frequently lubricated whenever the gears are being used (8) Backgear Spindle. Use the oil gun frequently, whenever the reduction gear is used (9) Apron Reservoir. Use the oil gun. This supply is distributed to the handwheel and rack pinion shafts and also feeds the reduction gear (10) Saddle. Use the oil gun on both nipples; one over the front shears, one at the rear (11) Topslide Ways. Clean and apply an oil

of SAE 30 viscosity (12) Cross-slide Ways. Clean and apply an oil of SAE 30 viscosity (13) Tailstock Barrel. Use the oil gun on nipples shown

### Lubricate occasionally

(2) Swing Head Pin and Eccentric. Apply oil of SAE 30 viscosity (14) Leadscrew Brackets. Use the oil gun on both nipples *(15) Leadscrew. Clean with a stiff brush and apply oil SAE 30 viscosity *(16) Rack. Apply oil of SAE 30 viscosity *(17) Cross-slide and Topslide Feedscrews. Oil occasionally from underneath, using oil of SAE 30 viscosity

**Myford supply and recommend Esso Nuto H32 Oil for** general lubrication. Where SAE 30 viscosity oil is specified, any good motor oil of this number will be satisfactory. *For items marked with an asterick, numbers 5, 7, 15, 16, 17, Rocol MTS 1000 grease should be used in those territories where it is availablez

223

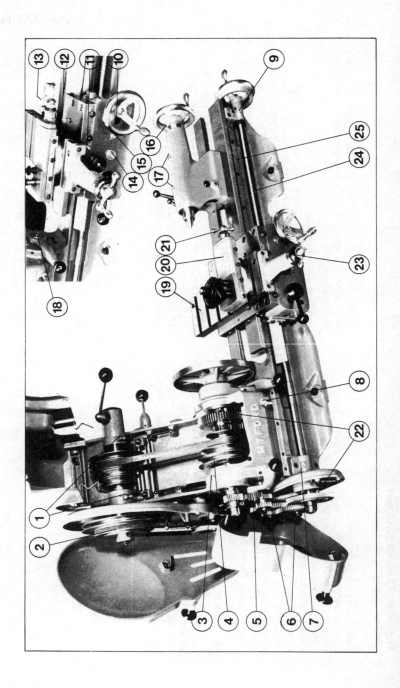

**Myford ML Super 7 Lubrication Chart**
*Use Esso Nuto H32 except where otherwise specified.*

(1) Countershaft Bearings. Replenish the two oil cups daily. (2) Cone Clutch. With the clutch disengaged apply two or three drops of oil weekly (3) Headstock Rear Bearing. Lubricate with the oil gun daily (4) Headstock Pulley. Lubricate with the oil gun twice daily whenever the reduction gear is in use (5) Tumbler Gears. Lubricate with the oil gun twice daily (6) Changewheel Studs. Lubricate with an oil can twice daily (7) LH Leadscrew Bracket. Lubricate with the oil gun weekly (8) Headstock Front Bearing. Replenish the oil cup twice daily (9) RH Leadscrew Bracket. Lubricate with the oil gun weekly (10) Apron Reservoir. Remove the filler plug and top up to overflowing weekly (11) Intermediate Gear/Clutch shaft. Lubricate with oil gun daily (12) Saddle, Front Shear. Lubricate with oil gun daily (13) Saddle, Rear Shear. Lubricate with oil gun daily (14) Apron Bevel Gear Bearing. Lubricate with oil gun daily (15) Leadscrew Bevel Gear Bearing. Lubricate with oil gun daily (16) Tailstock Thrust. Lubricate with oil gun daily (17) Tailstock Barrel. Lubricate with oil gun daily (18) Backgear Spindle. When backgear is in use lubricate with oil gun twice daily (19) Cross Slide Ways. Clean, and apply an oil of viscosity of SAE 30 weekly (20) Top Slide Ways. Clean, and apply an oil of viscosity SAE30 weekly *(21) Top Slide Feed Screw. Using oil of viscosity SAE30, lubricate from underneath twice weekly *(22) Backgears and Change gear teeth. Lubricate with oil of viscosity SAE30 daily *(23) Cross Slide Feedscrew. Using oil of viscosity SAE30, lubricate from underneath twice weekly *(24) Leadscrew. Clean with a stiff brush and apply oil of viscosity SAE30 weekly *(25) Rack. Lubricate with oil of viscosity SAE30 weekly

**Myford supply and recommend Esso Nuto H32 oil or** equivalent for general lubrication. Where oil of viscosity SAE 30 is specified, any good motor oil of this number will be satisfactory

As an alternative to motor oil of viscosity SAE30 use an industrial oil of viscosity I.S.O. VG68

*For items marked with an asterisk, numbers 21, 22, 23, 24, 25 Rocol MTS1000 grease should be used in those territories where it is available

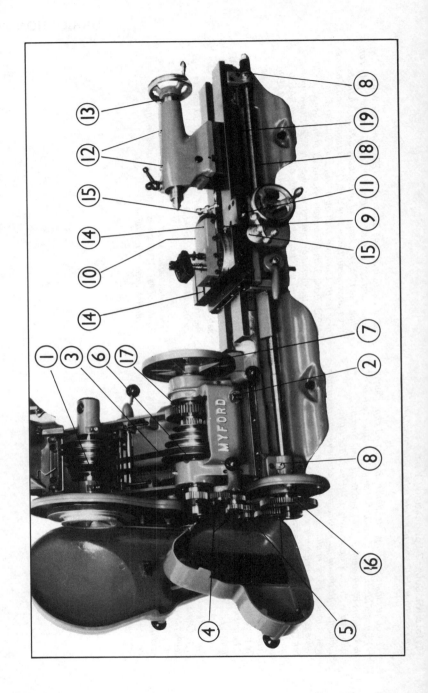

Myford ML7-R Lubrication Chart
Except where otherwise specified use Esso Nuto H32

(1) Countershaft Bearings. Replenish the two oil cups daily (2) Headstock front bearing. Replenish the oil cup twice daily (3) Headstock rear bearing. Lubricate with the oil gun daily (4) Tumbler gear studs. Lubricate with the oil gun twice daily (5) Changewheel studs. Lubricate with the oil gun twice daily (6) Headstock pulley. Lubricate with the oil gun twice daily whenever the reduction gear is in use (7) Backgear spindle. Lubricate with the oil gun twice daily whenever the reduction gear is in use (8) Leadscrew brackets, L.H. and R.H. Lubricate with the oil gun weekly (9) Saddle, front shear. Lubricate with the oil gun daily (10) Saddle, rear shear. Lubricate with the oil gun daily (11) Apron reservoir. Replenish with the oil gun daily. This lubricates the handwheel and rack and pinion shafts, also the reduction gear (12) Tailstock barrel. Lubricate with the oil gun daily (13) Tailstock thrust. Lubricate with the oil gun daily (14) Cross-slide and topslide ways. Clean and apply

an oil of viscosity SAE30 weekly * (15) Cross-slide and topslide feedscrews. Using oil of viscosity SAE30 lubricate underneath twice weekly * (16) Change gear teeth. Lubricate with oil of viscosity SAE30 daily * (17) Reduction gear teeth. Lubricate with oil of viscosity SAE30 daily whenever the reduction gear is in use * (18) Leadscrew. Clean with a stiff brush and apply oil of viscosity SAE30 weekly * (19) Rack. Lubricate with oil of viscosity SAE30 weekly

Myford supply and recommend Esso Nuto H32 (formerly Nuto H44) or equivalent for general lubrication. Where oil of viscosity SAE30 is specified, any good motor oil of this number will be satisfactory

*For items marked with an asterisk, numbers 15, 16, 17, 18 and 19, Rocol MTS1000 grease should be used in those territories where it is available

227

# Index

# MYFORD

# MYFORD